Programming Massively Parallel Processors

A Hands-on Approach

Programming
Massively Parallel
Processors
A Hands-on Approach

David B. Kirk and Wen-mei W. Hwu

ELSEVIER

AMSTERDAM • BOSTON • HEIDELBERG • LONDON
NEW YORK • OXFORD • PARIS • SAN DIEGO
SAN FRANCISCO • SINGAPORE • SYDNEY • TOKYO

Morgan Kaufmann Publishers is an imprint of Elsevier

MORGAN KAUFMANN

Morgan Kaufmann Publishers is an imprint of Elsevier.
30 Corporate Drive, Suite 400, Burlington, MA 01803, USA

This book is printed on acid-free paper.

Notices

Knowledge and best practice in this field are constantly changing. As new research and experience broaden our understanding, changes in research methods, professional practices, or medical treatment may become necessary.

Practitioners and researchers must always rely on their own experience and knowledge in evaluating and using any information, methods, compounds, or experiments described herein. In using such information or methods they should be mindful of their own safety and the safety of others, including parties for whom they have a professional responsibility.

To the fullest extent of the law, neither the Publisher nor the authors, contributors, or editors, assume any liability for any injury and/or damage to persons or property as a matter of products liability, negligence or otherwise, or from any use or operation of any methods, products, instructions, or ideas contained in the material herein.

Library of Congress Cataloging-in-Publication Data
Application Submitted

British Library Cataloguing-in-Publication Data
A catalogue record for this book is available from the British Library.

ISBN: 978-0-12-381472-2

For information on all Morgan Kaufmann publications,
visit our Web site at www.mkp.com or www.elsevierdirect.com

Printed in United States of America
10   11   12   13   14   5   4   3   2   1

Working together to grow libraries in developing countries

www.elsevier.com | www.bookaid.org | www.sabre.org

ELSEVIER   BOOK AID International   Sabre Foundation

Contents

Preface

WHY WE WROTE THIS BOOK

Mass-market computing systems that combine multicore CPUs and many-core GPUs have brought terascale computing to the laptop and petascale computing to clusters. Armed with such computing power, we are at the dawn of pervasive use of computational experiments for science, engineering, health, and business disciplines. Many will be able to achieve breakthroughs in their disciplines using computational experiments that are of unprecedented level of scale, controllability, and observability. This book provides a critical ingredient for the vision: teaching parallel programming to millions of graduate and undergraduate students so that computational thinking and parallel programming skills will be as pervasive as calculus.

We started with a course now known as ECE498AL. During the Christmas holiday of 2006, we were frantically working on the lecture slides and lab assignments. David was working the system trying to pull the early GeForce 8800 GTX GPU cards from customer shipments to Illinois, which would not succeed until a few weeks after the semester began. It also became clear that CUDA would not become public until a few weeks after the start of the semester. We had to work out the legal agreements so that we can offer the course to students under NDA for the first few weeks. We also needed to get the words out so that students would sign up since the course was not announced until after the preenrollment period.

We gave our first lecture on January 16, 2007. Everything fell into place. David commuted weekly to Urbana for the class. We had 52 students, a couple more than our capacity. We had draft slides for most of the first 10 lectures. Wen-mei's graduate student, John Stratton, graciously volunteered as the teaching assistant and set up the lab. All students signed NDA so that we can proceed with the first several lectures until CUDA became public. We recorded the lectures but did not release them on the Web until February. We had graduate students from physics, astronomy, chemistry, electrical engineering, mechanical engineering as well as computer science and computer engineering. The enthusiasm in the room made it all worthwhile.

Since then, we have taught the course three times in one-semester format and two times in one-week intensive format. The ECE498AL course has become a permanent course known as ECE408 of the University of Illinois, Urbana-Champaign. We started to write up some early chapters of this book when we offered ECE498AL the second time. We tested these chapters in our spring 2009 class and our 2009 Summer School. The first four chapters were also tested in an MIT class taught by Nicolas Pinto in spring 2009. We also shared these early chapters on the web and received valuable feedback from numerous individuals. We were encouraged by the feedback we received and decided to go for a full book. Here, we humbly present our first edition to you.

TARGET AUDIENCE

The target audience of this book is graduate and undergraduate students from all science and engineering disciplines where computational thinking and parallel programming skills are needed to use pervasive terascale computing hardware to achieve breakthroughs. We assume that the reader has at least some basic C programming experience and thus are more advanced programmers, both within and outside of the field of Computer Science. We especially target computational scientists in fields such as mechanical engineering, civil engineering, electrical engineering, bioengineering, physics, and chemistry, who use computation to further their field of research. As such, these scientists are both experts in their domain as well as advanced programmers. The book takes the approach of building on basic C programming skills, to teach parallel programming in C. We use C for CUDA™, a parallel programming environment that is supported on NVIDIA GPUs, and emulated on less parallel CPUs. There are approximately 200 million of these processors in the hands of consumers and professionals, and more than 40,000 programmers actively using CUDA. The applications that you develop as part of the learning experience will be able to be run by a very large user community.

HOW TO USE THE BOOK

We would like to offer some of our experience in teaching ECE498AL using the material detailed in this book.

A Three-Phased Approach

In ECE498AL the lectures and programming assignments are balanced with each other and organized into three phases:

Phase 1: One lecture based on Chapter 3 is dedicated to teaching the basic CUDA memory/threading model, the CUDA extensions to the C language, and the basic programming/debugging tools. After the lecture, students can write a naïve parallel matrix multiplication code in a couple of hours.

Phase 2: The next phase is a series of 10 lectures that give students the *conceptual* understanding of the CUDA memory model, the CUDA threading model, GPU hardware performance features, modern computer system architecture, and the common data-parallel programming patterns needed to develop a high-performance parallel application. These lectures are based on Chapters 4 through 7. The performance of their matrix multiplication codes increases by about 10 times through this period. The students also complete assignments on convolution, vector reduction, and prefix scan through this period.

Phase 3: Once the students have established solid CUDA programming skills, the remaining lectures cover computational thinking, a broader range of parallel execution models, and parallel programming principles. These lectures are based on Chapters 8 through 11. (The voice and video recordings of these lectures are available on-line (http://courses.ece. illinois.edu/ece498/al).)

Tying It All Together: The Final Project

While the lectures, labs, and chapters of this book help lay the intellectual foundation for the students, what brings the learning experience together is the final project. The final project is so important to the course that it is prominently positioned in the course and commands nearly 2 months' focus. It incorporates five innovative aspects: mentoring, workshop, clinic, final report, and symposium. (While much of the information about final project is available at the ECE498AL web site (http://courses.ece.illinois. edu/ece498/al), we would like to offer the thinking that was behind the design of these aspects.)

Students are encouraged to base their final projects on problems that represent current challenges in the research community. To seed the process, the instructors recruit several major computational science research groups to propose problems and serve as mentors. The mentors are asked to contribute a one-to-two-page project specification sheet that briefly describes the significance of the application, what the mentor would like to accomplish with the student teams on the application, the technical skills (particular type of Math, Physics, Chemistry courses) required to understand and work on the application, and a list of web and traditional resources that students can draw upon for technical background, general information, and building blocks, along with specific URLs or ftp paths to particular implementations and coding examples. These project specification sheets also provide students with learning experiences in defining their own research projects later in their careers. (Several examples are available at the ECE498AL course web site.)

Students are also encouraged to contact their potential mentors during their project selection process. Once the students and the mentors agree on a project, they enter into a close relationship, featuring frequent consultation and project reporting. We the instructors attempt to facilitate the collaborative relationship between students and their mentors, making it a very valuable experience for both mentors and students.

The Project Workshop

The main vehicle for the whole class to contribute to each other's final project ideas is the project workshop. We usually dedicate six of the lecture slots to project workshops. The workshops are designed for students' benefit. For example, if a student has identified a project, the workshop serves as a venue to present preliminary thinking, get feedback, and recruit teammates. If a student has not identified a project, he/she can simply attend the presentations, participate in the discussions, and join one of the project teams. Students are not graded during the workshops, in order to keep the atmosphere nonthreatening and enable them to focus on a meaningful dialog with the instructor(s), teaching assistants, and the rest of the class.

The workshop schedule is designed so the instructor(s) and teaching assistants can take some time to provide feedback to the project teams and so that students can ask questions. Presentations are limited to 10 min so there is time for feedback and questions during the class period. This limits the class size to about 36 presenters, assuming 90-min lecture slots. All presentations are preloaded into a PC in order to control the schedule strictly and maximize feedback time. Since not all students present at the workshop, we have been able to accommodate up to 50 students in each class, with extra workshop time available as needed.

The instructor(s) and TAs must make a commitment to attend all the presentations and to give useful feedback. Students typically need most help in answering the following questions. First, are the projects too big or too small for the amount of time available? Second, is there existing work in the field that the project can benefit from? Third, are the computations being targeted for parallel execution appropriate for the CUDA programming model?

The Design Document

Once the students decide on a project and form a team, they are required to submit a design document for the project. This helps them think through the project steps before they jump into it. The ability to do such planning will be important to their later career success. The design document should discuss the background and motivation for the project, application-level objectives and potential impact, main features of the end application, an overview of their design, an implementation plan, their performance goals, a verification plan and acceptance test, and a project schedule.

The teaching assistants hold a project clinic for final project teams during the week before the class symposium. This clinic helps ensure that students are on-track and that they have identified the potential roadblocks early in the process. Student teams are asked to come to the clinic with an initial draft of the following three versions of their application: (1) The best CPU sequential code in terms of performance, with SSE2 and other optimizations that establish a strong serial base of the code for their speedup comparisons; (2) The best CUDA parallel code in terms of performance. This version is the main output of the project; (3) A version of CPU sequential code that is based on the same algorithm as version 3, using single precision. This version is used by the students to characterize the parallel algorithm overhead in terms of extra computations involved.

Student teams are asked to be prepared to discuss the key ideas used in each version of the code, any floating-point precision issues, any comparison against previous results on the application, and the potential impact on the field if they achieve tremendous speedup. From our experience, the optimal schedule for the clinic is 1 week before the class symposium. An earlier time typically results in less mature projects and less meaningful sessions. A later time will not give students sufficient time to revise their projects according to the feedback.

The Project Report

Students are required to submit a project report on their team's key findings. Six lecture slots are combined into a whole-day class symposium. During the symposium, students use presentation slots proportional to the size of the teams. During the presentation, the students highlight the best parts of their project report for the benefit of the whole class. The presentation accounts for a significant part of students' grades. Each student must answer questions directed to him/her as individuals, so that different grades can be assigned to individuals in the same team. The symposium is a major opportunity for students to learn to produce a concise presentation that motivates their peers to read a full paper. After their presentation, the students also submit a full report on their final project.

ONLINE SUPPLEMENTS

The lab assignments, final project guidelines, and sample project specifications are available to instructors who use this book for their classes. While this book provides the intellectual contents for these classes, the additional material will be crucial in achieving the overall education goals. We would like to invite you to take advantage of the online material that accompanies this book, which is available at the Publisher's Web site www.elsevierdirect.com/9780123814722.

Finally, we encourage you to submit your feedback. We would like to hear from you if you have any ideas for improving this book and the supplementary online material. Of course, we also like to know what you liked about the book.

David B. Kirk and Wen-mei W. Hwu

Acknowledgments

We especially acknowledge Ian Buck, the father of CUDA and John Nickolls, the lead architect of Tesla GPU Computing Architecture. Their teams created an excellent infrastructure for this course. Ashutosh Rege and the NVIDIA DevTech team contributed to the original slides and contents used in ECE498AL course. Bill Bean, Simon Green, Mark Harris, Manju Hedge, Nadeem Mohammad, Brent Oster, Peter Shirley, Eric Young, and Cyril Zeller provided review comments and corrections to the manuscripts. Nadeem Mohammad organized the NVIDIA review efforts and also helped to plan Chapter 11 and Appendix B. Calisa Cole helped with cover. Nadeem's heroic efforts have been critical to the completion of this book.

We also thank Jensen Huang for providing a great amount of financial and human resources for developing the course. Tony Tamasi's team contributed heavily to the review and revision of the book chapters. Jensen also took the time to read the early drafts of the chapters and gave us valuable feedback. David Luebke has facilitated the GPU computing resources for the course. Jonah Alben has provided valuable insight. Michael Shebanow and Michael Garland have given guest lectures and contributed materials.

John Stone and Sam Stone in Illinois contributed much of the base material for the case study and OpenCL chapters. John Stratton and Chris Rodrigues contributed some of the base material for the computational thinking chapter. I-Jui "Ray" Sung, John Stratton, Xiao-Long Wu, Nady Obeid contributed to the lab material and helped to revise the course material as they volunteered to serve as teaching assistants on top of their research. Laurie Talkington and James Hutchinson helped to dictate early lectures that served as the base for the first five chapters. Mike Showerman helped build two generations of GPU computing clusters for the course. Jeremy Enos worked tirelessly to ensure that students have a stable, user-friendly GPU computing cluster to work on their lab assignments and projects.

We acknowledge Dick Blahut who challenged us to create the course in Illinois. His constant reminder that we needed to write the book helped keep us going. Beth Katsinas arranged a meeting between Dick Blahut and NVIDIA Vice President Dan Vivoli. Through that gathering, Blahut was introduced to David and challenged David to come to Illinois and create the course with Wen-mei.

We also thank Thom Dunning of the University of Illinois and Sharon Glotzer of the University of Michigan, Co-Directors of the multiuniversity Virtual School of Computational Science and Engineering, for graciously hosting the summer school version of the course. Trish Barker, Scott Lathrop, Umesh Thakkar, Tom Scavo, Andrew Schuh, and Beth McKown all helped organize the summer school. Robert Brunner, Klaus Schulten, Pratap Vanka, Brad Sutton, John Stone, Keith Thulborn, Michael Garland, Vlad Kindratenko, Naga Govindaraj, Yan Xu, Arron Shinn, and Justin Haldar contributed to the lectures and panel discussions at the summer school.

Nicolas Pinto tested the early versions of the first chapters in his MIT class and assembled an excellent set of feedback comments and corrections. Steve Lumetta and Sanjay Patel both taught versions of the course and gave us valuable feedback. John Owens graciously allowed us to use some of his slides. Tor Aamodt, Dan Connors, Tom Conte, Michael Giles, Nacho Navarro and numerous other instructors and their students worldwide have provided us with valuable feedback. Michael Giles reviewed the semi-final draft chapters in detail and identified many typos and inconsistencies.

We especially thank our colleagues Kurt Akeley, Al Aho, Arvind, Dick Blahut, Randy Bryant, Bob Colwell, Ed Davidson, Mike Flynn, John Hennessy, Pat Hanrahan, Nick Holonyak, Dick Karp, Kurt Keutzer, Dave Liu, Dave Kuck, Yale Patt, David Patterson, Bob Rao, Burton Smith, Jim Smith, and Mateo Valero who have taken the time to share their insight with us over the years.

We are humbled by the generosity and enthusiasm of all the great people who contributed to the course and the book.

David B. Kirk and Wen-mei W. Hwu

To Caroline, Rose, and Leo
To Sabrina, Amanda, Bryan, and Carissa
For enduring our absence while working on the course and the book

Introduction

1

INTRODUCTION

Microprocessors based on a single central processing unit (CPU), such as those in the Intel® Pentium® family and the AMD® Opteron™ family, drove rapid performance increases and cost reductions in computer applications for more than two decades. These microprocessors brought giga (billion) floating-point operations per second (GFLOPS) to the desktop and hundreds of GFLOPS to cluster servers. This relentless drive of performance improvement has allowed application software to provide more functionality, have better user interfaces, and generate more useful results. The users, in turn, demand even more improvements once they become accustomed to these improvements, creating a positive cycle for the computer industry.

During the drive, most software developers have relied on the advances in hardware to increase the speed of their applications under the hood; the same software simply runs faster as each new generation of processors is introduced. This drive, however, has slowed since 2003 due to energy-consumption and heat-dissipation issues that have limited the increase of the clock frequency and the level of productive activities that can be performed in each clock period within a single CPU. Virtually all microprocessor vendors have switched to models where multiple processing units, referred to as *processor cores*, are used in each chip to increase the

1

processing power. This switch has exerted a tremendous impact on the software developer community [Sutter 2005].

Traditionally, the vast majority of software applications are written as sequential programs, as described by von Neumann [1945] in his seminal report. The execution of these programs can be understood by a human sequentially stepping through the code. Historically, computer users have become accustomed to the expectation that these programs run faster with each new generation of microprocessors. Such expectation is no longer strictly valid from this day onward. A sequential program will only run on one of the processor cores, which will not become significantly faster than those in use today. Without performance improvement, application developers will no longer be able to introduce new features and capabilities into their software as new microprocessors are introduced, thus reducing the growth opportunities of the entire computer industry.

Rather, the applications software that will continue to enjoy performance improvement with each new generation of microprocessors will be parallel programs, in which multiple threads of execution cooperate to complete the work faster. This new, dramatically escalated incentive for parallel program development has been referred to as the *concurrency revolution* [Sutter 2005]. The practice of parallel programming is by no means new. The high-performance computing community has been developing parallel programs for decades. These programs run on large-scale, expensive computers. Only a few elite applications can justify the use of these expensive computers, thus limiting the practice of parallel programming to a small number of application developers. Now that all new microprocessors are parallel computers, the number of applications that must be developed as parallel programs has increased dramatically. There is now a great need for software developers to learn about parallel programming, which is the focus of this book.

1.1 GPUs AS PARALLEL COMPUTERS

Since 2003, the semiconductor industry has settled on two main trajectories for designing microprocessor [Hwu 2008]. The *multicore* trajectory seeks to maintain the execution speed of sequential programs while moving into multiple cores. The multicores began as two-core processors, with the number of cores approximately doubling with each semiconductor process generation. A current exemplar is the recent Intel® Core™ i7 microprocessor, which has four processor cores, each of which is an out-of-order, multiple-instruction issue processor implementing the full x86 instruction set; the microprocessor supports hyperthreading with two hardware threads and is designed to maximize the execution speed of sequential programs.

In contrast, the *many-core* trajectory focuses more on the execution throughput of parallel applications. The many-cores began as a large number of much smaller cores, and, once again, the number of cores doubles with each generation. A current exemplar is the NVIDIA® GeForce® GTX 280 graphics processing unit (GPU) with 240 cores, each of which is a heavily multithreaded, in-order, single-instruction issue processor that shares its control and instruction cache with seven other cores. Many-core processors, especially the GPUs, have led the race of floating-point performance since 2003. This phenomenon is illustrated in Figure 1.1. While the performance improvement of general-purpose microprocessors has slowed significantly, the GPUs have continued to improve relentlessly. As of 2009, the ratio between many-core GPUs and multicore CPUs for peak floating-point calculation throughput is about 10 to 1. These are not necessarily achievable application speeds but are merely the raw speed that the execution resources can potentially support in these chips: 1 teraflops (1000 gigaflops) versus 100 gigaflops in 2009.

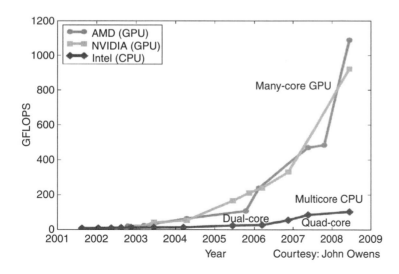

FIGURE 1.1

Enlarging performance gap between GPUs and CPUs.

Such a large performance gap between parallel and sequential execution has amounted to a significant "electrical potential" buildup, and at some point something will have to give. We have reached that point now. To date, this large performance gap has already motivated many applications developers to move the computationally intensive parts of their software to GPUs for execution. Not surprisingly, these computationally intensive parts are also the prime target of parallel programming—when there is more work to do, there is more opportunity to divide the work among cooperating parallel workers.

One might ask why there is such a large performance gap between many-core GPUs and general-purpose multicore CPUs. The answer lies in the differences in the fundamental design philosophies between the two types of processors, as illustrated in Figure 1.2. The design of a CPU is optimized for sequential code performance. It makes use of sophisticated control logic to allow instructions from a single thread of execution to execute in parallel or even out of their sequential order while maintaining the appearance of sequential execution. More importantly, large cache memories are provided to reduce the instruction and data access latencies of large complex applications. Neither control logic nor cache memories contribute to the peak calculation speed. As of 2009, the new general-purpose, multicore microprocessors typically have four large processor cores designed to deliver strong sequential code performance.

Memory bandwidth is another important issue. Graphics chips have been operating at approximately 10 times the bandwidth of contemporaneously available CPU chips. In late 2006, the GeForce® 8800 GTX, or simply

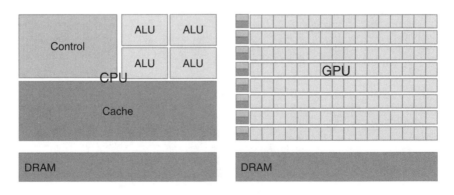

FIGURE 1.2

CPUs and GPUs have fundamentally different design philosophies.

G80, was capable of moving data at about 85 gigabytes per second (GB/s) in and out of its main dynamic random access memory (DRAM). Because of frame buffer requirements and the relaxed memory model—the way various system software, applications, and input/output (I/O) devices expect their memory accesses to work—general-purpose processors have to satisfy requirements from legacy operating systems, applications, and I/O devices that make memory bandwidth more difficult to increase. In contrast, with simpler memory models and fewer legacy constraints, the GPU designers can more easily achieve higher memory bandwidth. The more recent NVIDIA® GT200 chip supports about 150 GB/s. Microprocessor system memory bandwidth will probably not grow beyond 50 GB/s for about 3 years, so CPUs will continue to be at a disadvantage in terms of memory bandwidth for some time.

The design philosophy of the GPUs is shaped by the fast growing video game industry, which exerts tremendous economic pressure for the ability to perform a massive number of floating-point calculations per video frame in advanced games. This demand motivates the GPU vendors to look for ways to maximize the chip area and power budget dedicated to floating-point calculations. The prevailing solution to date is to optimize for the execution throughput of massive numbers of threads. The hardware takes advantage of a large number of execution threads to find work to do when some of them are waiting for long latency memory accesses, thus minimizing the control logic required for each execution thread. Small cache memories are provided to help control the bandwidth requirements of these applications so multiple threads that access the same memory data do not need to all go to the DRAM. As a result, much more chip area is dedicated to the floating-point calculations.

It should be clear now that GPUs are designed as numeric computing engines, and they will not perform well on some tasks on which CPUs are designed to perform well; therefore, one should expect that most applications will use both CPUs and GPUs, executing the sequential parts on the CPU and numerically intensive parts on the GPUs. This is why the CUDA™ (Compute Unified Device Architecture) programming model, introduced by NVIDIA in 2007, is designed to support joint CPU/GPU execution of an application.[1]

---

[1] See Chapter 2 for more background on the evolution of GPU computing and the creation of CUDA.

It is also important to note that performance is not the only decision factor when application developers choose the processors for running their applications. Several other factors can be even more important. First and foremost, the processors of choice must have a very large presence in the marketplace, referred to as the installation base of the processor. The reason is very simple. The cost of software development is best justified by a very large customer population. Applications that run on a processor with a small market presence will not have a large customer base. This has been a major problem with traditional parallel computing systems that have negligible market presence compared to general-purpose microprocessors. Only a few elite applications funded by government and large corporations have been successfully developed on these traditional parallel computing systems. This has changed with the advent of many-core GPUs. Due to their popularity in the PC market, hundreds of millions of GPUs have been sold. Virtually all PCs have GPUs in them. The G80 processors and their successors have shipped more than 200 million units to date. This is the first time that massively parallel computing has been feasible with a mass-market product. Such a large market presence has made these GPUs economically attractive for application developers.

Other important decision factors are practical form factors and easy accessibility. Until 2006, parallel software applications usually ran on data-center servers or departmental clusters, but such execution environments tend to limit the use of these applications. For example, in an application such as medical imaging, it is fine to publish a paper based on a 64-node cluster machine, but actual clinical applications on magnetic resonance imaging (MRI) machines are all based on some combination of a PC and special hardware accelerators. The simple reason is that manufacturers such as GE and Siemens cannot sell MRIs with racks of clusters to clinical settings, but this is common in academic departmental settings. In fact, the National Institutes of Health (NIH) refused to fund parallel programming projects for some time; they felt that the impact of parallel software would be limited because huge cluster-based machines would not work in the clinical setting. Today, GE ships MRI products with GPUs, and NIH funds research using GPU computing.

Yet another important consideration in selecting a processor for executing numeric computing applications is the support for the Institute of Electrical and Electronics Engineers (IEEE) floating-point standard. The standard makes it possible to have predictable results across processors from different vendors. While support for the IEEE floating-point standard was not strong in early GPUs, this has also changed for new generations of GPUs since the introduction of the G80. As we will discuss in Chapter 7, GPU support for the IEEE floating-point standard has become comparable to that of the CPUs. As a result, one can expect that more numerical applications will be ported to GPUs and yield comparable values as the CPUs. Today, a major remaining issue is that the floating-point arithmetic units of the GPUs are primarily single precision. Applications that truly require double-precision floating point were not suitable for GPU execution; however, this has changed with the recent GPUs, whose double-precision execution speed approaches about half that of single precision, a level that high-end CPU cores achieve. This makes the GPUs suitable for even more numerical applications.

Until 2006, graphics chips were very difficult to use because programmers had to use the equivalent of graphic application programming interface (API) functions to access the processor cores, meaning that OpenGL® or Direct3D® techniques were needed to program these chips. This technique was called GPGPU, short for general-purpose programming using a graphics processing unit. Even with a higher level programming environment, the underlying code is still limited by the APIs. These APIs limit the kinds of applications that one can actually write for these chips. That's why only a few people could master the skills necessary to use these chips to achieve performance for a limited number of applications; consequently, it did not become a widespread programming phenomenon. Nonetheless, this technology was sufficiently exciting to inspire some heroic efforts and excellent results.

Everything changed in 2007 with the release of CUDA [NVIDIA 2007]. NVIDIA actually devoted silicon area to facilitate the ease of parallel programming, so this did not represent a change in software alone; additional hardware was added to the chip. In the G80 and its successor chips for parallel computing, CUDA programs no longer go through the graphics interface at all. Instead, a new general-purpose parallel programming interface on the silicon chip serves the requests of CUDA programs. Moreover, all of the other software layers were redone, as well, so the programmers can use the familiar C/C++ programming tools. Some of our students tried to do their lab assignments using the old OpenGL-based programming interface, and their experience helped them to greatly appreciate the improvements that eliminated the need for using the graphics APIs for computing applications.

1.2 ARCHITECTURE OF A MODERN GPU

Figure 1.3 shows the architecture of a typical CUDA-capable GPU. It is organized into an array of highly threaded streaming multiprocessors (SMs). In Figure 1.3, two SMs form a building block; however, the number of SMs in a building block can vary from one generation of CUDA GPUs to another generation. Also, each SM in Figure 1.3 has a number of streaming processors (SPs) that share control logic and instruction cache. Each GPU currently comes with up to 4 gigabytes of graphics double data rate (GDDR) DRAM, referred to as *global memory* in Figure 1.3. These GDDR DRAMs differ from the system DRAMs on the CPU motherboard in that they are essentially the frame buffer memory that is used for graphics. For graphics applications, they hold video images, and texture information for three-dimensional (3D) rendering, but for computing they function as very-high-bandwidth, off-chip memory, though with somewhat more latency than typical system memory. For massively parallel applications, the higher bandwidth makes up for the longer latency.

The G80 that introduced the CUDA architecture had 86.4 GB/s of memory bandwidth, plus an 8-GB/s communication bandwidth with the CPU. A CUDA application can transfer data from the system memory at 4 GB/s and at the same time upload data back to the system memory at 4 GB/s. Altogether, there is a combined total of 8 GB/s. The communication bandwidth is much lower than the memory bandwidth and may seem like a limitation; however, the PCI Express® bandwidth is comparable to the CPU front-side bus bandwidth to the system memory, so it's really not the limitation it would seem at first. The communication bandwidth is also expected to grow as the CPU bus bandwidth of the system memory grows in the future.

The massively parallel G80 chip has 128 SPs (16 SMs, each with 8 SPs). Each SP has a multiply–add (MAD) unit and an additional multiply unit. With 128 SPs, that's a total of over 500 gigaflops. In addition, special-function units perform floating-point functions such as square root (SQRT), as well as transcendental functions. With 240 SPs, the GT200 exceeds 1 teraflops. Because each SP is massively threaded, it can run thousands of threads per application. A good application typically runs 5000–12,000 threads simultaneously on this chip. For those who are used to simultaneous multithreading, note that Intel CPUs support 2 or 4 threads, depending on the machine model, per core. The G80 chip supports up to 768 threads per SM, which sums up to about 12,000 threads for this chip. The more recent GT200 supports 1024 threads per SM and up to about 30,000 threads

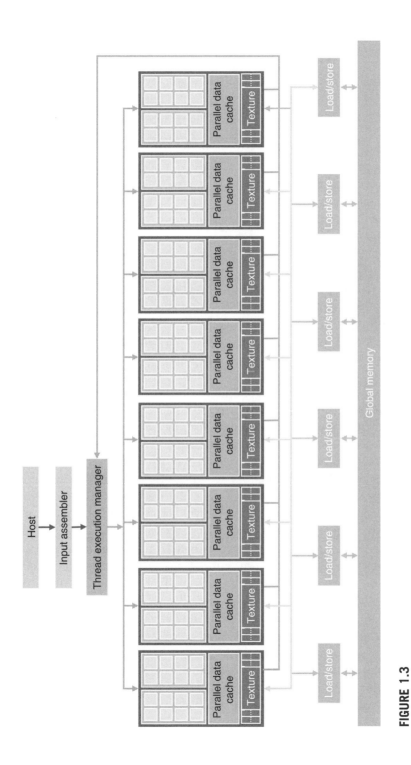

FIGURE 1.3

Architecture of a CUDA-capable GPU.

for the chip. Thus, the level of parallelism supported by GPU hardware is increasing quickly. It is very important to strive for such levels of parallelism when developing GPU parallel computing applications.

1.3 WHY MORE SPEED OR PARALLELISM?

As we stated in Section 1.1, the main motivation for massively parallel programming is for applications to enjoy a continued increase in speed in future hardware generations. One might ask why applications will continue to demand increased speed. Many applications that we have today seem to be running quite fast enough. As we will discuss in the case study chapters, when an application is suitable for parallel execution, a good implementation on a GPU can achieve more than 100 times ($100\times$) speedup over sequential execution. If the application includes what we call *data parallelism*, it is often a simple task to achieve a $10\times$ speedup with just a few hours of work. For anything beyond that, we invite you to keep reading!

Despite the myriad computing applications in today's world, many exciting mass-market applications of the future will be what we currently consider to be *supercomputing applications*, or *superapplications*. For example, the biology research community is moving more and more into the molecular level. Microscopes, arguably the most important instrument in molecular biology, used to rely on optics or electronic instrumentation, but there are limitations to the molecular-level observations that we can make with these instruments. These limitations can be effectively addressed by incorporating a computational model to simulate the underlying molecular activities with boundary conditions set by traditional instrumentation. From the simulation we can measure even more details and test more hypotheses than can ever be imagined with traditional instrumentation alone. These simulations will continue to benefit from the increasing computing speed in the foreseeable future in terms of the size of the biological system that can be modeled and the length of reaction time that can be simulated within a tolerable response time. These enhancements will have tremendous implications with regard to science and medicine.

For applications such as video and audio coding and manipulation, consider our satisfaction with digital high-definition television (HDTV) versus older National Television System Committee (NTSC) television. Once we experience the level of details offered by HDTV, it is very hard to go back to older technology. But, consider all the processing that is necessary for that HDTV. It is a very parallel process, as are 3D imaging and visualization. In the future, new functionalities such as view synthesis and high-resolution display of low-resolution videos will demand that televisions have more computing power.

Among the benefits offered by greater computing speed are much better user interfaces. Consider the Apple® iPhone® interfaces; the user enjoys a much more natural interface with the touch screen compared to other cell phone devices, even though the iPhone has a limited-size window. Undoubtedly, future versions of these devices will incorporate higher definition, three-dimensional perspectives, voice and computer vision based interfaces, requiring even more computing speed.

Similar developments are underway in consumer electronic gaming. Imagine driving a car in a game today; the game is, in fact, simply a prearranged set of scenes. If your car bumps into an obstacle, the course of your vehicle does not change; only the game score changes. Your wheels are not bent or damaged, and it is no more difficult to drive, regardless of whether you bumped your wheels or even lost a wheel. With increased computing speed, the games can be based on dynamic simulation rather than prearranged scenes. We can expect to see more of these realistic effects in the future—accidents will damage your wheels, and your online driving experience will be much more realistic. Realistic modeling and simulation of physics effects are known to demand large amounts of computing power.

All of the new applications that we mentioned involve simulating a concurrent world in different ways and at different levels, with tremendous amounts of data being processed. And, with this huge quantity of data, much of the computation can be done on different parts of the data in parallel, although they will have to be reconciled at some point. Techniques for doing so are well known to those who work with such applications on a regular basis. Thus, various granularities of parallelism do exist, but the programming model must not hinder parallel implementation, and the data delivery must be properly managed. CUDA includes such a programming model along with hardware support that facilitates parallel implementation. We aim to teach application developers the fundamental techniques for managing parallel execution and delivering data.

How many times speedup can be expected from parallelizing these super-application? It depends on the portion of the application that can be parallelized. If the percentage of time spent in the part that can be parallelized is 30%, a 100× speedup of the parallel portion will reduce the execution time by 29.7%. The speedup for the entire application will be only 1.4×. In fact, even an infinite amount of speedup in the parallel portion can only slash less 30% off execution time, achieving no more than 1.43× speedup.

On the other hand, if 99% of the execution time is in the parallel portion, a 100× speedup will reduce the application execution to 1.99% of the original time. This gives the entire application a 50× speedup; therefore, it is very important that an application has the vast majority of its execution in the parallel portion for a massively parallel processor to effectively speedup its execution.

Researchers have achieved speedups of more than 100× for some applications; however, this is typically achieved only after extensive optimization and tuning after the algorithms have been enhanced so more than 99.9% of the application execution time is in parallel execution. In general, straightforward parallelization of applications often saturates the memory (DRAM) bandwidth, resulting in only about a 10× speedup. The trick is to figure out how to get around memory bandwidth limitations, which involves doing one of many transformations to utilize specialized GPU on-chip memories to drastically reduce the number of accesses to the DRAM. One must, however, further optimize the code to get around limitations such as limited on-chip memory capacity. An important goal of this book is to help you to fully understand these optimizations and become skilled in them.

Keep in mind that the level of speedup achieved over CPU execution can also reflect the suitability of the CPU to the application. In some applications, CPUs perform very well, making it more difficult to speed up performance using a GPU. Most applications have portions that can be much better executed by the CPU. Thus, one must give the CPU a fair chance to perform and make sure that code is written in such a way that GPUs *complement* CPU execution, thus properly exploiting the heterogeneous parallel computing capabilities of the combined CPU/GPU system. This is precisely what the CUDA programming model promotes, as we will further explain in the book.

Figure 1.4 illustrates the key parts of a typical application. Much of the code of a real application tends to be sequential. These portions are considered to be the pit area of the peach; trying to apply parallel computing techniques to these portions is like biting into the peach pit—not a good feeling! These portions are very difficult to parallelize. CPUs tend to do a very good job on these portions. The good news is that these portions, although they can take up a large portion of the code, tend to account for only a small portion of the execution time of superapplications.

Then come the meat portions of the peach. These portions are easy to parallelize, as are some early graphics applications. For example, most of today's medical imaging applications are still running on combinations of

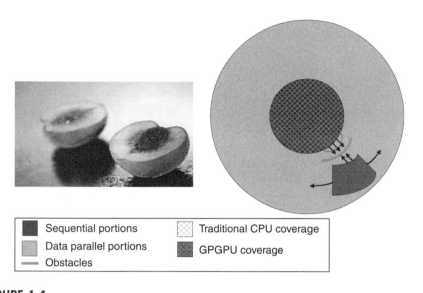

FIGURE 1.4

Coverage of sequential and parallel application portions.

microprocessor clusters and special-purpose hardware. The cost and size benefit of the GPUs can drastically improve the quality of these applications. As illustrated in Figure 1.4, early GPGPUs cover only a small portion of the meat section, which is analogous to a small portion of the most exciting applications coming in the next 10 years. As we will see, the CUDA programming model is designed to cover a much larger section of the peach meat portions of exciting applications.

1.4 PARALLEL PROGRAMMING LANGUAGES AND MODELS

Many parallel programming languages and models have been proposed in the past several decades [Mattson 2004]. The ones that are the most widely used are the Message Passing Interface (MPI) for scalable cluster computing and OpenMP™ for shared-memory multiprocessor systems. MPI is a model where computing nodes in a cluster do not share memory [MPI 2009]; all data sharing and interaction must be done through explicit message passing. MPI has been successful in the high-performance scientific computing domain. Applications written in MPI have been known to run successfully on cluster computing systems with more than 100,000 nodes. The amount of effort required to port an application into MPI, however, can be extremely high due to lack of shared memory across computing nodes. CUDA, on the other hand, provides shared memory for parallel execution in the GPU to address this difficulty. As for CPU and GPU communication, CUDA currently provides very limited shared memory capability between the CPU and the GPU. Programmers need to manage the data transfer between the CPU and GPU in a manner similar to "one-sided" message passing, a capability whose absence in MPI has been historically considered as a major weakness of MPI.

OpenMP supports shared memory, so it offers the same advantage as CUDA in programming efforts; however, it has not been able to scale beyond a couple hundred computing nodes due to thread management overheads and cache coherence hardware requirements. CUDA achieves much higher scalability with simple, low-overhead thread management and no cache coherence hardware requirements. As we will see, however, CUDA does not support as wide a range of applications as OpenMP due to these scalability tradeoffs. On the other hand, many superapplications fit well into the simple thread management model of CUDA and thus enjoy the scalability and performance.

Aspects of CUDA are similar to both MPI and OpenMP in that the programmer manages the parallel code constructs, although OpenMP compilers do more of the automation in managing parallel execution. Several ongoing research efforts aim at adding more automation of parallelism management and performance optimization to the CUDA tool chain. Developers who are experienced with MPI and OpenMP will find CUDA easy to learn. Especially, many of the performance optimization techniques are common among these models.

More recently, several major industry players, including Apple, Intel, AMD/ATI, and NVIDIA, have jointly developed a standardized programming model called OpenCL™ [Khronos 2009]. Similar to CUDA, the OpenCL programming model defines language extensions and runtime APIs to allow programmers to manage parallelism and data delivery in massively parallel processors. OpenCL is a standardized programming model in that applications developed in OpenCL can run without modification on all processors that support the OpenCL language extensions and API.

The reader might ask why the book is not based on OpenCL. The main reason is that OpenCL was still in its infancy when this book was written. The level of programming constructs in OpenCL is still at a lower level than CUDA and much more tedious to use. Also, the speed achieved in an application expressed in OpenCL is still much lower than in CUDA on the platforms that support both. Because programming massively parallel processors is motivated by speed, we expect that most who program massively parallel processors will continue to use CUDA for the foreseeable future. Finally, those who are familiar with both OpenCL and CUDA know that there is a remarkable similarity between the key features of OpenCL and CUDA; that is, a CUDA programmer should be able to learn OpenCL programming with minimal effort. We will give a more detailed analysis of these similarities later in the book.

1.5 OVERARCHING GOALS

Our primary goal is to teach you, the reader, how to program massively parallel processors to achieve high performance, and our approach will not require a great deal of hardware expertise. Someone once said that if you don't care about performance parallel programming is very easy. You can literally write a parallel program in an hour. But, we're going to dedicate many pages to materials on how to do *high-performance* parallel programming, and we believe that it will become easy once you develop the right insight and go about it the right way. In particular, we will focus on *computational thinking* techniques that will enable you to think about problems in ways that are amenable to high-performance parallel computing.

Note that hardware architecture features have constraints. High-performance parallel programming on most of the chips will require some knowledge of how the hardware actually works. It will probably take 10 more years before we can build tools and machines so most programmers can work without this knowledge. We will not be teaching computer architecture as a separate topic; instead, we will teach the essential computer architecture knowledge as part of our discussions on high-performance parallel programming techniques.

Our second goal is to teach parallel programming for correct functionality and reliability, which constitute a subtle issue in parallel computing. Those who have worked on parallel systems in the past know that achieving initial performance is not enough. The challenge is to achieve it in such a way that you can debug the code and support the users. We will show that with the CUDA programming model that focuses on data parallelism, one can achieve both high performance and high reliability in their applications.

Our third goal is achieving scalability across future hardware generations by exploring approaches to parallel programming such that future machines, which will be more and more parallel, can run your code faster than today's machines. We want to help you to master parallel programming so your programs can scale up to the level of performance of new generations of machines.

Much technical knowledge will be required to achieve these goals, so we will cover quite a few principles and patterns of parallel programming in this book. We cannot guarantee that we will cover all of them, however, so we have selected several of the most useful and well-proven techniques to cover in detail. To complement your knowledge and expertise, we include a list of recommended literature. We are now ready to give you a quick overview of the rest of the book.

1.6 ORGANIZATION OF THE BOOK

Chapter 2 reviews the history of GPU computing. It begins with a brief summary of the evolution of graphics hardware toward greater programmability and then discusses the historical GPGPU movement. Many of the current features and limitations of CUDA GPUs have their roots in these historic developments. A good understanding of these historic developments will help the reader to better understand the current state and the future trends of hardware evolution that will continue to impact the types of applications that will benefit from CUDA.

Chapter 3 introduces CUDA programming. This chapter relies on the fact that students have had previous experience with C programming. It first introduces CUDA as a simple, small extension to C that supports heterogeneous CPU/GPU joint computing and the widely used single-program, multiple-data (SPMD) parallel programming model. It then covers the thought processes involved in: (1) identifying the part of application programs to be parallelized, (2) isolating the data to be used by the parallelized code by using an API function to allocate memory on the parallel computing device, (3) using an API function to transfer data to the parallel computing device, (4) developing a kernel function that will be executed by individual threads in the parallelized part, (5) launching a kernel function for execution by parallel threads, and (6) eventually transferring the data back to the host processor with an API function call. Although the objective of Chapter 3 is to teach enough concepts of the CUDA programming model so the readers can write a simple parallel CUDA program, it actually covers several basic skills needed to develop a parallel application based on any parallel programming model. We use a running example of matrix–matrix multiplication to make this chapter concrete.

Chapters 4 through 7 are designed to give the readers more in-depth understanding of the CUDA programming model. Chapter 4 covers the thread organization and execution model required to fully understand the execution behavior of threads and basic performance concepts. Chapter 5 is dedicated to the special memories that can be used to hold CUDA variables for improved program execution speed. Chapter 6 introduces the major factors that contribute to the performance of a CUDA kernel function. Chapter 7 introduces the floating-point representation and concepts such as precision and accuracy. Although these chapters are based on CUDA, they help the readers build a foundation for parallel programming in general. We believe that humans understand best when we learn from the bottom up; that is, we must first learn the concepts in the context of a particular programming model, which provides us with a solid footing to generalize our knowledge to other programming models. As we do so, we can draw on our concrete experience from the CUDA model. An in-depth experience with the CUDA model also enables us to gain maturity, which will help us learn concepts that may not even be pertinent to the CUDA model.

Chapters 8 and 9 are case studies of two real applications, which take the readers through the thought processes of parallelizing and optimizing their applications for significant speedups. For each application, we begin by identifying alternative ways of formulating the basic structure of the parallel execution and follow up with reasoning about the advantages and disadvantages of each alternative. We then go through the steps of code transformation necessary to achieve high performance. These two chapters help the readers put all the materials from the previous chapters together and prepare for their own application development projects.

Chapter 10 generalizes the parallel programming techniques into problem decomposition principles, algorithm strategies, and computational thinking. It does so by covering the concept of organizing the computation tasks of a program so they can be done in parallel. We begin by discussing the translational process of organizing abstract scientific concepts into computational tasks, an important first step in producing quality application software, serial or parallel. The chapter then addresses parallel algorithm structures and their effects on application performance, which is grounded in the performance tuning experience with CUDA. The chapter concludes with a treatment of parallel programming styles and models, allowing the readers to place their knowledge in a wider context. With this chapter, the readers can begin to generalize from the SPMD programming style to other styles of parallel programming, such as loop parallelism in OpenMP and fork–join in p-thread programming. Although we do not go into these alternative parallel programming styles, we expect that the readers will be able to learn to program in any of them with the foundation gained in this book.

Chapter 11 introduces the OpenCL programming model from a CUDA programmer's perspective. The reader will find OpenCL to be extremely similar to CUDA. The most important difference arises from OpenCL's use of API functions to implement functionalities such as kernel launching and thread identification. The use of API functions makes OpenCL more tedious to use; nevertheless, a CUDA programmer has all the knowledge and skills necessary to understand and write OpenCL programs. In fact, we believe that the best way to teach OpenCL programming is to teach CUDA first. We demonstrate this with a chapter that relates all major OpenCL features to their corresponding CUDA features. We also illustrate the use of these features by adapting our simple CUDA examples into OpenCL.

Chapter 12 offers some concluding remarks and an outlook for the future of massively parallel programming. We revisit our goals and summarize how the chapters fit together to help achieve the goals. We then present a brief survey of the major trends in the architecture of massively parallel processors and how these trends will likely impact parallel programming in the future. We conclude with a prediction that these fast advances in massively parallel computing will make it one of the most exciting areas in the coming decade.

References and Further Reading

Hwu, W. W., Keutzer, K., & Mattson, T. (2008). The concurrency challenge. *IEEE Design and Test of Computers*, July/August, 312–320.

Khronos Group. (2009). *The OpenCL Specification Version 1.0*. Beaverton, OR: Khronos Group. (http://www.khronos.org/registry/cl/specs/opencl-1.0.29.pdf).

Mattson, T. G., Sanders, B. A., & Massingill, B. L. (2004). *Patterns of parallel programming*. Upper Saddle River, NJ: Addison-Wesley.

Message Passing Interface Forum. (2009). *MPI: A Message-Passing Interface Standard, Version 2.2*. Knoxville: University of Tennessee. (http://www.mpi-forum.org/docs/mpi-2.2/mpi22-report.pdf).

NVIDIA. (2007). *CUDA programming guide*. Santa Clara, CA: NVIDIA Corp.

OpenMP Architecture Review Board. (2005). *OpenMP Application Program Interface*. (http://www.openmp.org/mp-documents/spec25.pdf).

Sutter, H., & Larus, J. (2005). Software and the concurrency revolution. *ACM Queue*, *3*(7), 54–62.

von Neumann, J. (1945). *First draft of a report on the EDVAC*. Contract No. W-670-ORD-4926, U.S. Army Ordnance Department and University of Pennsylvania (reproduced in Goldstine H. H. (Ed.), (1972). *The computer: From Pascal to von Neumann*. Princeton, NJ: Princeton University Press).

Wing, J. (2006). Computational thinking. *Communications of the ACM*, *49*(3), 33–35.

History of GPU Computing

2

CHAPTER CONTENTS

INTRODUCTION

To CUDA™ and OpenCL™ programmers, graphics processing units (GPUs) are massively parallel numeric computing processors programmed in C with extensions. One needs not understand graphics algorithms or terminology in order to be able to program these processors. However, understanding the graphics heritage of these processors illuminates the strengths and weaknesses of these processors with respect to major computational patterns. In particular, the history helps to clarify the rationale behind major architectural design decisions of modern programmable GPUs: massive multithreading, relatively small cache memories compared to central processing units (CPUs), and bandwidth-centric memory interface design. Insights into the historical developments will also likely give the reader the context needed to project the future evolution of GPUs as computing devices.

2.1 EVOLUTION OF GRAPHICS PIPELINES

Three-dimensional (3D) graphics pipeline hardware evolved from the large expensive systems of the early 1980s to small workstations and then PC accelerators in the mid- to late 1990s. During this period, the performance-leading graphics subsystems decreased in price from $50,000 to $200. During the same period, the performance increased from 50 million pixels per second to 1 billion pixels per second and from 100,000 vertices per second to 10 million vertices per second. Although these advancements have much to do with the relentlessly shrinking feature sizes of semiconductor devices, they also have resulted from innovations in graphics algorithms and hardware design that have shaped the native hardware capabilities of modern GPUs.

The remarkable advancement of graphics hardware performance has been driven by the market demand for high-quality, real-time graphics in computer applications. In an electronic gaming application, for example, one needs to render ever more complex scenes at an ever-increasing resolution at a rate of 60 frames per second. The net result is that over the last 30 years graphics architecture has evolved from being a simple pipeline for drawing wire-frame diagrams to a highly parallel design consisting of several deep parallel pipelines capable of rendering the complex interactive imagery of 3D scenes. Concurrently, many of the hardware functionalities involved became far more sophisticated and user programmable.

2.1.1 The Era of Fixed-Function Graphics Pipelines

From the early 1980s to the late 1990s, the leading performance graphics hardware was fixed-function pipelines that were configurable but not programmable. In that same era, major graphics application programming interface (API) libraries became popular. An API is a standardized layer of software (i.e., a collection of library functions) that allows applications (such as games) to use software or hardware services and functionality. An API, for example, can allow a game to send commands to a graphics processing unit to draw objects on a display. One such API is DirectX™, Microsoft's proprietary API for media functionality. The Direct3D® component of DirectX™ provides interface functions to graphics processors. The other major API is OpenGL®, an open standard API supported by multiple vendors and popular in professional workstation applications. This era of fixed-function graphics pipeline roughly corresponds to the first seven generations of DirectX™.

Figure 2.1 shows an example of fixed-function graphics pipeline in early NVIDIA® GeForce® GPUs. The host interface receives graphics commands and data from the CPU. The commands are typically given by application programs by calling an API function. The host interface typically contains a specialized direct memory access (DMA) hardware to efficiently transfer

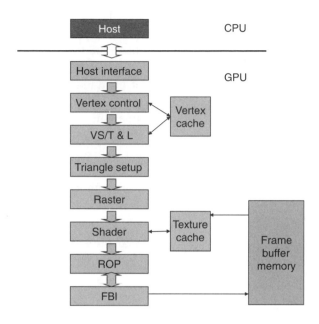

FIGURE 2.1

A fixed-function NVIDIA GeForce graphics pipeline.

bulk data to and from the host system memory to the graphics pipeline. The host interface also communicates back the status and result data of executing the commands.

Before we describe the other stages of the pipeline, we should clarify that the term *vertex* usually refers to the corner of a polygon. The GeForce graphics pipeline is designed to render triangles, so the term *vertex* is typically used in this case to refer to the corners of a triangle. The surface of an object is drawn as a collection of triangles. The finer the sizes of the triangles are, the better the quality of the picture typically becomes. The vertex control stage in Figure 2.1 receives parameterized triangle data from the CPU. The vertex control stage then converts the triangle data into a form that the hardware understands and places the prepared data into the vertex cache.

The vertex shading, transform, and lighting (VS/T&L) stage in Figure 2.1 transforms vertices and assigns per-vertex values (e.g., colors, normals, texture coordinates, tangents). The shading is done by the pixel shader hardware. The vertex shader can assign a color to each vertex, but color is not applied to triangle pixels until later. The triangle setup stage further creates edge equations that are used to interpolate colors and other per-vertex data (such as texture coordinates) across the pixels touched by the triangle. The raster stage determines which pixels are contained in each triangle. For each of these pixels, the raster stage interpolates per-vertex values necessary for shading the pixel, including the color, position, and texture position that will be shaded (painted) on the pixel.

The shader stage in Figure 2.1 determines the final color of each pixel. This can be generated as a combined effect of many techniques: interpolation of vertex colors, texture mapping, per-pixel lighting mathematics, reflections, and more. Many effects that make the rendered images more realistic are incorporated in the shader stage. Figure 2.2 illustrates texture mapping, one of the shader stage functionalities. It shows an example in which a world map texture is mapped onto a sphere object. Note that the sphere object is described as a large collection of triangles. Although the shader stage must perform only a small number of coordinate transform

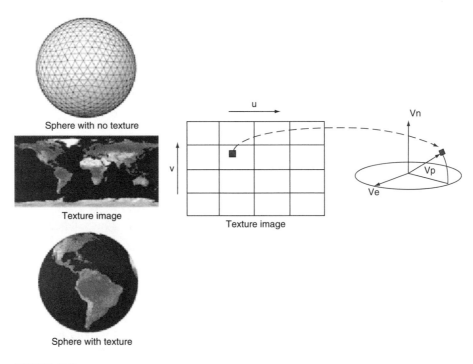

FIGURE 2.2

Texture mapping example: painting a world map texture image onto a globe object.

calculations to identify the exact coordinates of the texture point that will be painted on a point in one of the triangles that describes the sphere object, the sheer number of pixels covered by the image requires the shader stage to perform a very large number of coordinate transforms for each frame.

The raster operation (ROP) stage in Figure 2.2 performs the final raster operations on the pixels. It performs color raster operations that blend the color of overlapping/adjacent objects for transparency and antialiasing effects. It also determines the visible objects for a given viewpoint and discards the occluded pixels. A pixel becomes occluded when it is blocked by pixels from other objects according to the given view point.

Figure 2.3 illustrates antialiasing, one of the ROP stage operations. Notice the three adjacent triangles with a black background. In the aliased output, each pixel assumes the color of one of the objects or the background. The limited resolution makes the edges look crooked and the shapes of the objects distorted. The problem is that many pixels are partly in one object and partly in another object or the background. Forcing these pixels to assume the color of one of the objects introduces distortion into the edges of the objects. The antialiasing operation gives each pixel a color that is blended, or linearly combined, from the colors of all the objects and background that partially overlap the pixel. The contribution of each object to the color of the pixel is the amount of the pixel that the object overlaps.

Finally, the frame buffer interface (FBI) stage in Figure 2.1 manages memory reads from and writes to the display frame buffer memory. For high-resolution displays, there is a very high bandwidth requirement in

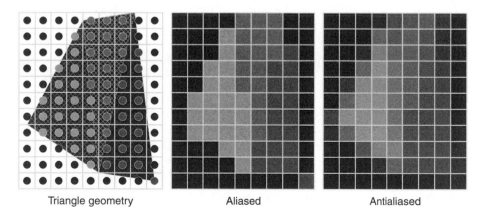

| Triangle geometry | Aliased | Antialiased |

FIGURE 2.3

Example of antialiasing operations.

accessing the frame buffer. Such bandwidth is achieved by two strategies. One is that graphics pipelines typically use special memory designs that provide higher bandwidth than the system memories. Second, the FBI simultaneously manages multiple memory channels that connect to multiple memory banks. The combined bandwidth improvement of multiple channels and special memory structures gives the frame buffers much higher bandwidth than their contemporaneous system memories. Such high memory bandwidth has continued to this day and has become a distinguishing feature of modern GPU design.

For two decades, each generation of hardware and its corresponding generation of API brought incremental improvements to the various stages of the graphics pipeline. Although each generation introduced additional hardware resources and configurability to the pipeline stages, developers were growing more sophisticated and asking for more new features than could be reasonably offered as built-in fixed functions. The obvious next step was to make some of these graphics pipeline stages into programmable processors.

2.1.2 Evolution of Programmable Real-Time Graphics

In 2001, the NVIDIA GeForce 3 took the first step toward achieving true general shader programmability. It exposed the application developer to what had been the private internal instruction set of the floating-point vertex engine (VS/T&L stage). This coincided with the release of Microsoft's DirectX 8 and OpenGL vertex shader extensions. Later GPUs, at the time of DirectX 9, extended general programmability and floating-point capability to the pixel shader stage and made texture accessible from the vertex shader stage. The ATI Radeon™ 9700, introduced in 2002, featured a programmable 24-bit floating-point pixel shader processor programmed with DirectX 9 and OpenGL. The GeForce FX added 32-bit floating-point pixel processors. These programmable pixel shader processors were part of a general trend toward unifying the functionality of the different stages as seen by the application programmer. The GeForce 6800 and 7800 series were built with separate processor designs dedicated to vertex and pixel processing. The XBox® 360 introduced an early unified processor GPU in 2005, allowing vertex and pixel shaders to execute on the same processor.

In graphics pipelines, certain stages do a great deal of floating-point arithmetic on completely independent data, such as transforming the positions of triangle vertices or generating pixel colors. This *data independence* as the dominating application characteristic is a key difference between the design assumption for GPUs and CPUs. A single frame, rendered in 1/60th of a second, might have a million triangles and 6 million pixels. The opportunity to use hardware parallelism to exploit this data independence is tremendous.

The specific functions executed at a few graphics pipeline stages vary with rendering algorithms. Such variation has motivated the hardware designers to make those pipeline stages programmable. Two particular programmable stages stand out: the vertex shader and the pixel shader. Vertex shader programs map the positions of triangle vertices onto the screen, altering their position, color, or orientation. Typically, a vertex shader thread reads a floating-point (x, y, z, w) vertex position and computes a floating-point (x, y, z) screen position. Geometry shader programs operate on primitives defined by multiple vertices, changing them or generating additional primitives. Vertex shader programs and geometry shader programs execute on the vertex shader (VS/T&L) stage of the graphics pipeline.

A shader program calculates the floating-point red, green, blue, alpha (RGBA) color contribution to the rendered image at its pixel sample (x, y) image position. These programs execute on the shader stage of the graphics pipeline. For all three types of graphics shader programs, program instances can be run in parallel, because each works on independent data, produces independent results, and has no side effects. This property has motivated the design of the programmable pipeline stages into massively parallel processors.

Figure 2.4 shows an example of a programmable pipeline that employs a vertex processor and a fragment (pixel) processor. The programmable vertex processor executes the programs designated to the vertex shader stage, and the programmable fragment processor executes the programs designated to the (pixel) shader stage. Between these programmable graphics pipeline stages are dozens of fixed-function stages that perform well-defined tasks far more efficiently than a programmable processor could and which would benefit far less from programmability. For example, between the vertex processing stage and the pixel (fragment) processing stage is a *rasterizer* (rasterization and interpolation), a complex state machine that determines exactly which pixels (and portions thereof) lie within each geometric primitive's boundaries. Together, the mix of programmable and fixed-function stages is engineered to balance extreme performance with user control over the rendering algorithms.

Common rendering algorithms perform a single pass over input primitives and access other memory resources in a highly coherent manner. That is, these algorithms tend to simultaneously access contiguous memory locations, such as all triangles or all pixels in a neighborhood. As a result, these algorithms exhibit excellent efficiency in memory bandwidth utilization

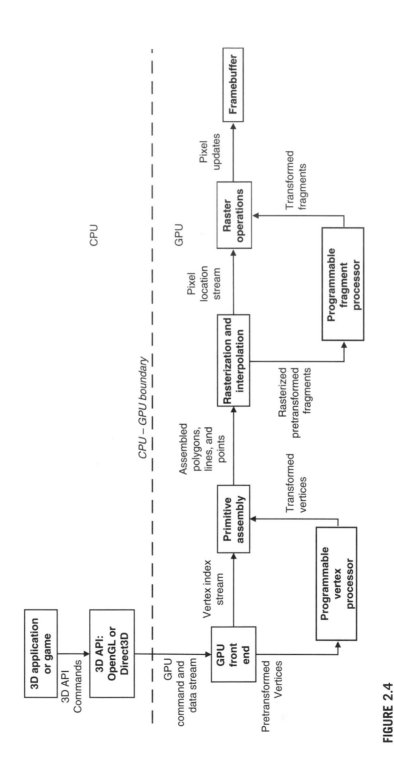

FIGURE 2.4

Example of a separate vertex processor and fragment processor in a programmable graphics pipeline.

and are largely insensitive to memory latency. Combined with a pixel shader workload that is usually compute limited, these characteristics have guided GPUs along a different evolutionary path than CPUs. In particular, whereas the CPU die area is dominated by cache memories, GPUs are dominated by floating-point datapath and fixed-function logic. GPU memory interfaces emphasize bandwidth over latency (as latency can be readily hidden by massively parallel execution); indeed, bandwidth is typically many times higher than that for a CPU, exceeding 100 GB/s in more recent designs.

2.1.3 Unified Graphics and Computing Processors

Introduced in 2006, the GeForce 8800 GPU mapped the separate programmable graphics stages to an array of unified processors; the logical graphics pipeline is physically a recirculating path that visits these processors three times, with much fixed-function graphics logic between visits. This is illustrated in Figure 2.5. The unified processor array allows dynamic partitioning of the array to vertex shading, geometry processing, and pixel processing. Because different rendering algorithms present wildly different loads among the three programmable stages, this unification allows the same pool of execution resources to be dynamically allocated to different pipeline stages and achieve better load balance.

The GeForce 8800 hardware corresponds to the DirectX 10 API generation. By the DirectX 10 generation, the functionality of vertex and pixel shaders had been made identical to the programmer, and a new logical stage was introduced, the geometry shader, to process all the vertices of a primitive rather than vertices in isolation. The GeForce 8800 was designed with DirectX 10 in mind. Developers were coming up with more sophisticated shading algorithms, and this motivated a sharp increase in the available shader operation rate, particularly floating-point operations. NVIDIA pursued a processor design with higher operating clock frequency than what was allowed by standard-cell methodologies in order to deliver the desired operation throughput as area efficiently as possible. High-clock-speed design requires substantially greater engineering effort, thus favoring the design of one processor array rather than two (or three, given the new geometry stage). It became worthwhile to take on the engineering challenges of a unified processor—load balancing and recirculation of a logical pipeline onto threads of the processor array—while seeking the benefits of one processor design. Such design paved the way for using the programmable GPU processor array for general numeric computing.

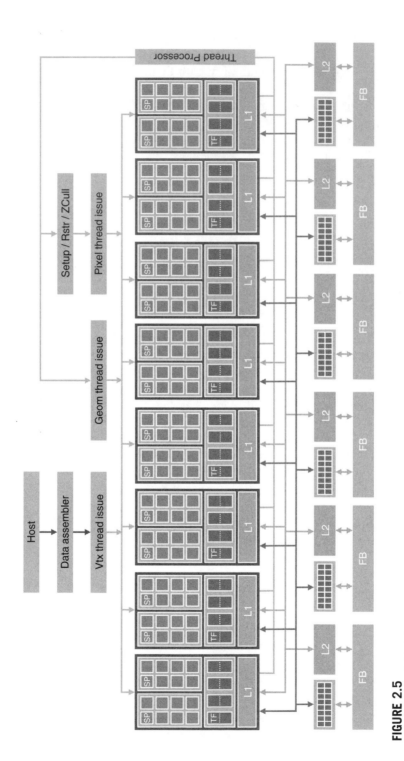

FIGURE 2.5

Unified programmable processor array of the GeForce 8800 GTX graphics pipeline.

2.1.4 **GPGPU: An Intermediate Step**

While the GPU hardware designs evolved toward more unified processors, they increasingly resembled high-performance parallel computers. As DirectX 9-capable GPUs became available, some researchers took notice of the raw performance growth path of GPUs and began to explore the use of GPUs to solve compute-intensive science and engineering problems; however, DirectX 9 GPUs had been designed only to match the features required by the graphics APIs. To access the computational resources, a programmer had to cast his or her problem into native graphics operations so the computation could be launched through OpenGL or DirectX API calls. To run many simultaneous instances of a compute function, for example, the computation had to be written as a pixel shader. The collection of input data had to be stored in texture images and issued to the GPU by submitting triangles (with clipping to a rectangle shape if that was what was desired). The output had to be cast as a set of pixels generated from the raster operations.

The fact that the GPU processor array and frame buffer memory interface were designed to process graphics data proved too restrictive for general numeric applications. In particular, the output data of the shader programs are single pixels whose memory locations have been predetermined; thus, the graphics processor array is designed with very restricted memory reading and writing capability. Figure 2.6 illustrates the limited

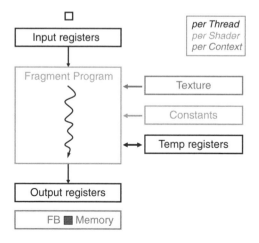

FIGURE 2.6

The restricted input and output capabilities of a shader programming model.

memory access capability of early programmable shader processor arrays; shader programmers needed to use texture to access arbitrary memory locations for their input data. More importantly, shaders did not have the means to perform writes with calculated memory addresses, referred to as *scatter operations*, to memory. The only way to write a result to memory was to emit it as a pixel color value, and configure the frame buffer operation stage to write (or blend, if desired) the result to a two-dimensional frame buffer.

Furthermore, the only way to get a result from one pass of computation to the next was to write all parallel results to a pixel frame buffer, then use that frame buffer as a texture map input to the pixel fragment shader of the next stage of the computation. There was also no user-defined data types; most data had to be stored in one-, two-, or four-component vector arrays. Mapping general computations to a GPU in this era was quite awkward. Nevertheless, intrepid researchers demonstrated a handful of useful applications with painstaking efforts. This field was called "GPGPU," for general-purpose computing on GPUs.

2.2 GPU COMPUTING

While developing the Tesla™ GPU architecture, NVIDIA realized its potential usefulness would be much greater if programmers could think of the GPU like a processor. NVIDIA selected a programming approach in which programmers would explicitly declare the data-parallel aspects of their workload.

For the DirectX™ 10 generation of graphics, NVIDIA had already begun work on a high-efficiency floating-point and integer processor that could run a variety of simultaneous workloads to support the logical graphics pipeline. The designers of the Tesla GPU architecture took another step. The shader processors became fully programmable processors with large instruction memory, instruction cache, and instruction sequencing control logic. The cost of these additional hardware resources was reduced by having multiple shader processors to share their instruction cache and instruction sequencing control logic. This design style works well with graphics applications because the same shader program needs to be applied to a massive number of vertices or pixels. NVIDIA added memory load and store instructions with random byte addressing capability to support the requirements of compiled C programs. To nongraphics application programmers, the Tesla GPU architecture introduced a more generic parallel programming model with a hierarchy of parallel threads, barrier synchronization, and atomic operations to dispatch and manage highly parallel computing work. NVIDIA also developed the CUDA C/C++ compiler, libraries, and runtime software to enable programmers to readily access the new data-parallel computation model and develop applications. Programmers no longer need to use the graphics API to access the GPU parallel computing capabilities. The G80 chip was based on the Tesla architecture and was used in the GeForce 8800 GTX, which was followed later by G92 and GT200.

2.2.1 Scalable GPUs

Scalability has been an attractive feature of graphics systems from the beginning. In the early days, workstation graphics systems gave customers a choice in pixel horsepower by varying the number of pixel processor circuit boards installed. Prior to the mid-1990s, PC graphics scaling was almost nonexistent. There was one option: the VGA controller. As 3D-capable accelerators began to appear, there was room in the market for a range of offerings. In 1998, 3dfx introduced multiboard scaling with their original Scan Line Interleave (SLI) on their Voodoo2, which held the performance crown for its time. Also in 1998, NVIDIA introduced distinct products as variants on a single architecture with Riva TNT Ultra (high-performance) and Vanta (low-cost), first by speed binning and packaging, then with separate chip designs (GeForce 2 GTS and GeForce 2 MX). At present, for a given architecture generation, four or five separate chip designs are needed to cover the range of desktop PC performance and price points. In addition, there are separate segments in notebook and workstation systems. After acquiring 3dfx in 2001, NVIDIA continued the multi-GPU SLI concept; for example, the GeForce 6800 provides multi-GPU scalability transparently to both the programmer and the user. Functional behavior is identical across the scaling range; one application will run unchanged on any implementation of an architectural family.

By switching to the multicore trajectory, CPUs are scaling to higher transistor counts by increasing the number of nearly-constant-performance cores on a die rather than simply increasing the performance of a single core. At this writing, the industry is transitioning from quad-core to hex- and oct-core CPUs. Programmers are forced to find four- to eight-fold parallelism to fully utilize these processors. Many of them resort to coarse-grained parallelism strategies where different tasks of an application are performed in parallel. Such applications must be rewritten often to have more parallel tasks for each successive doubling of core count. In contrast, the highly multithreaded GPUs encourage the use of massive, fine-grained data parallelism in CUDA. Efficient threading support in GPUs allows applications to expose a much larger amount of parallelism than available hardware execution resources with little or no penalty. Each doubling of GPU core count provides more hardware execution resources that exploit more of the exposed parallelism for higher performance; that is, the GPU parallel programming model for graphics and parallel computing is designed for transparent and portable scalability. A graphics program or CUDA program is written once and runs on a GPU with any number of processor cores.

2.2.2 Recent Developments

Academic and industrial work on applications using CUDA has produced hundreds of examples of successful CUDA programs. Many of these programs run the application tens or hundreds of times faster than multicore CPUs are capable of running them. With the introduction of tools such as MCUDA [Stratton 2008], the parallel threads of a CUDA program can also run efficiently on a multicore CPU, although at a lower speed than on GPUs due to lower levels of floating-point execution resources. Examples of these applications include n-body simulation, molecular modeling, computational finance, and oil/gas reservoir simulation. Although many of these use single-precision floating-point arithmetic, some problems require double precision. The arrival of double-precision floating point in GPUs enabled an even broader range of applications to benefit from GPU acceleration.

For an exhaustive list and examples of current developments in applications that are accelerated by GPUs, visit CUDA Zone at http://www.nvidia.com/CUDA. For resources in developing research applications, see CUDA Research at http://www.cuda-research.org.

2.3 FUTURE TRENDS

Naturally, the number of processor cores will continue to increase in proportion to increases in available transistors as silicon processes improve. In addition, GPUs will continue to enjoy vigorous architectural evolution. Despite their demonstrated high performance on data parallel applications, GPU core processors are still of relatively simple design. More aggressive techniques will be introduced with each successive architecture to increase the actual utilization of the calculating units. Because scalable parallel computing on GPUs is still a young field, novel applications are rapidly being created. By studying them, GPU designers will discover and implement new machine optimizations. Chapter 12 provides more details of such future trends.

References and Further Reading

Akeley, K. (1993). Reality engine graphics. *Computer Graphics (SIGGRAPH 93)*, *27*, 109–116.

Akeley, K., & Jermoluk, T. (1988). High-performance polygon rendering. *Computer Graphics (SIGGRAPH 88)*, *22*(4), 239–246.

Blelloch, G. B. (1990). Prefix sums and their applications. In J. H. Reif (Ed.), *Synthesis of parallel algorithms*. San Francisco, CA: Morgan Kaufmann.

Blythe, D. (2006). The Direct3D 10 System. *ACM Transactions on Graphics*, *25* (3), 724–734.

Buck, I., Foley, T., Horn, D., Sugerman, J., Fatahlian, K., Houston, M., et al. (2004). Brooks for GPUs: Stream computing on graphics hardware. *ACM Transactions on Graphics*, *23*(3), 777–786 (http://doi.acm.org/10.1145/1186562.1015800).

Elder, G. (2002). Radeon 9700. In *Proceedings of the ACM eurographics/SIGGRAPH workshop on graphics hardware 2002* (http://www.graphicshardware.org/previous/www_2002/presentations/Hot3D-RADEON9700.ppt).

Fernando, R. (Ed.), *GPU gems: Programming techniques, tips, and tricks for real-time graphics*. Reading, MA: Addison-Wesley (http://developer.nvidia.com/object/gpu_gems_home.html).

Fernando, R., & Kilgard, M. J. (2003). *The Cg tutorial: The definitive guide to programmable real-time graphics*. Reading, MA: Addison-Wesley.

Foley, J., van Dam, A., Feiner, S., & Hughes, J. *Interactive computer graphics: Principles and practice, C edition* (2nd ed.). Reading, MA: Addison-Wesley.

Hillis, W. D., & Steele, G. L. (1986). Data parallel algorithms. *Communications of the ACM*, *29*(12), 1170–1183 (http://doi.acm.org/10.1145/7902.7903).

IEEE 754R Working Group. (2006). *Standard for floating-point arithmetic P754 (Draft)*. Piscataway, NJ: Institute of Electrical and Electronics Engineers (http://www.validlab.com/754R/drafts/archive/2006-10-04.pdf).

Industrial Light and Magic. (2003). *OpenEXR*. San Mateo, CA: Industrial Light and Magic (www.openexr.com).

Intel. (2007). *Intel 64 and IA-32 Architectures optimization reference manual*. Order No. 248966-016. Santa Clara, CA: Intel Corp. (http://www3.intel.com/design/processor/manuals/248966.pdf).

Kessenich, J., Baldwin, D., & Rost, R. (2006). *The OpenGL® shading language, Language Version 1.20*. Madison, AL: 3Dlabs, Inc. (http://www.opengl.org/documentation/specs/).

Kirk, D., & Voorhies, D. (1990). The rendering architecture of the DN10000VS. *Computer Graphics (SIGGRAPH 1990)*, *24*(4), 299–307.

Lindholm, E., Kilgard, M. J., & Moreton, H. (2001). A user-programmable vertex engine. In *Proceedings of the 28th annual ACM conference on computer graphics and interactive techniques* (pp. 149–158). Reading, MA: ACM Press/Addison-Wesley.

Lindholm, E., Nickolls, J., Oberman, S., & Montrym, J. (2008). NVIDIA Tesla: A unified graphics and computing architecture. *IEEE Micro*, 28(2), 39–55.

Microsoft. (2003). *Microsoft DirectX 9 programmable graphics pipeline.* Redmond, WA: Microsoft Press.

Microsoft. (2009). *Microsoft DirectX specification.* Redmond, WA: Microsoft Press (http://msdn.microsoft.com/directx/).

Montrym, J., Baum, D., Dignam, D., & Migdal, C. (1997). InfiniteReality: A real-time graphics system. In G. O. Owen, T. Whitted, & B. Mones-Hattal (Eds.), *Proceedings of the 24th annual ACM conference on computer graphics and interactive techniques* (pp. 293–301). Reading, MA: ACM Press/Addison-Wesley.

Montrym, J., & Moreton, H. (2005). The GeForce 6800. *IEEE Micro*, 25(2), 41–51.

Moore, G. E. (1965). Cramming more components onto integrated circuits. *Electronics*, 38(8), 114–117.

Nguyen, H. (Ed.), (2008). *GPU Gems 3.* Reading, MA: Addison-Wesley.

Nickolls, J., Buck, I., Garland, M., & Skadron, K. (2008). Scalable parallel programming with CUDA. *ACM Queue*, 6(2), 40–53.

NVIDIA. (2007a). *NVIDIA CUDA—Compute unified device architecture, programming guide, Version 1.1* (http://developer.download.nvidia.com/compute/cuda/1_1/NVIDIA_CUDA_Programming_Guide_1.1.pdf).

NVIDIA. (2007b). *NVIDIA compute—PTX: Parallel thread execution, ISA Version 1.1* (http://www.nvidia.com/object/io_1195170102263.html).

NVIDIA. (2009). *CUDA Zone* (http://www.nvidia.com/CUDA).

Nyland, L., Harris, M., & Prins, J. (2007). Fast N-body simulation with CUDA. In H. Nguyen (Ed.), *GPU Gems 3.* Reading, MA: Addison-Wesley.

Oberman, S. F., & Siu, M. Y. (2005). A high-performance area-efficient multifunction interpolator. In *Proceedings of the 17th IEEE symposium on computer arithmetic* (pp. 272–279). Cape Cod, MA.

Patterson, D. A., & Hennessy, J. L. (2004). *Computer organization and design: The hardware/software interface* (3rd ed.). San Francisco, CA: Morgan Kaufmann.

Pharr, M. (Ed.) (2005). *GPU Gems 2: Programming techniques for high-performance graphics and general-purpose computation.* Reading, MA: Addison Wesley.

Satish, N., Harris, M., & Garland, M. *Designing efficient sorting algorithms for manycore GPUs. Proc. 23rd IEEE int'l parallel & distributed processing symposium,* May 2009.

Segal, M., & Akeley, K. (2006). *The OpenGL® graphics system: A specification, Version 2.1.* Mountain View, CA: Silicon Graphics (http://www.opengl.org/documentation/specs/).

Sengupta, S., Harris, M., Zhang, Y., & Owens, J. D. (2007). Scan primitives for GPU computing. In T. Aila & M. Segal (Eds.), *Graphics hardware* (pp. 97–106). San Diego, CA: ACM Press.

Stratton, J. A., Stone, S. S., & Hwu, W. W. (2008). MCUDA: An efficient imple-
mentation of CUDA kernels for multi-core CPUs. In *Proceedings of the 21st
International Workshop on Languages and Compilers for Parallel Computing
(LCPC)*. Canada: Edmonton.

Volkov, V., & Demmel, J. (2008). *LU, QR and Cholesky factorizations using vector
capabilities of GPUs*. Technical report no. UCB/EECS-2008-49. Berkeley:
EECS Department, University of California (http://www.eecs.berkeley.edu/
Pubs/TechRpts/2008/EECS-2008-49.html).

Williams, S., Oliker, L., Vuduc, R., Shalf, J., Yelick, K., & Demmel, J. (2008).
Optimization of sparse matrix-vector multiplication on emerging multicore
platforms. In *Parallel computing—Special issue on revolutionary technologies
for acceleration of emerging petascale applications*.

Introduction to CUDA

3

CHAPTER CONTENTS

INTRODUCTION

To a CUDA™ programmer, the computing system consists of a *host*, which is a traditional central processing unit (CPU), such as an Intel® architecture microprocessor in personal computers today, and one or more *devices*, which are massively parallel processors equipped with a large number of arithmetic execution units. In modern software applications, program sections often exhibit a rich amount of data parallelism, a property allowing many arithmetic operations to be safely performed on program data structures in a simultaneous manner. The CUDA devices accelerate the execution of these applications by harvesting a large amount of data parallelism. Because data parallelism plays such an important role in CUDA, we will first discuss the concept of data parallelism before introducing the basic features of CUDA.

3.1 DATA PARALLELISM

Many software applications that process a large amount of data and thus incur long execution times on today's computers are designed to model real-world, physical phenomena. Images and video frames are snapshots of a physical world where different parts of a picture capture simultaneous, independent physical events. Rigid body physics and fluid dynamics model natural forces and movements that can be independently evaluated within small time steps. Such independent evaluation is the basis of data parallelism in these applications.

As we mentioned earlier, data parallelism refers to the program property whereby many arithmetic operations can be safely performed on the data structures in a simultaneous manner. We illustrate the concept of data parallelism with a matrix–matrix multiplication (matrix multiplication, for brevity) example in Figure 3.1. In this example, each element of the product matrix **P** is generated by performing a dot product between a row of input matrix **M** and a column of input matrix **N**. In Figure 3.1, the highlighted element of matrix **P** is generated by taking the dot product of the highlighted row of matrix **M** and the highlighted column of matrix **N**. Note that the dot product operations for computing different matrix **P** elements can be simultaneously performed. That is, none of these dot products will affect

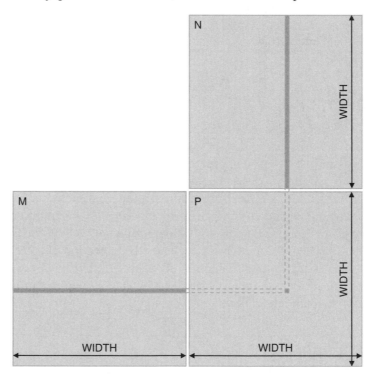

FIGURE 3.1

Data parallelism in matrix multiplication.

the results of each other. For large matrices, the number of dot products can be very large; for example, a 1000 × 1000 matrix multiplication has 1,000,000 independent dot products, each involving 1000 multiply and 1000 accumulate arithmetic operations. Therefore, matrix multiplication of large dimensions can have very large amount of data parallelism. By executing many dot products in parallel, a CUDA device can significantly accelerate the execution of the matrix multiplication over a traditional host CPU. The data parallelism in real applications is not always as simple as that in our matrix multiplication example. In a later chapter, we will discuss these more sophisticated forms of data parallelism.

3.2 CUDA PROGRAM STRUCTURE

A CUDA program consists of one or more phases that are executed on either the host (CPU) or a device such as a GPU. The phases that exhibit little or no data parallelism are implemented in host code. The phases that exhibit rich amount of data parallelism are implemented in the device code. A CUDA program is a unified source code encompassing both host and device code. The NVIDIA® C compiler (nvcc) separates the two during the compilation process. The host code is straight ANSI C code; it is further compiled with the host's standard C compilers and runs as an ordinary CPU process. The device code is written using ANSI C extended with keywords for labeling data-parallel functions, called *kernels*, and their associated data structures. The device code is typically further compiled by the nvcc and executed on a GPU device. In situations where no device is available or the kernel is more appropriately executed on a CPU, one can also choose to execute kernels on a CPU using the emulation features in CUDA software development kit (SDK) or the MCUDA tool [Stratton 2008].

The kernel functions (or, simply, kernels) typically generate a large number of threads to exploit data parallelism. In the matrix multiplication example, the entire matrix multiplication computation can be implemented as a kernel where each thread is used to compute one element of output matrix **P**. In this example, the number of threads used by the kernel is a function of the matrix dimension. For a 1000 × 1000 matrix multiplication, the kernel that uses one thread to compute one **P** element would generate 1,000,000 threads when it is invoked. It is worth noting that CUDA threads are of much lighter weight than the CPU threads. CUDA programmers can assume that these threads take very few cycles to generate and schedule due to efficient hardware support. This is in contrast with the CPU threads that typically require thousands of clock cycles to generate and schedule.

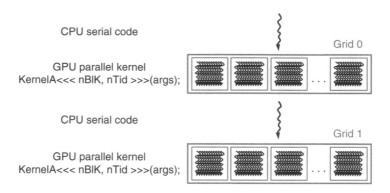

FIGURE 3.2

Execution of a CUDA program.

The execution of a typical CUDA program is illustrated in Figure 3.2. The execution starts with host (CPU) execution. When a kernel function is invoked, or *launched*, the execution is moved to a device (GPU), where a large number of threads are generated to take advantage of abundant data parallelism. All the threads that are generated by a kernel during an invocation are collectively called a *grid*. Figure 3.2 shows the execution of two grids of threads. We will discuss how these grids are organized soon. When all threads of a kernel complete their execution, the corresponding grid terminates, and the execution continues on the host until another kernel is invoked.

3.3 A MATRIX–MATRIX MULTIPLICATION EXAMPLE

At this point, it is worthwhile to introduce a code example that concretely illustrates the CUDA program structure. Figure 3.3 shows a simple main function skeleton for the matrix multiplication example. For simplicity, we assume that the matrices are square in shape, and the dimension of each matrix is specified by the parameter `Width`.

The main program first allocates the **M**, **N**, and **P** matrices in the host memory and then performs I/O to read in **M** and **N** in Part 1. These are ANSI C operations, so we are not showing the actual code for the sake of brevity. The detailed code of the main function and some user-defined ANSI C functions is shown in Appendix A. Similarly, after completing the matrix multiplication, Part 3 of the main function performs I/O to write the product matrix **P** and to free all the allocated matrices. The details of Part 3 are also shown in Appendix A. Part 2 is the main focus of our

```
int main(void) {
1.  // Allocate and initialize the matrices M, N, P
    // I/O to read the input matrices M and N
....

2.  // M * N on the device
    MatrixMultiplication(M, N, P, Width);


3.  // I/O to write the output matrix P
    // Free matrices M, N, P
...
return 0;
}
```

FIGURE 3.3

A simple main function for the matrix multiplication example.

example. It calls a function, `MatrixMultiplication()`, to perform matrix multiplication on a device.

Before we explain how to use a CUDA device to execute the matrix multiplication function, it is helpful to first review how a conventional CPU-only matrix multiplication function works. A simple version of a CPU-only matrix multiplication function is shown in Figure 3.4. The `MatrixMultiplication()` function implements a straightforward algorithm that consists of three loop levels. The innermost loop iterates over variable k and steps through one row of matrix **M** and one column of matrix **N**. The loop calculates a dot product of the row of **M** and the column of **N** and generates one element of **P**. Immediately after the innermost loop, the **P** element generated is written into the output **P** matrix.

The index used for accessing the **M** matrix in the innermost loop is `i*Width+k`. This is because the **M** matrix elements are placed into the system memory that is ultimately accessed with a linear address. That is, every location in the system memory has an address that ranges from 0 to the largest memory location. For C programs, the placement of a 2-dimensional matrix into this linear addressed memory is done according to the row-major convention, as illustrated in Figure 3.5.[1] All elements of a row are placed into consecutive memory locations. The rows are then placed one after another. Figure 3.5 shows an example where a 4×4 matrix is

---

[1]Note that FORTRAN adopts the column–major placement approach: All elements of a column are first placed into consecutive locations, and all columns are then placed in their numerical order.

```
void MatrixMultiplication(float* M, float* N, float* P, int Width)
{
   for (int i = 0; i < Width; ++i)
      for (int j = 0; j < Width; ++j) {
         float sum = 0;
         for (int k  = 0; k < Width; ++k) {
            float a = M[i * width + k];
            float b = N[k * width + j];
            sum += a * b;
         }
         P[i * Width + j] = sum;
      }
}
```

FIGURE 3.4

A simple matrix multiplication function with only host code.

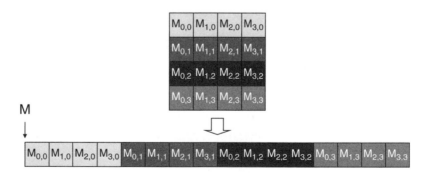

FIGURE 3.5

Placement of two-dimensional array elements into the linear address system memory.

placed into 16 consecutive locations, with all elements of row 0 first followed by the four elements of row 1, etc. Therefore, the index for an **M** element in row i and column k is `i*Width+k`. The `i*Width` term skips over all elements of the rows before row i. The k term then selects the proper element within the section for row i.

The outer two (i and j) loops in Figure 3.4 jointly iterate over all rows of **M** and all columns of **N**; each joint iteration performs a row–column dot product to generate one **P** element. Each i value identifies a row. By systematically iterating all **M** rows and all **N** columns, the function generates all **P** elements. We now have a complete matrix multiplication function that executes solely on the CPU. Note that all of the code that we have shown so far is in standard C.

Assume that a programmer now wants to port the matrix multiplication function into CUDA. A straightforward way to do so is to modify the `MatrixMultiplication()` function to move the bulk of the calculation to a CUDA device. The structure of the revised function is shown in Figure 3.6. Part 1 of the function allocates device (GPU) memory to hold copies of the **M**, **N**, and **P** matrices and copies these matrices over to the device memory. Part 2 invokes a kernel that launches parallel execution of the actual matrix multiplication on the device. Part 3 copies the product matrix **P** from the device memory back to the host memory.

Note that the revised `MatrixMultiplication()` function is essentially an outsourcing agent that ships input data to a device, activates the calculation on the device, and collects the results from the device. The agent does so in such

```
void MatrixMultiplication(float* M, float* N, float* P, int Width)
{
  int size = Width * Width * sizeof(float);
  float* Md, Nd, Pd;
  ...
1. // Allocate device memory for M, N, and P
   // copy M and N to allocated device memory locations

2. // Kernel invocation code - to have the device to perform
   // the actual matrix multiplication

3. // copy P from the device memory
   // Free device matrices
}
```

FIGURE 3.6

Outline of a revised host code `MatrixMultiplication()` that moves the matrix multiplication to a device.

a way that the main program does not have to even be aware that the matrix multiplication is now actually done on a device. The details of the revised function, as well as the way to compose the kernel function, will serve as illustrations as we introduce the basic features of the CUDA programming model.

3.4 DEVICE MEMORIES AND DATA TRANSFER

In CUDA, the host and devices have separate memory spaces. This reflects the reality that devices are typically hardware cards that come with their own dynamic random access memory (DRAM). For example, the NVIDIA T10 processor comes with up to 4 GB (billion bytes, or gigabytes) of DRAM. In order to execute a kernel on a device, the programmer needs to allocate memory on the device and transfer pertinent data from the host memory to the allocated device memory. This corresponds to Part 1 of Figure 3.6. Similarly, after device execution, the programmer needs to transfer result data from the device memory back to the host memory and free up the device memory that is no longer needed. This corresponds to Part 3 of Figure 3.6. The CUDA runtime system provides application programming interface (API) functions to perform these activities on behalf of the programmer. From this point on, we will simply say that a piece of data is transferred from host to device as shorthand for saying that the piece of data is transferred from the host memory to the device memory. The same holds for the opposite data transfer direction.

Figure 3.7 shows an overview of the CUDA device memory model for programmers to reason about the allocation, movement, and usage of the various memory types of a device. At the bottom of the figure, we see global memory and constant memory. These are the memories that the host code can transfer data to and from the device, as illustrated by the bidirectional arrows between these memories and the host. Constant memory allows read-only access by the device code and is described in Chapter 5. For now, we will focus on the use of global memory. Note that the host memory is not explicitly shown in Figure 3.7 but is assumed to be contained in the host.[2]

The CUDA memory model is supported by API functions that help CUDA programmers to manage data in these memories. Figure 3.8 shows the API functions for allocating and deallocating device global memory. The function `cudaMalloc()` can be called from the host code to allocate

---

[2]Note that we have omitted the texture memory from Figure 3.7 for simplicity. We will introduce texture memory later.

- Device code can:
    - R/W per-thread registers
    - R/W per-thread local memory
    - R/W per-block shared memory
    - R/W per-grid global memory
    - Read only per-grid constant memory

- Host code can
    - Transfer data to/from per-grid global and constant memories

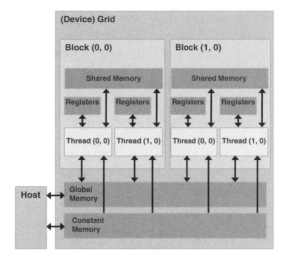

FIGURE 3.7

Overview of the CUDA device memory model.

- cudaMalloc()
    - Allocates object in the device global memory
    - Two parameters
        - **Address of a pointer** to the allocated object
        - **Size of** of allocated object in terms of bytes
- cudaFree()
    - Frees object from device global memory
        - Pointer to freed object

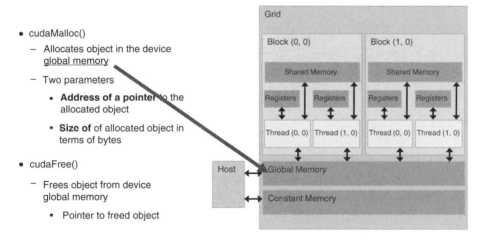

FIGURE 3.8

CUDA API functions for device global memory management.

a piece of global memory for an object. The reader should be able to notice the striking similarity between cudaMalloc() and the standard C runtime library malloc(). This is intentional; CUDA is C with minimal extensions. CUDA uses the standard C runtime library malloc() function to manage the host memory and adds cudaMalloc() as an extension to the C runtime library. By keeping the interface as close to the original C runtime libraries as possible, CUDA minimizes the time that a C programmer needs to relearn the use of these extensions.

The first parameter of the cudaMalloc() function is the address of a pointer variable that must point to the allocated object after allocation. The address of the pointer variable should be cast to (void **) because the function expects a generic pointer value; the memory allocation function is a generic function that is not restricted to any particular type of objects. This address allows the cudaMalloc() function to write the address of the allocated object into the pointer variable.[3] The second parameter of the cudaMalloc() function gives the size of the object to be allocated, in terms of bytes. The usage of this second parameter is consistent with the size parameter of the C malloc() function.

We now use a simple code example illustrating the use of cudaMalloc(). This is a continuation of the example in Figure 3.6. For clarity, we will end a pointer variable with the letter "d" to indicate that the variable is used to point to an object in the device memory space. The programmer passes the address of **Md** (i.e., &Md) as the first parameter after casting it to a void pointer; that is, **Md** is the pointer that points to the device global memory region allocated for the **M** matrix. The size of the allocated array will be Width*Width*4 (the size of a single-precision floating number). After the computation, cudaFree() is called with pointer **Md** as input to free the storage space for the **M** matrix from the device global memory:

```
float *Md
int size = Width * Width * sizeof(float);
cudaMalloc((void**)&Md, size);
...
cudaFree(Md);
```

The reader should complete Part 1 of the MatrixMultiplication() example in Figure 3.6 with similar declarations of an **Nd** and a **Pd** pointer variable as

---

[3]Note that cudaMalloc() has a different format from the C malloc() function. The C Malloc() function returns a pointer to the allocated object. It takes only one parameter that specifies the size of the allocated object. The cudaMalloc() function writes to the pointer variable whose address is given as the first parameter. As a result, the cudaMalloc() function takes two parameters. The two-parameter format of cuda-Malloc() allows it to use the return value to report any errors in the same way as other CUDA API functions.

well as their corresponding `cudaMalloc()` calls. Furthermore, Part 3 in Figure 3.6 can be completed with the `cudaFree()` calls for **Nd** and **Pd**.

Once a program has allocated device global memory for the data objects, it can request that data be transferred from host to device. This is accomplished by calling one of the CUDA API functions, `cudaMemcpy()`, for data transfer between memories. Figure 3.9 shows the API function for such a data transfer. The `cudaMemcpy()` function takes four parameters. The first parameter is a pointer to the destination location for the copy operation. The second parameter points to the source data object to be copied. The third parameter specifies the number of bytes to be copied. The fourth parameter indicates the types of memory involved in the copy: from host memory to host memory, from host memory to device memory, from device memory to host memory, and from device memory to device memory. For example, the memory copy function can be used to copy data from one location of the device memory to another location of the device memory. Please note that `cudaMemcpy()` cannot be used to copy between different GPUs in multi-GPU systems.

For the matrix multiplication example, the host code calls the `cudaMemcpy()` function to copy the **M** and **N** matrices from the host memory to the device memory before the multiplication and then to copy the **P** matrix from the device memory to the host memory after the multiplication is done.

- cudaMemcpy()

  - **Memory** data transfer
  - Requires four parameters

    - Pointer to destination
    - Pointer to source
    - Number of bytes copied

    - Type of transfer

      - Host to Host
      - Host to Device
      - Device to Host
      - Device to Device

  - Transfer is asynchronous

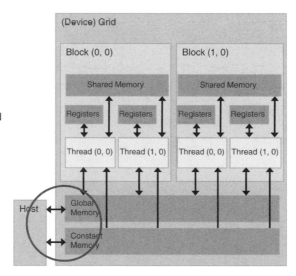

FIGURE 3.9

CUDA API functions for data transfer between memories.

Assume that **M**, **P**, **Md**, **Pd**, and size have already been set as we discussed before; the two function calls are shown below. Note that the two symbolic constants, `cudaMemcpyHostToDevice` and `cudaMemcpyDeviceToHost`, are recognized, predefined constants of the CUDA programming environment. The same function can be used to transfer data in both directions by properly ordering the source and destination pointers and using the appropriate constant for the transfer type:

```
cudaMemcpy(Md, M, size, cudaMemcpyHostToDevice);
cudaMemcpy(P, Pd, size, cudaMemcpyDeviceToHost);
```

To summarize, the main program in Figure 3.3 calls `MatrixMultiplication()`, which is also executed on the host. `MatrixMultiplication()`, as outlined in Figure 3.6, is responsible for allocating device memory, performing data transfers, and activating the kernel that performs the actual matrix multiplication. We often refer to this type of host code as the *stub function* for invoking a kernel. After the matrix multiplication, `MatrixMultiplication()` also copies result data from device to the host. We show a more fleshed out version of the `MatrixMultiplication()` function in Figure 3.10.

Compared to Figure 3.6, the revised `MatrixMultiplication()` function is complete in Part 1 and Part 3. Part 1 allocates device memory for **Md**,

```
void MatrixMultiplication(float* M, float* N, float* P, int Width)
{
   int size = Width * Width * sizeof(float);
   float* Md, Nd, Pd;

1. // Transfer M and N to device memory
   cudaMalloc((void**) &Md, size);
   cudaMemcpy(Md, M, size, cudaMemcpyHostToDevice);
   cudaMalloc((void**) &Nd, size);
   cudaMemcpy(Nd, N, size, cudaMemcpyHostToDevice);

   // Allocate P on the device
   cudaMalloc((void**) &Pd, size);

2. // Kernel invocation code - to be shown later
   ...
3. // Transfer P from device to host
   cudaMemcpy(P, Pd, size, cudaMemcpyDeviceToHost);
   // Free device matrices
   cudaFree(Md); cudaFree(Nd); cudaFree (Pd);
   }
```

FIGURE 3.10

The revised `MatrixMultiplication()` function.

Nd, and **Pd**, the device counterparts of **M**, **N**, and **P**, and transfers **M** to **Md** and **N** to **Nd**. This is accomplished with calls to the `cudaMalloc()` and `cudaMemcpy()` functions. The readers are encouraged to write their own function calls with the appropriate parameter values and compare their code with that shown in Figure 3.10. Part 2 invokes the kernel and will be described in the following text. Part 3 reads the product data from device memory to host memory so the value will be available to `main()`. This is accomplished with a call to the `cudaMemcpy()` function. It then frees **Md**, **Nd**, and **Pd** from the device memory, which is accomplished with calls to the `cudaFree()` functions.

3.5 KERNEL FUNCTIONS AND THREADING

We are now ready to discuss more about the CUDA kernel functions and the effect of invoking these kernel functions. In CUDA, a kernel function specifies the code to be executed by all threads during a parallel phase. Because all of these threads execute the same code, CUDA programming is an instance of the well-known single-program, multiple-data (SPMD) parallel programming style [Atallah 1998], a popular programming style for massively parallel computing systems.[4]

Figure 3.11 shows the kernel function for matrix multiplication. The syntax is ANSI C with some notable extensions. First, there is a CUDA-specific keyword "__global__" in front of the declaration of `MatrixMulKernel()`. This keyword indicates that the function is a kernel and that it can be called from a host functions to generate a grid of threads on a device.

In general, CUDA extends C function declarations with three qualifier keywords. The meanings of these keywords are summarized in Figure 3.12. The __global__ keyword indicates that the function being declared is a CUDA kernel function. The function will be executed on the device and can only be called from the host to generate a grid of threads on a device. We will show the host code syntax for calling a kernel function later in Figure 3.14. Besides __global__, there are two other keywords that can be used in front of a function declaration. Figure 3.12 summarizes the

---

[4]Note that SPMD is not the same as single instruction, multiple data (SIMD). In an SPMD system, the parallel processing units execute the same program on multiple parts of the data; however, these processing units do not have to be executing the same instruction at the same time. In an SIMD system, all processing units are executing the same instruction at any instant.

```
// Matrix multiplication kernel - thread specification
__global__ void MatrixMulKernel(float* Md, float* Nd, float* Pd, int Width)
{
   // 2D Thread ID
   int tx = threadIdx.x;
   int ty = threadIdx.y;

   // Pvalue stores the Pd element that is computed by the thread
   float Pvalue = 0;

   for (int k = 0; k < Width; ++k)
   {
      float Mdelement = Md[ty * Width + k];
      float Ndelement = Nd[k * Width + tx];
      Pvalue += Mdelement * Ndelement;
   }

   // Write the matrix to device memory each thread writes one element
   Pd[ty * Width + tx] = Pvalue;
}
```

FIGURE 3.11

The matrix multiplication kernel function.

	Executed on the:	Only callable from the:
__device__ float DeviceFunc()	device	device
__global__ void KernelFunc()	device	host
__host__ float HostFunc()	host	host

FIGURE 3.12

CUDA extensions to C functional declaration.

meaning of these keywords. The __device__ keyword indicates that the function being declared is a CUDA device function. A device function executes on a CUDA device and can only be called from a kernel function or another device function. Device functions can have neither recursive function calls nor indirect function calls through pointers in them. The __host__ keyword indicates that the function being declared is a CUDA host function. A host function is simply a traditional C function that executes on the host and can only be called from another host function. By default, all functions in a CUDA program are host functions if they do not have any of the CUDA keywords in their declaration. This makes sense, as many CUDA applications are ported from CPU-only execution environments. The programmer would add kernel functions and device functions during the porting process. The original functions remain as host functions. Having all functions default into host functions spares the programmer the tedious work of changing all original function declarations.

Note that one can use both __host__ and __device__ in a function declaration. This combination triggers the compilation system to generate two versions of the same function. One is executed on the host and can only be called from a host function. The other is executed on the device and can only be called from a device or kernel function. This supports a common use when the same function source code can be simply recompiled to generate a device version. Many user library functions will likely fall into this category.

Other notable extensions of ANSI C, in Figure 3.11, are the keywords threadIdx.x and threadIdx.y, which refer to the thread indices of a thread. Note that all threads execute the same kernel code. There needs to be a mechanism to allow them to distinguish themselves and direct themselves toward the particular parts of the data structure that they are designated to work on. These keywords identify predefined variables that allow a thread to access the hardware registers at runtime that provide the identifying coordinates to the thread. Different threads will see different values in their threadIdx.x and threadIdx.y variables. For simplicity, we will refer to a thread as $Thread_{threadIdx.x,\ threadIdx.y}$. Note that the coordinates reflect a multidimensional organization for the threads. We will come back to this point soon.

A quick comparison of Figure 3.4 and Figure 3.11 reveals an important insight for CUDA kernel functions and CUDA kernel invocation. The kernel function in Figure 3.11 has only one loop, which corresponds to the innermost loop in Figure 3.4. The readers should ask where the other two levels of outer loops go. The answer is that the outer two loop levels are now replaced with the grid of threads. The entire grid forms the equivalent of the two-level loop. Each thread in the grid corresponds to one of the iterations of the original two-level loop. The original loop variables i and j are now replaced with $threadIdx.x$ and $threadIdx.y$. Instead of having the loop increment the values of i and j for use in each loop iteration, the CUDA threading hardware generates all of the $threadIdx.x$ and $threadIdx.y$ values for each thread.

In Figure 3.11, each thread uses its $threadIdx.x$ and $threadIdx.y$ to identify the row of **Md** and the column of **Nd** to perform the dot product operation. It should be clear that these indices simply take over the role of variables i and j in Figure 3.8. Note that we assigned $threadIdx.x$ to the automatic C variable tx and $threadIdx.y$ to variable ty for brevity in

Figure 3.8. Each thread also uses its *threadIdx.x* and *threadIdx.y* values to select the **Pd** element that it is responsible for; for example, *Thread$_{2,3}$* will perform a dot product between column 2 of **Nd** and row 3 of **Md** and write the result into element (2,3) of **Pd**. This way, the threads collectively generate all the elements of the **Pd** matrix.

When a kernel is invoked, or *launched*, it is executed as *grid* of parallel threads. In Figure 3.13, the launch of Kernel 1 creates Grid 1. Each CUDA thread grid typically is comprised of thousands to millions of lightweight GPU threads per kernel invocation. Creating enough threads to fully utilize the hardware often requires a large amount of data parallelism; for example, each element of a large array might be computed in a separate thread.

Threads in a grid are organized into a two-level hierarchy, as illustrated in Figure 3.13. For simplicity, a small number of threads are shown in Figure 3.13. In reality, a grid will typically consist of many more threads. At the top level, each grid consists of one or more thread blocks. All blocks in a grid have the same number of threads. In Figure 3.13, Grid 1 is organized as a 2×2 array of 4 blocks. Each block has a unique two-dimensional coordinate given by the CUDA specific keywords `blockIdx.x` and `blockIdx.y`. All thread blocks must have the same number of threads organized in the same manner.

- A thread block is a batch of threads that can cooperate with each other by:

  — Synchronizing their execution
    - For hazard-free shared memory accesses

  — Efficiently sharing data through a low-latency shared memory

- Two threads from two different blocks cannot cooperate

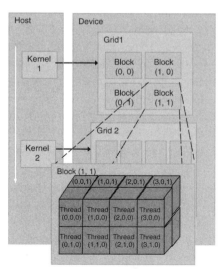

FIGURE 3.13

CUDA thread organization.

Each thread block is, in turn, organized as a three-dimensional array of threads with a total size of up to 512 threads. The coordinates of threads in a block are uniquely defined by three thread indices: threadIdx.x, threadIdx.y, and threadIdx.z. Not all applications will use all three dimensions of a thread block. In Figure 3.13, each thread block is organized into a 4×2×2 three-dimensional array of threads. This gives Grid 1 a total of 4×16 = 64 threads. This is obviously a simplified example.

In the matrix multiplication example, a grid is invoked to compute the product matrix. The code in Figure 3.11 does not use any block index in accessing input and output data. Threads with the same threadIdx values from different blocks would end up accessing the same input and output data elements. As a result, the kernel can use only one thread block. The threadIdx.x and threadIdx.y values are used to organize the block into a two-dimensional array of threads. Because a thread block can have only up to 512 threads, and each thread calculates one element of the product matrix in Figure 3.11, the code can only calculate a product matrix of up to 512 elements. This is obviously not acceptable. As we explained before, the product matrix must have millions of elements in order to have a sufficient amount of data parallelism to benefit from execution on a device. We will address this issue in Chapter 4 using multiple blocks.

When the host code invokes a kernel, it sets the grid and thread block dimensions via *execution configuration* parameters. This is illustrated in Figure 3.14. Two struct variables of type dim3 are declared. The first is for describing the configuration of blocks, which are defined as 16×16 groups of threads. The second variable, dimGrid, describes the configuration of the grid. In this example, we only have one (1×1) block in each grid. The final line of code invokes the kernel. The special syntax between the name of the kernel function and the traditional C parameters of the function is a CUDA extension to ANSI C. It provides the dimensions of the grid in terms of number of blocks and the dimensions of the blocks in terms of number of threads.

```
// Setup the execution configuration
dim3 dimBlock(Width, Width);
dim3 dimGrid(1, 1);

// Launch the device computation threads!
MatrixMulKernel<<<dimGrid, dimBlock>>>(Md, Nd, Pd, Width);
```

FIGURE 3.14

Example of host code that launches a kernel.

3.6 SUMMARY

This chapter serves as a quick overview of the CUDA programming model. CUDA extends the C language to support parallel computing. The extensions discussed in this chapter are summarized below.

3.6.1 Function declarations

CUDA extends the C function declaration syntax to support heterogeneous parallel computing. The extensions are summarized in Figure 3.12. Using one of __global__, __device__, or __host__, a CUDA programmer can instruct the compiler to generate a kernel function, a device function, or a host function. If both __host__ and __device__ are used in a function declaration, the compiler generates two versions of the function, one for the device and one for the host. If a function declaration does not have any CUDA extension keyword, the function defaults into a host function.

3.6.2 Kernel launch

CUDA extends C function call syntax with kernel execution configuration parameters surrounded by <<< and >>>. These execution configuration parameters are only used during a call to a kernel function, or a kernel launch. We discussed the execution configuration parameters that define the dimensions of the grid and the dimensions of each block. The reader should refer to the *CUDA Programming Guide* [NVIDIA 2007] for more details regarding the kernel launch extensions as well as other types of execution configuration parameters.

3.6.3 Predefined variables

CUDA kernels can access a set of predefined variables that allow each thread to distinguish among themselves and to determine the area of data each thread is to work on. We discussed the threadIdx variable in this chapter. In Chapter 4, we will further discuss blockIdx, gridDim, and blockDim variables.[5]

---

[5]Note that the gridDim and blockDim variables are built-in, predefined variables that are accessible in kernel functions. They should not be confused with the user defined dimGrid and dimBlock variables that are used in the host code for the purpose of setting up the configuration parameters. The value of these configuration parameters will ultimately become the values of gridDim and blockDim once the kernel has been launched.

3.6.4 **Runtime API**

CUDA supports a set of API functions to provide services to CUDA programs. The services that we discussed in this chapter are `cudaMalloc()` and `cudaMemcpy()` functions. These functions allocate device memory and transfer data between the host and device on behalf of the calling program. The reader is referred to the *CUDA Programming Guide* [NVIDIA 2007] for other CUDA API functions.

Our goal for this chapter is to introduce the fundamental concepts of the CUDA programming model and the essential CUDA extensions to C for writing a simple CUDA program. The chapter is by no means a comprehensive account of all CUDA features. Some of these features will be covered in the rest of the book; however, our emphasis will be on key concepts rather than details. In general, we would like to encourage the reader to always consult the *CUDA Programming Guide* for more details on the concepts that we cover.

References and Further Reading

Atallah, M. J. (Ed.), (1998). *Algorithms and theory of computation handbook.* Boca Raton, FL: CRC Press.

NVIDIA. (2009). *CUDA programming guide 2.3.* Santa Clara, CA: NVIDIA.

Stratton, J. A., Stone, S. S., & Hwu, W. W. (2008). MCUDA: An efficient implementation of CUDA kernels for multi-core CPUs. In *Proceedings of the 21st International Workshop on languages and compilers for parallel computing (LCPC).* Canada: Edmonton.

CUDA Threads

4

CHAPTER CONTENTS

INTRODUCTION

Fine-grained, data-parallel threads are the fundamental means of parallel execution in CUDA™. As we explained in Chapter 3, launching a CUDA kernel function creates a grid of threads that all execute the kernel function. That is, the kernel function specifies the C statements that are executed by each individual thread created when the kernel is launched at runtime. This chapter presents more details on the organization, resource assignment, and scheduling of threads in a grid. A CUDA programmer who understands these details is well equipped to write and to understand high-performance CUDA applications.

4.1 CUDA THREAD ORGANIZATION

Because all threads in a grid execute the same kernel function, they rely on unique coordinates to distinguish themselves from each other and to identify the appropriate portion of the data to process. These threads are organized into a two-level hierarchy using unique coordinates—`blockIdx` (for block index) and `threadIdx` (for thread index)—assigned to them by the CUDA runtime system. The `blockIdx` and `threadIdx` appear as built-in, preinitialized variables that can be accessed within kernel functions.

When a thread executes the kernel function, references to the `blockIdx` and `threadIdx` variables return the coordinates of the thread. Additional built-in variables, `gridDim` and `blockDim`, provide the dimension of the grid and the dimension of each block respectively.

Figure 4.1 shows a simple example of CUDA thread organization. The grid in this example consists of N thread blocks, each with a `blockIdx.x` value that ranges from 0 to $N-1$. Each block, in turn, consists of M threads, each with a `threadIdx.x` value that ranges from 0 to $M-1$. All blocks at the grid level are organized as a one-dimensional (1D) array; all threads within each block are also organized as a 1D array. Each grid has a total of $N*M$ threads.

The black box of each thread block in Figure 4.1 shows a fragment of the kernel code. The code fragment uses the `threadID = blockIdx.x * blockDim.x + threadIdx` to identify the part of the input data to read from and the part of the output data structure to write to. Thread 3 of Block 0 has a `threadID` value of $0*M + 3 = 3$. Thread 3 of Block 5 has a `threadID` value of $5*M + 3$.

Assume a grid has 128 blocks ($N = 128$) and each block has 32 threads ($M = 32$). In this example, access to `blockDim` in the kernel returns 32. There are a total of $128*32 = 4096$ threads in the grid. Thread 3 of Block 0 has a threaded value of $0*32 + 3 = 3$. Thread 3 of Block 5 has a threaded value of $5*32 + 3 = 163$. Thread 15 of Block 102 has a threaded value of 3279. The reader should verify that every one of the 4096 threads has its own unique threaded value. In Figure 4.1, the kernel code uses threadID variable to index into the `input[]`and the `output[]`arrays. If we assume that both arrays are declared with 4096 elements, then each thread will take one of the input elements and produce one of the output elements.

In general, a grid is organized as a 2D array of blocks. Each block is organized into a 3D array of threads. The exact organization of a grid is determined by the execution configuration provided at kernel launch. The first parameter of the execution configuration specifies the dimensions of the grid in terms of number of blocks. The second specifies the dimensions of each block in terms of number of threads. Each such parameter is a `dim3` type, which is essentially a C `struct` with three unsigned integer fields: x, y, and z. Because grids are 2D arrays of block dimensions, the third field of the grid dimension parameter is ignored; it should be set to 1 for clarity. The following host code can be used to launch the kernel whose organization is shown in Figure 4.1:

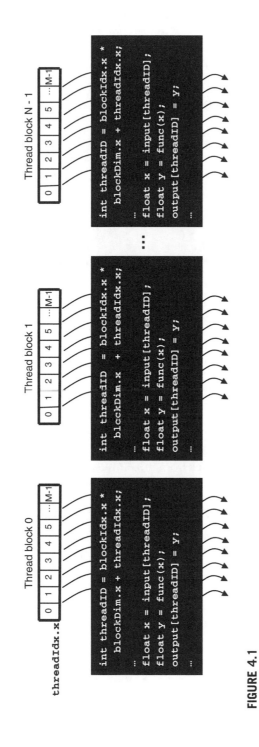

FIGURE 4.1

Overview of CUDA thread organization.

```
dim3 dimGrid(128, 1, 1);
dim3 dimBlock(32, 1, 1);
KernelFunction<<<dimGrid, dimBlock>>>(...);
```

The first two statements initialize the execution configuration parameters. Because the grid and the blocks are 1D arrays, only the first dimension of dimBlock and dimGrid are used. The other dimensions are set to 1. The third statement is the actual kernel launch. The execution configuration parameters are between <<< and >>>. Note that scalar values can also be used for the execution configuration parameters if a grid or block has only one dimension; for example, the same grid can be launched with one statement:

```
KernelFunction<<<128, 32>>>(...);
```

The values of gridDim.x and gridDim.y can range from 1 to 65,535. The values of gridDim.x and gridDim.y can be calculated based on other variables at kernel launch time. Once a kernel is launched, its dimensions cannot change. All threads in a block share the same blockIdx value. The blockIdx.x value ranges between 0 and gridDim.x − 1, and the blockIdx.y value between 0 and gridDim.y− 1.

Figure 4.2 shows a small 2D grid that is launched with the following host code:

```
dim3 dimGrid(2, 2, 1);
dim3 dimBlock(4, 2, 2);
KernelFunction<<<dimGrid, dimBlock>>>(...);
```

The grid consists of four blocks organized into a 2×2 array. Each block in Figure 4.2 is labeled with (blockIdx.x, blockIdx.y); for example, Block(1,0) has blockIdx.x = 1 and blockIdx.y = 0.

In general, blocks are organized into 3D arrays of threads. All blocks in a grid have the same dimensions. Each threadIdx consists of three components: the x coordinate threadIdx.x, the y coordinate threadIdx.y, and the z coordinate threadIdx.z. The number of threads in each dimension of a block is specified by the second execution configuration parameter given at the kernel launch. With the kernel, this configuration parameter can be accessed as a predefined struct variable, blockDim. The total size of a block is limited to 512 threads, with flexibility in distributing these elements into the three dimensions as long as the total number of threads does not exceed 512. For example, (512, 1, 1), (8, 16, 2), and (16, 16, 2) are all allowable blockDim values, but (32, 32, 1) is not allowable because the total number of threads would be 1024.

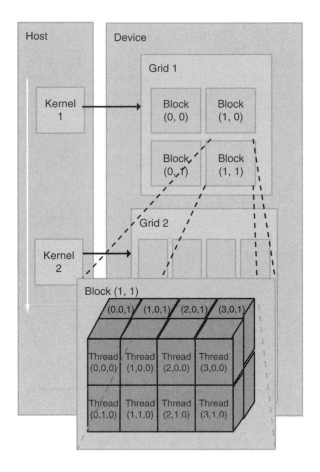

FIGURE 4.2

A multidimensional example of CUDA grid organization.

Figure 4.2 also illustrates the organization of threads within a block. In this example, each block is organized into 4×2×2 arrays of threads. Because all blocks within a grid have the same dimensions, we only need to show one of them. Figure 4.2 expands block (1, 1) to show its 16 threads; for example, thread (2, 1, 0) has `threadIdx.x = 2`, `threadIdx.y = 1`, and `threadIdx.z = 0`. Note that, in this example, we have 4 blocks of 16 threads each, with a grand total of 64 threads in the grid. We have used these small numbers to keep the illustration simple. Typical CUDA grids contain thousands to millions of threads.

4.2 USING `blockIdx` AND `threadIdx`

From the programmer's point of view, the main functionality of `blockIdx` and `threadIdx` variables is to provide threads with a means to distinguish among themselves when executing the same kernel. One common usage for `threadIdx` and `blockIdx` is to determine the area of data that a thread is to work on. This was illustrated by the simple matrix multiplication code in Figure 3.11, where the dot product loop uses `threadIdx.x` and `threadIdx.y` to identify the row of **Md** and column of **Nd** to work on. We will now cover more sophisticated usage of these variables.

One limitation of the simple code in Figure 3.11 is that it can only handle matrices of up to 16 elements in each dimension. This limitation comes from the fact that the kernel function does not use `blockIdx`. As a result, we are limited to using only one block of threads. Even if we used more blocks, threads from different blocks would end up calculating the same **Pd** element if they have the same `threadIdx` value. Recall that each block can have up to 512 threads. With each thread calculating one element of **Pd**, we can calculate up to 512 **Pd** elements with the code. For square matrices, we are limited to 16×16 because 32×32 requires more than 512 threads per block.

In order to accommodate larger matrices, we need to use multiple thread blocks. Figure 4.3 shows the basic idea of such an approach. Conceptually, we break **Pd** into square tiles. All the **Pd** elements of a tile are computed by a block of threads. By keeping the dimensions of these **Pd** tiles small, we keep the total number of threads in each block under 512, the maximal allowable block size. In Figure 4.3, for simplicity, we abbreviate `threadIdx.x` and `threadIdx.y` as `tx` and `ty`. Similarly, we abbreviate `blockIdx.x` and `blockIdx.y` as `bx` and `by`.

Each thread still calculates one **Pd** element. The difference is that it must use its `blockIdx` values to identify the tile that contains its element before it uses its `threadIdx` values to identify its element inside the tile. That is, each thread now uses both `threadIdx` and `blockIdx` to identify the **Pd** element to work on. This is portrayed in Figure 4.3, where the `bx`, `by`, `tx`, and `ty` values of threads calculating the **Pd** elements are marked in both *x* and *y* dimensions. All threads calculating the **Pd** elements within a tile have the same `blockIdx` values.

Assume that the dimensions of a block are square and are specified by the variable `TILE_WIDTH`. Each dimension of **Pd** is now divided into sections of `TILE_WIDTH` elements each, as shown on the left and top edges of Figure 4.3. Each block handles such a section. Thus, a thread can find the *x* index of its **Pd** element as (bx*TILE_WIDTH + tx) and the *y* index as (by*TILE_WIDTH + ty). That is, thread (tx, ty) in block (bx, by) is to use row (by*TILE_WIDTH + ty) of **Md** and column (bx*TILE_WIDTH + tx) of **Nd** to calculate the **Pd** element at column (bx*TILE_WIDTH + tx) and row (by*TILE_WIDTH + ty).

Figure 4.4 shows a small example of using multiple blocks to calculate **Pd**. For simplicity, we use a very small TILE_WIDTH value (2) so we can fit the entire example in one picture. The **Pd** matrix is now divided into 4 tiles. Each dimension of **Pd** is now divided into sections of 2 elements. Each block needs to calculate 4 **Pd** elements. We can do so by creating blocks that are organized into 2×2 arrays of threads, with each thread calculating

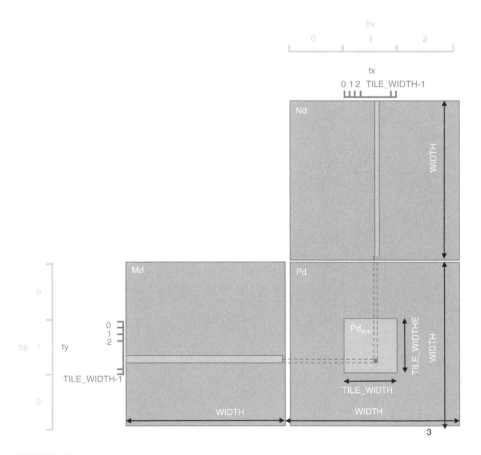

FIGURE 4.3

Matrix multiplication using multiple blocks by tiling **Pd**.

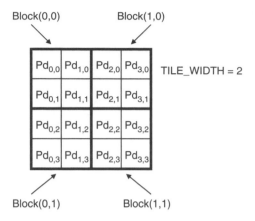

FIGURE 4.4

A simplified example of using multiple blocks to calculate **Pd**.

one **Pd** element. In the example, thread (0, 0) of block (0, 0) calculates $Pd_{0,0}$, whereas thread (0, 0) of block (1, 0) calculates $Pd_{2,0}$. It is easy to verify that one can identify the **Pd** element calculated by thread (0, 0) of block (1, 0) with the formula given above: `Pd[bx* TILE_WIDTH + tx]` `[by* TILE_WIDTH + ty]` = `Pd[1*2 + 0][0*2 + 0]` = `Pd[2][0]`. The reader should work through the index derivation for as many threads as it takes to become comfortable with the concept.

Once we have identified the indices for the **Pd** element to be calculated by a thread, we also have identified the row (y) index of **Md** and the column (x) index of **Nd** for input values. As shown in Figure 4.3, the row index of **Md** used by thread (`tx`, `ty`) of block (`bx`, `by`) is (`by*TILE_WIDTH + ty`). The column index of **Nd** used by the same thread is (`bx*TILE_WIDTH + tx`). We are now ready to revise the kernel of Figure 3.11 into a version that uses multiple blocks to calculate **Pd**.

Figure 4.5 illustrates the multiplication actions in each thread block. For the small matrix multiplication, threads in block (0, 0) produce four dot products: Thread (0, 0) generates $Pd_{0,0}$ by calculating the dot product of row 0 of **Md** and column 0 of **Nd**. Thread (1, 0) generates $Pd_{1,0}$ by calculating the dot product of row 0 of **Md** and column 1 of **Nd**. The arrows of $Pd_{0,0}$, $Pd_{1,0}$, $Pd_{0,1}$, and $Pd_{1,1}$ shows the row and column used for generating their result value.

Figure 4.6 shows a revised matrix multiplication kernel function that uses multiple blocks. In Figure 4.6, each thread uses its `blockIdx` and `threadIdx` values to identify the row index (`Row`) and the column index

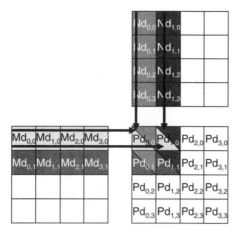

FIGURE 4.5

Matrix multiplication actions of one thread block.

(`Col`) of the **Pd** element that it is responsible for. It then performs a dot product on the row of **Md** and column of **Nd** to generate the value of the **Pd** element. It eventually writes the **Pd** value to the appropriate global memory location. Note that this kernel can handle matrices of up to $16 \times 65{,}535$ elements in each dimension. In the situation where matrices larger than this new limit are to be multiplied, one can divide the **Pd** matrix into submatrices of a size permitted by the kernel. Each submatrix would still be

```
__global__ void MatrixMulKernel(float* Md, float* Nd, float* Pd, int Width)
{
  // Calculate the row index of the Pd element and M
  int Row = blockIdx.y*TILE_WIDTH + threadIdx.y;
  // Calculate the column idenx of Pd and N
  int Col = blockIdx.x*TILE_WIDTH + threadIdx.x;

  float Pvalue = 0;
  // each thread computes one element of the block sub-matrix
  for (int k = 0; k < Width; ++k)
    Pvalue += Md[Row*Width+k] * Nd[k*Width+Col];

  Pd[Row*Width+Col] = Pvalue;
}
```

FIGURE 4.6

Revised matrix multiplication kernel using multiple blocks.

```
// Setup the execution configuration
  dim3 dimGrid(Width/TILE_WIDTH, Width/TILE_WIDTH);
  dim3 dimBlock(TILE_WIDTH, TILE_WIDTH);


// Launch the device computation threads!
MatrixMulKernel<<<dimGrid, dimBlock>>>(Md, Nd, Pd, Width);
```

FIGURE 4.7

Revised host code for launching the revised kernel.

processed by an ample number of blocks (65,535 × 65,535). All of these blocks can run in parallel with each other and will fully utilize parallel execution resources of any processors in the foreseeable future.

Figure 4.7 shows the revised host code to be used in the `MatrixMultiplication()` stub function to launch the revised kernel. Note that the `dimGrid` now receives the value of `Width/TILE_WIDTH` for both the *x* dimension and the *y* dimension. The revised code now launches the `MatrixMulKernel()` with multiple blocks. Note that the code treats the Md, Nd, and Pd arrays as 1D array with row major layout. The calculation of the indices used to access Md, Nd, and Pd is the same as that in Section 3.3.

4.3 SYNCHRONIZATION AND TRANSPARENT SCALABILITY

CUDA allows threads in the same block to coordinate their activities using a barrier synchronization function, `__syncthreads()`. When a kernel function calls `__syncthreads()`, the thread that executes the function call will be held at the calling location until every thread in the block reaches the location. This ensures that all threads in a block have completed a phase of their execution of the kernel before any moves on to the next phase. We will discuss an important use of `__syncthreads()` in Chapter 5.

Barrier synchronization is a simple and popular method of coordinating parallel activities. In real life, we often use barrier synchronization to coordinate parallel activities of multiple persons; for example, assume that four friends go to a shopping mall in a car. They can all go to different stores to buy their own clothes. This is a parallel activity and is much more efficient than if they all remain as a group and sequentially visit the stores to shop for their clothes. However, barrier synchronization is needed before they leave the mall. They have to wait until all four friends have returned to the car before they can leave. Without barrier synchronization, one or more persons could be left at the mall when the car leaves, which could seriously damage their friendship!

In CUDA, a __syncthreads() statement must be executed by all threads in a block. When a __syncthreads() statement is placed in an *if* statement, either all threads in a block execute the path that includes the __syncthreads() or none of them does. For an *if–then–else* statement, if each path has a __syncthreads() statement, then either all threads in a block execute the __syncthreads() on the *then* path or all of them execute the *else* path. The two __syncthreads() are different barrier synchronization points. If a thread in a block executes the *then* path and another executes the *else* path, then they would be waiting at different barrier synchronization points. They would end up waiting for each other forever.

The ability to synchronize also imposes execution constraints on threads within a block. These threads should execute in close time proximity with each other to avoid excessively long waiting times. CUDA runtime systems satisfy this constraint by assigning execution resources to all threads in a block as a unit; that is, when a thread of a block is assigned to an execution resource, all other threads in the same block are also assigned to the same resource. This ensures the time proximity of all threads in a block and prevents excessive waiting time during barrier synchronization.

This leads us to a major tradeoff in the design of CUDA barrier synchronization. By not allowing threads in different blocks to perform barrier synchronization with each other, the CUDA runtime system can execute blocks in any order relative to each other because none of them must wait for each other. This flexibility enables scalable implementations as shown in Figure 4.8. In a low-cost implementation with only a few execution resources, one can execute a small number of blocks at the same time

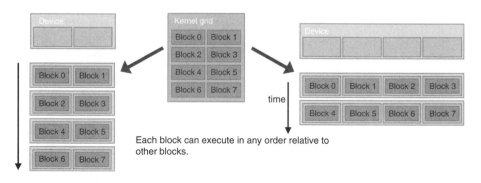

Each block can execute in any order relative to other blocks.

FIGURE 4.8

Transparent scalability for CUDA programs allowed by the lack of synchronization constraints between blocks.

(shown as executing two blocks a time on the left-hand side of Figure 4.8). In a high-end implementation with more execution resources, one can execute a large number of blocks at the same time (shown as executing four blocks at a time on the right-hand side of Figure 4.8). The ability to execute the same application code at a wide range of speeds allows the production of a wide range of implementations according to the cost, power, and performance requirements of particular market segments. A mobile processor, for example, may execute an application slowly but at extremely low power consumption, and a desktop processor may execute the same application at a higher speed while consuming more power. Both execute exactly the same application program with no change to the code. The ability to execute the same application code on hardware with different numbers of execution resources is referred to as *transparent scalability*, which reduces the burden on application developers and improves the usability of applications.

4.4 THREAD ASSIGNMENT

Once a kernel is launched, the CUDA runtime system generates the corresponding grid of threads. These threads are assigned to execution resources on a block-by-block basis. In the current generation of hardware, the execution resources are organized into streaming multiprocessors (SMs); for example, the NVIDIA® GT200 implementation has 30 streaming multiprocessors, 2 of which are shown in Figure 4.9. Up to 8 blocks can be assigned to each SM in the GT200 design as long as there are enough resources to satisfy the needs of all of the blocks. In situations with an insufficient amount of any one or more types of resources needed for the simultaneous execution of 8 blocks, the CUDA runtime automatically reduces the number of blocks assigned to each SM until the resource usage is under the limit. With 30 SMs in the GT200 processor, up to 240 blocks can be simultaneously assigned to them. Most grids contain many more than 240 blocks. The runtime system maintains a list of blocks that need to execute and assigns new blocks to SMs as they complete the execution of blocks previously assigned to them.

Figure 4.9 shows an example in which three thread blocks are assigned to each SM. One of the SM resource limitations is the number of threads that can be simultaneously tracked and scheduled. Hardware resources are required for SMs to maintain the thread, block IDs, and track their execution status. In the GT200 design, up to 1024 threads can be assigned to each SM. This could

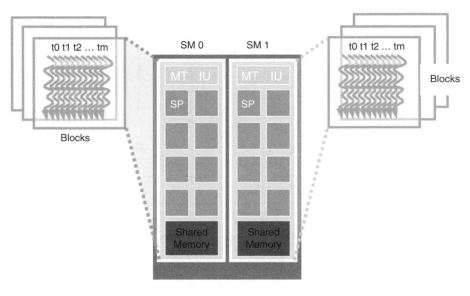

FIGURE 4.9

Thread block assignment to streaming multiprocessors (SMs).

be in the form of 4 blocks of 256 threads each, 8 blocks of 128 threads each, etc. It should be obvious that 16 blocks of 64 threads each is not possible, as each SM can only accommodate up to 8 blocks. Because the GT200 has 30 SMs, up to 30,720 threads can be simultaneously residing in the SMs for execution. The number of threads that can be assigned to each SM increased from the G80 to the GT200. Each SM in G80 can accommodate 768 threads, and, because the G80 has 16 SMs, up to 12,288 threads can be simultaneously residing in the SMs for execution. The transparent scalability of CUDA allows the same application code to run unchanged on G80 and GT200.

4.5 THREAD SCHEDULING AND LATENCY TOLERANCE

Thread scheduling is strictly an implementation concept and thus must be discussed in the context of specific hardware implementations. In the GT200 implementation, once a block is assigned to a streaming multiprocessor, it is further divided into 32-thread units called *warps*. The size of warps is implementation specific. In fact, warps are not part of the CUDA specification; however, knowledge of warps can be helpful in understanding and optimizing the performance of CUDA applications on particular generations of CUDA devices. The warp is the unit of thread scheduling in SMs.

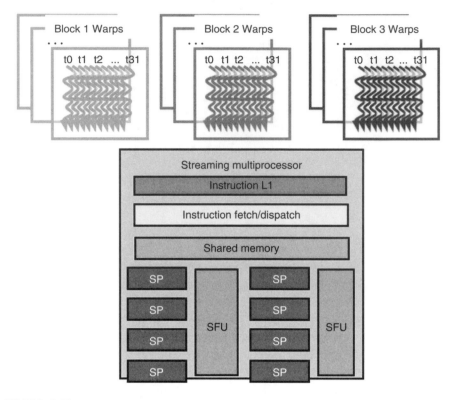

FIGURE 4.10

Blocks partitioned into warps for thread scheduling.

Figure 4.10 shows the division of blocks into warps in the GT200. Each warp consists of 32 threads of consecutive `threadIdx` values: Threads 0 through 31 form the first warp, threads 32 through 63 the second warp, and so on. In this example, three blocks (Block 1, Block 2, and Block 3) are all assigned to an SM. Each of the three blocks is further divided into warps for scheduling purposes.

We can calculate the number of warps that reside in an SM for a given block size and a given number of blocks assigned to each SM. In Figure 4.10, for example, if each block has 256 threads, then we can determine that each block has 256/32 or 8 warps. With 3 blocks in each SM, we have $8 \times 3 = 24$ warps in each SM. This is, in fact, the maximal number of warps that can reside in each SM in the G80, as there can be no more than 768 threads in each SM, which amounts to $768/32 = 24$ warps. This number increases to 32 warps per SM for the GT200.

A legitimate question is why do we need to have so many warps in an SM if there are only 8 SPs in an SM? The answer is that this is how CUDA processors efficiently execute long-latency operations such as global memory accesses. When an instruction executed by the threads in a warp must wait for the result of a previously initiated long-latency operation, the warp is not selected for execution. Another resident warp that is no longer waiting for results is selected for execution. If more than one warp is ready for execution, a priority mechanism is used to select one for execution. This mechanism of filling the latency of expensive operations with work from other threads is often referred to as *latency hiding*.

Note that warp scheduling is also used for tolerating other types of long-latency operations such as pipelined floating-point arithmetic and branch instructions. With enough warps around, the hardware will likely find a warp to execute at any point in time, thus making full use of the execution hardware in spite of these long-latency operations. The selection of ready warps for execution does not introduce any idle time into the execution timeline, which is referred to as *zero-overhead thread scheduling*. With warp scheduling, the long waiting time of warp instructions is hidden by executing instructions from other warps. This ability to tolerate long-latency operations is the main reason why graphics processing units (GPUs) do not dedicate nearly as much chip area to cache memories and branch prediction mechanisms as central processing units (CPUs) do. As a result, GPUs can dedicate more of their chip area to floating-point execution resources.

We are now ready to do a simple exercise.[1] For matrix multiplication, should we use 8×8, 16×16, or 32×32 thread blocks for the GT200? To answer the question, we can analyze the pros and cons of each choice. If we use 8×8 blocks, each block would have only 64 threads, and we will need 1024/64 = 12 blocks to fully occupy an SM; however, because we are limited to 8 blocks in each SM, we will end up with only 64 × 8 = 512 threads in each SM. This means that the SM execution resources will likely be underutilized because there will be fewer warps to schedule around long-latency operations.

---

[1]Note that this is an overly simplified exercise. As we will explain in Chapter 5, the usage of other resources such as registers and shared memory must also be considered when determining the most appropriate block dimensions. This exercise highlights the interactions between the limit on the number of thread blocks and the limit on the number of threads that can be assigned to each SM.

The 16×16 blocks give 256 threads per block. This means that each SM can take $1024/256 = 4$ blocks. This is within the 8-block limitation. This is a good configuration because we will have full thread capacity in each SM and the maximal number of warps for scheduling around the long-latency operations. The 32×32 blocks exceed the limitation of up to 512 threads per block.

4.6 SUMMARY

The kernel execution configuration defines the dimensions of a grid and its blocks. Unique coordinates in `blockIdx` and `threadIdx` variables allow threads of a grid to identify themselves and their domains. It is the programmer's responsibility to use these variables in kernel functions so the threads can properly identify the portion of the data to process. This model of programming compels the programmer to organize threads and their data into hierarchical and multidimensional organizations.

Once a grid is launched, its blocks are assigned to streaming multiprocessors in arbitrary order, resulting in transparent scalability of CUDA applications. The transparent scalability comes with the limitation that threads in different blocks cannot synchronize with each other. The only safe way for threads in different blocks to synchronize with each other is to terminate the kernel and start a new kernel for the activities after the synchronization point.

Threads are assigned to SMs for execution on a block-by-block basis. For GT200 processors, each SM can accommodate up to 8 blocks or 1024 threads, whichever becomes a limitation first. Once a block is assigned to an SM, it is further partitioned into warps. At any time, the SM executes only a subset of its resident warps for execution. This allows the other warps to wait for long-latency operations without slowing down the overall execution throughput of the massive number of execution units.

4.7 EXERCISES

4.1 A student mentioned that he was able to multiply two 1024×1024 matrices using a tiled matrix multiplication code with 1024 thread blocks on the G80. He further mentioned that each thread in a thread block calculates one element of the result matrix. What would be your reaction and why?

4.2 The following kernel is executed on a large matrix, which is tiled into submatrices. To manipulate tiles, a new CUDA programmer has written the following device kernel to transpose each tile in the matrix. The tiles are of size BLOCK_SIZE by BLOCK_SIZE, and each of the dimensions of matrix A is known to be a multiple of BLOCK_SIZE. The kernel invocation and code are shown below. BLOCK_SIZE is known at compile time but could be set anywhere from 1 to 20.

```
dim3 blockDim(BLOCK_SIZE,BLOCK_SIZE);
dim3 gridDim(A_width/blockDim.x,A_height/blockDim.y);
BlockTranspose<<<gridDim, blockDim>>>(A, A_width, A_height);

__global__ void
BlockTranspose(float* A_elements, int A_width, int A_height)
{
  __shared__ float blockA[BLOCK_SIZE][BLOCK_SIZE];

  int baseIdx = blockIdx.x * BLOCK_SIZE + threadIdx.x;
  baseIdx += (blockIdx.y * BLOCK_SIZE + threadIdx.y) * A_width;

  blockA[threadIdx.y][threadIdx.x] = A_elements[baseIdx];
  A_elements[baseIdx] = blockA[threadIdx.x][threadIdx.y];
}
```

Out of the possible range of values for BLOCK_SIZE, for what values of BLOCK_SIZE will this kernel function correctly when executing on the device?

4.3 If the code does not execute correctly for all BLOCK_SIZE values, suggest a fix to the code to make it work for all BLOCK_SIZE values.

CUDA™ Memories

5

CHAPTER CONTENTS

INTRODUCTION

So far, we have learned to write a CUDA™ kernel function that is executed by a massive number of threads. The data to be processed by these threads are first transferred from the host memory to the device global memory. The threads then access their portion of the data from the global memory using their block IDs and thread IDs. We have also learned more details of the assignment and scheduling of threads for execution. Although this is a very good start, these simple CUDA kernels will likely achieve only a small fraction of the potential speed of the underlying hardware. The poor performance is due to the fact that global memory, which is typically implemented with dynamic random access memory (DRAM), tends to have long access latencies (hundreds of clock cycles) and finite access bandwidth. Although having many threads available for execution can theoretically tolerate long memory access latencies, one can easily run into a situation where traffic congestion in the global memory access paths prevents all but a few threads from making progress, thus rendering some of the streaming multiprocessors (SMs) idle. In order to circumvent such congestion, CUDA provides a number of additional methods for accessing memory that can remove the majority of data requests to the global memory. In this chapter, you will learn to use these memories to boost the execution efficiency of CUDA kernels.

5.1 IMPORTANCE OF MEMORY ACCESS EFFICIENCY

We can illustrate the effect of memory access efficiency by calculating the expected performance level of the matrix multiplication kernel code shown in Figure 4.6, replicated here in Figure 5.1. The most important part of the kernel in terms of execution time is the *for* loop that performs dot product calculations. In every iteration of this loop, two global memory accesses are performed for one floating-point multiplication and one floating-point addition. Thus, the ratio of floating-point calculation to the global memory access operation is 1 to 1, or 1.0. We will refer to this ratio as the *compute to global memory access (CGMA) ratio*, defined as the number of floating-point calculations performed for each access to the global memory within a region of a CUDA program.

The CGMA ratio has major implications on the performance of a CUDA kernel. For example, the NVIDIA® G80 supports 86.4 gigabytes per second (GB/s) of global memory access bandwidth. The highest achievable floating-point calculation throughput is limited by the rate at which the input data can be loaded from the global memory. With 4 bytes in each single-precision floating-point datum, one can expect to load not more than 21.6 (86.4/4) giga single-precision data per second. With a CGMA ratio of 1.0, the matrix multiplication kernel will execute at no more than 21.6 billion floating-point operations per second (gigaflops), as each floating

```
__global__ void MatrixMulKernel(float* Md, float* Nd, float* Pd, int Width)
{
// Calculate the row index of the Pd element and M
int Row = blockIdx.y*TILE_WIDTH + threadIdx.y;
// Calculate the column index of Pd and N
int Col = blockIdx.x*TILE_WIDTH + threadIdx.x;

float Pvalue = 0;
// each thread computes one element of the block sub-matrix
for (int k = 0; k < Width; ++k)
  Pvalue += Md[Row*Width+k] * Nd[k*Width+Col];

Pd[Row*Width+Col] = Pvalue;
}
```

FIGURE 5.1

Matrix multiplication kernel using multiple blocks (see Figure 4.6).

point operation requires one single-precision global memory datum. Although 21.6 gigaflops is a respectable number, it is only a tiny fraction of the peak performance of 367 gigaflops for the G80. We will need to increase the CGMA ratio to achieve a higher level of performance for the kernel.

5.2 CUDA DEVICE MEMORY TYPES

CUDA supports several types of memory that can be used by programmers to achieve high CGMA ratios and thus high execution speeds in their kernels. Figure 5.2 shows these CUDA device memories. At the bottom of the figure, we see global memory and constant memory. These types of memory can be written (W) and read (R) by the host by calling application programming interface (API) functions. We have already introduced global memory in Chapter 3. The constant memory supports short-latency, high-bandwidth, read-only access by the device when all threads simultaneously access the same location.

Registers and shared memory in Figure 5.2 are on-chip memories. Variables that reside in these types of memory can be accessed at very high speed in a highly parallel manner. Registers are allocated to individual threads; each thread can only access its own registers. A kernel function

- Device code can:
  - R/W per-thread registers
  - R/W per-thread local memory
  - R/W per-block shared memory
  - R/W per-grid global memory
  - Read only per-grid constant memory
- Host code can
  - Transfer data to/from per-grid global and constant memories

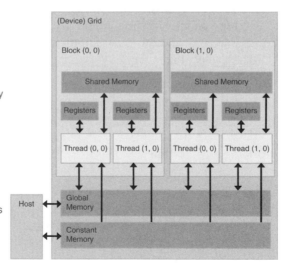

FIGURE 5.2

Overview of the CUDA device memory model.

typically uses registers to hold frequently accessed variables that are private to each thread. Shared memory is allocated to thread blocks; all threads in a block can access variables in the shared memory locations allocated to the block. Shared memory is an efficient means for threads to cooperate by sharing their input data and the intermediate results of their work. By declaring a CUDA variable in one of the CUDA memory types, a CUDA programmer dictates the visibility and access speed of the variable.

Table 5.1 presents the CUDA syntax for declaring program variables into the various types of device memory. Each such declaration also gives its declared CUDA variable a scope and lifetime. Scope identifies the range of threads that can access the variable: by a single thread only, by all threads of a block, or by all threads of all grids. If the scope of a variable is a single thread, a private version of the variable will be created for every thread; each thread can only access its private version of the variable. For example, if a kernel declares a variable whose scope is a thread and it is launched with 1 million threads, then 1 million versions of the variable will be created so each thread initializes and uses its own version of the variable.

Lifetime specifies the portion of the program's execution duration when the variable is available for use: either within a kernel's invocation or throughout the entire application. If a variable's lifetime is within a kernel invocation, it must be declared within the kernel function body and will be available for use only by the kernel's code. If the kernel is invoked several times, the contents of the variable are not maintained across these invocations. Each invocation must initialize the variable in order to use them. On the other hand, if a variable's lifetime is throughout the entire

Table 5.1 CUDA Variable Type Qualifiers

Variable Declaration	Memory	Scope	Lifetime
Automatic variables other than arrays	Register	Thread	Kernel
Automatic array variables	Local	Thread	Kernel
`__device__, __shared__, int SharedVar;`	Shared	Block	Kernel
`__device__, int GlobalVar;`	Global	Grid	Application
`__device__, __constant__, int ConstVar;`	Constant	Grid	Application

application, it must be declared outside of any function body. The contents of the variable are maintained throughout the execution of the application and are available to all kernels.

As shown in Table 5.1, all automatic scalar variables declared in kernel and device functions are placed into registers. We refer to variables that are not arrays as *scalar* variables. The scopes of these automatic variables are within individual threads. When a kernel function declares an automatic variable, a private copy of that variable is generated for every thread that executes the kernel function. When a thread terminates, all of its automatic variables also cease to exist. In Figure 5.1, variables tx, ty, and Pvalue are all automatic variables and fall into this category. Note that accessing these variables is extremely fast and parallel, but one must be careful not to exceed the limited capacity of the register storage in the hardware implementations. We will address this point in Chapter 6.

Automatic array variables are not stored in registers.[1] Instead, they are stored into the global memory and incur long access delays and potential access congestions. The scope of these arrays is, like automatic scalar variables, limited to individual threads. That is, a private version of each automatic array is created for and used by every thread. Once a thread terminates its execution, the contents of its automatic array variables also cease to exist. From our experience, one seldom needs to use automatic array variables in kernel functions and device functions.

If a variable declaration is preceded by the keyword __shared__ (each __ consists of two _ characters), it declares a shared variable in CUDA. One can also add an optional __device__ in front of __shared__ in the declaration to achieve the same effect. Such declarations typically reside within a kernel function or a device function. The scope of a shared variable[2] is within a thread block; that is, all threads in a block see the same version of a shared variable. A private version of the shared variable is created for and used by each thread block during kernel execution. The lifetime of a shared variable is within the duration of the kernel. When a kernel terminates its execution, the contents of its shared variables cease to exist. Shared variables are an efficient means for threads within a block to collaborate with each other. Accessing shared memory is extremely fast

---

[1]There are some exceptions to this rule. The compiler may decide to store an automatic array into registers if all accesses are done with constant index values.

[2]The "extern_shared_SharedArray[]" notation allows the size of a shared memory array to be determined at runtime. Interested readers are referred to the CUDA Programming Guide for details.

and highly parallel. CUDA programmers often use shared memory to hold the portion of global memory data that are heavily used in an execution phase of the kernel. One may need to adjust the algorithms used to create execution phases that focus heavily on small portions of the global memory data, as we will demonstrate with matrix multiplication in Section 5.3.

If a variable declaration is preceded by the keyword __constant__, it declares a constant variable in CUDA. One can also add an optional __device__ in front of __constant__ to achieve the same effect. Declaration of constant variables must be outside any function body. The scope of a constant variable is all grids, meaning that all threads in all grids see the same version of a constant variable. The lifetime of a constant variable is the entire application execution. Constant variables are often used for variables that provide input values to kernel functions. Constant variables are stored in the global memory but are cached for efficient access. With appropriate access patterns, accessing constant memory is extremely fast and parallel. Currently, the total size of constant variables in an application is limited at 65,536 bytes. One may need to break up the input data volume to fit within this limitation, as we will illustrate in Chapter 8.

A variable whose declaration is preceded only by the keyword __device__ is a global variable and will be placed in global memory. Accesses to a global variable are slow; however, global variables are visible to all threads of all kernels. Their contents also persist through the entire execution. Thus, global variables can be used as a means for threads to collaborate across blocks. One must, however, be aware of the fact that there is currently no way to synchronize between threads from different thread blocks or to ensure data consistency across threads when accessing global memory other than terminating the current kernel execution. Therefore, global variables are often used to pass information from one kernel invocation to another kernel invocation.

Note that there is a limitation on the use of pointers with CUDA variables declared in device memory. In general, pointers are used to point to data objects in global memory. There are two typical ways in which pointer usage arises in kernel and device functions. First, if an object is allocated by a host function, the pointer to the object is initialized by cudaMalloc() and can be passed to the kernel function as a parameter; for example, the parameters **Md**, **Nd**, and **Pd** in Figure 5.1 are such pointers. The second type of usage is to assign the address of a variable declared in the global memory to a pointer variable; for example, the statement {float*ptr = &GlobalVar;} in a kernel function assigns the address of GlobalVar into the automatic pointer variable ptr.

5.3 A STRATEGY FOR REDUCING GLOBAL MEMORY TRAFFIC

We have an intrinsic tradeoff in the use of device memories in CUDA. Global memory is large but slow, whereas the shared memory is small but fast. A common strategy is to partition the data into subsets called *tiles* such that each tile fits into the shared memory. The term *tile* draws on the analogy that a large wall (i.e., the global memory data) can often be covered by tiles (i.e., subsets that each can fit into the shared memory). An important criterion is that the kernel computations on these tiles can be done independently of each other. Note that not all data structures can be partitioned into tiles given an arbitrary kernel function.

The concept of tiling can be illustrated with the matrix multiplication example. Figure 5.3 shows a small example of matrix multiplication using multiple blocks. It corresponds to the kernel function in Figure 5.1. This example assumes that we use four 2×2 blocks to compute the **Pd** matrix. Figure 5.3 highlights the computation done by the four threads of block (0, 0). These four threads compute $\mathbf{Pd}_{0,0}$, $\mathbf{Pd}_{1,0}$, $\mathbf{Pd}_{0,1}$, and $\mathbf{Pd}_{1,1}$. The accesses to the **Md** and **Nd** elements by thread (0, 0) and thread (1, 0) of block (0, 0) are highlighted with black arrows.

Figure 5.4 shows the global memory accesses done by all threads in block(0,0). The threads are listed in the horizontal direction, with the time of access increasing downward in the vertical direction. Note that each

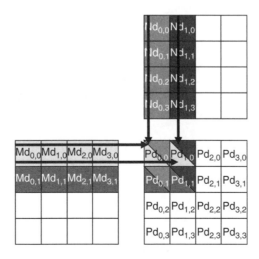

FIGURE 5.3

A small example of matrix multiplication using multiple blocks.

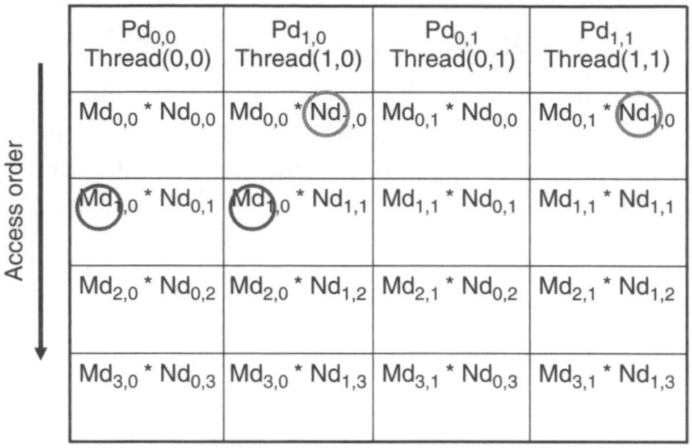

$Pd_{0,0}$ Thread(0,0)	$Pd_{1,0}$ Thread(1,0)	$Pd_{0,1}$ Thread(0,1)	$Pd_{1,1}$ Thread(1,1)
$Md_{0,0} * Nd_{0,0}$	$Md_{0,0} * Nd_{1,0}$	$Md_{0,1} * Nd_{0,0}$	$Md_{0,1} * Nd_{1,0}$
$Md_{1,0} * Nd_{0,1}$	$Md_{1,0} * Nd_{1,1}$	$Md_{1,1} * Nd_{0,1}$	$Md_{1,1} * Nd_{1,1}$
$Md_{2,0} * Nd_{0,2}$	$Md_{2,0} * Nd_{1,2}$	$Md_{2,1} * Nd_{0,2}$	$Md_{2,1} * Nd_{1,2}$
$Md_{3,0} * Nd_{0,3}$	$Md_{3,0} * Nd_{1,3}$	$Md_{3,1} * Nd_{0,3}$	$Md_{3,1} * Nd_{1,3}$

Access order

FIGURE 5.4

Global memory accesses performed by threads in block(0,0).

thread accesses four elements of **Md** and four elements of **Nd** during its execution. Among the four threads highlighted, there is a significant overlap in terms of the **Md** and **Nd** elements they access; for example, thread(0,0) and thread(1,0) both access $Md_{1,0}$ as well as the rest of row 0 of **Md**. Similarly, $thread_{1,0}$ and $thread_{1,1}$ both access $Nd_{1,0}$ as well as the rest of column 1 of **Nd**.

The kernel in Figure 5.1 is written so both thread(0,0) and thread(1,0) access these **Md** row 0 elements from the global memory. If we can somehow manage to have thread(0,0) and thread(1,0) collaborate so these **Md** elements are only loaded from global memory once, we can reduce the total number of accesses to the global memory by half. In general, we can see that every **Md** and **Nd** element is accessed exactly twice during the execution of block(0,0); therefore, if all four threads could collaborate in their accesses to global memory, we could potentially reduce the traffic to the global memory by half.

The reader should verify that the potential reduction in global memory traffic in the matrix multiplication example is proportional to the dimension of the blocks used. With $N \times N$ blocks, the potential reduction of global memory traffic would be N. That is, if we use 16×16 blocks, we could potentially reduce the global memory traffic to 1/16 through collaboration between threads.

We now present an algorithm where threads collaborate to reduce the traffic to the global memory. The basic idea is to have the threads collaboratively load **Md** and **Nd** elements into the shared memory before they individually use these elements in their dot product calculation. Keep in mind that the size of the shared memory is quite small and one must be careful not to exceed the capacity of the shared memory when loading these **Md** and **Nd** elements into the shared memory. This can be accomplished by dividing the **Md** and **Nd** matrices into smaller tiles. The size of these tiles is chosen so they can fit into the shared memory. In the simplest form, the tile dimensions equal those of the block, as illustrated in Figure 5.5.

In Figure 5.5, we divide **Md** and **Nd** into 2×2 tiles, as delineated by the thick lines. The dot product calculations performed by each thread are now divided into phases. In each phase, all threads in a block collaborate to load a tile of **Md** and a tile of **Nd** into the shared memory. This is done by having every thread in a block to load one **Md** element and one **Nd** element into the shared memory, as illustrated in Figure 5.6. Each row of Figure 5.6 shows the execution activities of a thread. (Note that time now progresses from left to right.) We only need to show the activities of threads in block(0,0); the other blocks all have the same behavior. The shared memory array for the **Md** elements is called **Mds**. The shared memory array for the **Nd** elements is called **Nds**. At the beginning of Phase 1, the four threads of block(0,0) collaboratively load a tile of **Md** into shared memory; thread(0,0) loads $Md_{0,0}$ into $Mds_{0,0}$, thread(1,0) loads $Md_{1,0}$ into $Mds_{1,0}$, thread(0,1) loads $Md_{0,1}$ into $Mds_{0,1}$, and thread(1,1) loads $Md_{1,1}$ into $Mds_{1,1}$. Look at the

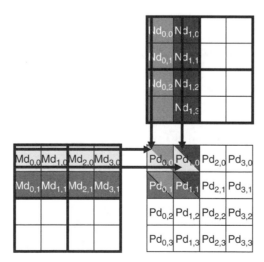

FIGURE 5.5

Tiling **Md** and **Nd** to utilize shared memory.

	Phase 1			Phase 2		
$T_{0,0}$	$Md_{0,0}$ ↓ $Mds_{0,0}$	$Nd_{0,0}$ ↓ $Nds_{0,0}$	$PValue_{0,0}$ += $Mds_{0,0}*Nds_{0,0}$ + $Mds_{1,0}*Nds_{0,1}$	$Md_{2,0}$ ↓ $Mds_{0,0}$	$Nd_{0,2}$ ↓ $Nds_{0,0}$	$PValue_{0,0}$ += $Mds_{0,0}*Nds_{0,0}$ + $Mds_{1,0}*Nds_{0,1}$
$T_{1,0}$	$Md_{1,0}$ ↓ $Mds_{1,0}$	$Nd_{1,0}$ ↓ $Nds_{1,0}$	$PValue_{1,0}$ += $Mds_{0,0}*Nds_{1,0}$ + $Mds_{1,0}*Nds_{1,1}$	$Md_{3,0}$ ↓ $Mds_{1,0}$	$Nd_{1,2}$ ↓ $Nds_{1,0}$	$PValue_{1,0}$ += $Mds_{0,0}*Nds_{1,0}$ + $Mds_{1,0}*Nds_{1,1}$
$T_{0,1}$	$Md_{0,1}$ ↓ $Mds_{0,1}$	$Nd_{0,1}$ ↓ $Nds_{0,1}$	$PdValue_{0,1}$ += $Mds_{0,1}*Nds_{0,0}$ + $Mds_{11}*Nds_{0,1}$	$Md_{2,1}$ ↓ $Mds_{0,1}$	$Nd_{0,3}$ ↓ $Nds_{0,1}$	$PdValue_{0,1}$ += $Mds_{0,1}*Nds_{0,0}$ + $Mds_{1,1}*Nds_{0,1}$
$T_{1,1}$	$Md_{1,1}$ ↓ $Mds_{1,1}$	$Nd_{1,1}$ ↓ $Nds_{1,1}$	$PdValue_{1,1}$ += $Mds_{0,1}*Nds_{1,0}$ + $Mds_{1,1}*Nds_{1,1}$	$Md_{3,1}$ ↓ $Mds_{1,1}$	$Nd_{1,3}$ ↓ $Nds_{1,1}$	$PdValue_{1,1}$ += $Mds_{0,1}*Nds_{1,0}$ + $Mds_{1,1}*Nds_{1,1}$

time ⟶

FIGURE 5.6

Execution phases of a tiled matrix multiplication.

second column of Figure 5.6. A tile of **Nd** is also loaded in a similar manner, as shown in the third column of Figure 5.6.

After the two tiles of **Md** and **Nd** are loaded into the shared memory, these values are used in the calculation of the dot product. Note that each value in the shared memory is used twice; for example, the $Md_{1,1}$ value, loaded by $thread_{1,1}$ into $Mds_{1,1}$, is used twice: once by $thread_{0,1}$ and once by $thread_{1,1}$. By loading each global memory value into shared memory so it can be used multiple times we reduce the number of accesses to the global memory. In this case, we reduce the number of accesses to the global memory by half. The reader should verify that the reduction is by a factor of N if the tiles are $N \times N$ elements.

Note that the calculation of each dot product in Figure 5.6 is now performed in two phases, shown as Phase 1 and Phase 2. In each phase, products of two pairs of the input matrix elements are accumulated into the `Pvalue` variable. The first phase calculation is shown in the fourth column of Figure 5.6; the second phase is in the seventh column. In general, if an input matrix is of dimension N and the tile size is `TILE_WIDTH`, the dot product would be performed in `N/TILE_WIDTH` phases. The creation of these phases is key to the reduction of accesses to the global memory. With each phase focusing on a small subset of the input matrix values, the threads can collaboratively load the subset into the shared memory and use the values in the shared memory to satisfy their overlapping input needs in the phase.

Note also that **Mds** and **Nds** are reused to hold the input values. In each phase, the same **Mds** and **Nds** are used to hold the subset of **Md** and **Nd** elements used in the phase. This allows a much smaller shared memory to serve most of the accesses to global memory. This is because each phase focuses on a small subset of the input matrix elements. Such focused access behavior is called *locality*. When an algorithm exhibits locality, there is an opportunity to use small, high-speed memories to serve most of the accesses and remove these accesses from the global memory. Locality is as important for achieving high performance in multicore central processing units (CPUs) as in many-core graphics processing units (GPUs). We will return to the concept of locality in Chapter 6.

We are now ready to present the tiled kernel function that uses shared memory to reduce the traffic to global memory. The kernel shown in Figure 5.7 implements the phases illustrated in Figure 5.6. In Figure 5.7, Line 1 and Line 2 declare **Mds** and **Nds** as shared memory variables.

```
__global__ void MatrixMulKernel(float* Md, float* Nd, float* Pd, int Width)
{
1.   __shared__ float Mds[TILE_WIDTH][TILE_WIDTH];
2.   __shared__ float Nds[TILE_WIDTH][TILE_WIDTH];

3.   int bx = blockIdx.x; int by = blockIdx.y;
4.   int tx = threadIdx.x; int ty = threadIdx.y;

// Identify the row and column of the Pd element to work on
5.   int Row = by * TILE_WIDTH + ty;
6.   int Col = bx * TILE_WIDTH + tx;

7.   float Pvalue = 0;
// Loop over the Md and Nd tiles required to compute the Pd element
8.   for (int m = 0; m < Width/TILE_WIDTH; ++m) {

// Collaborative loading of Md and Nd tiles into shared memory
9.     Mds[ty][tx] = Md[Row*Width + (m*TILE_WIDTH + tx)];
10.    Nds[ty][tx] = Nd[(m*TILE_WIDTH + ty)*Width + Col];
11.    __syncthreads();

12.    for (int k = 0; k < TILE_WIDTH; ++k)
13.      Pvalue += Mds[ty][k] * Nds[k][tx];
14.    __syncthreads();
     }
15. Pd[Row*Width + Col] = Pvalue;
}
```

FIGURE 5.7

Tiled matrix multiplication kernel using shared memories.

Recall that the scope of shared memory variables is a block. Thus, all threads of a block have access to the same **Mds** and **Nds** arrays. This is important, as all threads in a block must have access to the **Md** and **Nd** values loaded into **Mds** and **Nds** by their peers so they can use these values to satisfy their input needs.

Lines 3 and 4 save the `threadIdx` and `blockIdx` values into automatic variables and thus into registers for fast access. Recall that automatic scalar variables are placed into registers. Their scope is in each individual thread. That is, one private version of `tx`, `ty`, `bx`, and `by` is created by the runtime system for each thread. They will reside in registers that are accessible by one thread. They are initialized with the `threadIdx` and `blockIdx` values and used many times during the lifetime of thread. Once the thread ends, the values of these variables also cease to exist.

Lines 5 and 6 determine the row index and column index of the **Pd** element that the thread is to produce. As shown in Figure 5.8, the column (*x*) index of the **Pd** element to be produced by a thread can be calculated as `bx*TILE_WIDTH + tx`. This is because each block covers `TILE_WIDTH` elements in the *x* dimension. A thread in block `bx` would have bx blocks of threads, or `bx*TILE_WIDTH` threads, before it; they cover `bx*TILE_WIDTH` elements of **Pd**. Another `tx` thread within the same block would cover another `tx` element of **Pd**. Thus, the thread with `bx` and `tx` should be responsible for calculating the **Pd** element whose *x* index is `bx*TILE_WIDTH + tx`. For the example in Figure 5.5, the *x* index of the **Pd** element to be calculated by thread(1,0) of block(0,1) is 0*2 + 1 = 1. Similarly, the *y* index can be calculated as `by*TILE_WIDTH + ty`. In Figure 5.5, the *y* index of the **Pd** element to be calculated by thread(1,0) of block(0,1) is 1*2 + 0 = 2. Thus, the **Pd** element to be calculated by this thread is $Pd_{1,2}$.

Line 8 of Figure 5.7 marks the beginning of the loop that iterates through all the phases of calculating the final **Pd** element. Each iteration of the loop corresponds to one phase of the calculation shown in Figure 5.6. The `m` variable indicates the number of phases that have already been done for the dot product. Recall that each phase uses one tile of **Md** and one tile of **Nd** elements; therefore, at the beginning of each phase, `m*TILE_WIDTH` pairs of **Md** and **Nd** elements have been processed by previous phases.

Recall that all threads in a grid execute the same kernel function. The `threadIdx` variable allows them to identify the part of the data they are to process. Also recall that the thread with `by = blockIdx.y` and `ty = threadIdx.y` processes row (`by*TILE_WIDTH + ty`) of **Md**, as shown at the left side of Figure 5.8. Line 5 stores this number into the `Row` variable of each thread. Likewise, the thread with `bx = blockIdx.x` and

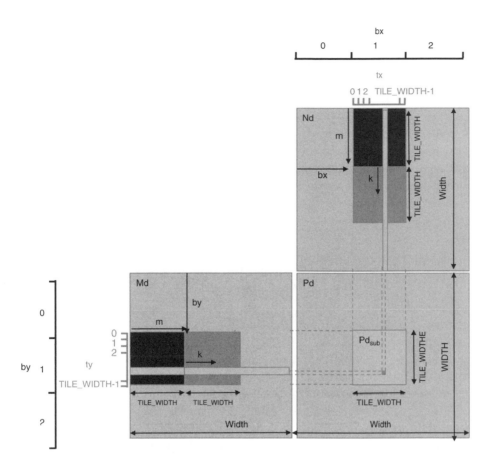

FIGURE 5.8

Calculation of the matrix indices in tiled multiplication.

$tx = threadIdx.x$ processes the column ($bx*TILE\_WIDTH + tx$) of **Nd**, as shown at the top of Figure 5.8. Line 6 stores this number into the Col variable of each thread. These variables will be used when the threads load **Md** and **Nd** elements into the shared memory.

In each phase, Line 9 loads the appropriate **Md** element into the shared memory. Because we already know the row index of **Md** and column index of **Nd** elements to be processed by the thread, we will focus on the column index of **Md** and row index of **Nd**. As shown in Figure 5.8, each block has $TILE\_WIDTH^2$ threads that will collaborate to load $TILE\_WIDTH^2$ **Md** elements into the shared memory. Thus, all we need to do is to assign each thread to load one **Md** element. This is conveniently done using the blockIdx and threadIdx. Note that the beginning index of the section of **Md** elements to be loaded is m*TILE_WIDTH; therefore, an easy approach is to have every thread load an element from that point identified by the threadIdx value. This is precisely what we have in Line 9, where each thread loads Md[Row*Width + (m*TILE_WIDTH + tx)]. Because the value of Row is a linear function of ty, each of the TILE_WIDTH^2 threads will load a unique **Md** element into the shared memory. Together, these threads will load the orange square subset of **Md** shown in Figure 5.8. The reader should use the small example in Figures 5.5 and 5.6 to verify that the address calculation works correctly.

Line 11 calls the __syncthreads() barrier synchronization function to make sure that all threads in the same block have completed loading the **Md** and **Nd** tiles into **Mds** and **Nds**. Once the tiles of **Md** and **Nd** are loaded in **Mds** and **Nds**, the loop in Line 12 performs the phases of the dot product based on these elements. The progression of the loop for thread (tx, ty) is shown in Figure 5.8, with the direction of the **Md** and **Nd** data usage marked with k, the loop variable in Line 12. Note that the data will be accessed from **Mds** and **Nds**, the shared memory arrays holding these **Md** and **Nd** elements. Line 14 calls the __syncthreads() barrier synchronization function to make sure that all threads of the block have completed using the **Mds** and **Nds** contents before any of them loops back to the next iteration and loads the next tile of **Md** and **Nd**.

The benefit of the tiled algorithm is substantial. For matrix multiplication, the global memory accesses are reduced by a factor of TILE_WIDTH. If one uses 16×16 tiles, we can reduce the global memory accesses by a factor of 16. This reduction allows the 86.4-GB/s global memory bandwidth to serve a much larger floating-point computation rate than the original algorithm. More specifically, the global memory bandwidth can now support $[(86.4/4) \times 16] = 345.6$ gigaflops, very close to the peak floating-point performance of the G80. This effectively removes global memory bandwidth as the major limiting factor of matrix multiplication performance.

5.4 MEMORY AS A LIMITING FACTOR TO PARALLELISM

Although CUDA registers, shared memory, and constant memory can be extremely effective in reducing the number of accesses to global memory, one must be careful not to exceed the capacity of these memories. Each CUDA device offers a limited amount of CUDA memory, which limits the number of threads that can simultaneously reside in the streaming multi-processors for a given application. In general, the more memory locations each thread requires, the fewer the number of threads that can reside in each SM and thus the fewer number of threads that can reside in the entire processor.

In the G80, each SM has 8K ($= 8192$) registers, which amounts to 128K ($= 131,072$) registers for the entire processor. This is a very large number, but it only allows each thread to use a very limited number of registers. Recall that each G80 SM can accommodate up to 768 threads. In order to fill this capacity, each thread can use only 8K/768 $= 10$ registers. If each thread uses 11 registers, the number of threads that can be executed concurrently in each SM will be reduced. Such reduction is done at the block granularity. For example, if each block contains 256 threads, the number of threads will be reduced 256 at a time; thus, the next lower number of threads from 768 would be 512, a 1/3 reduction of threads that can simultaneously reside in each SM. This can greatly reduce the number of warps available for scheduling, thus reducing the processor's ability to find useful work in the presence of long-latency operations.

Shared memory usage can also limit the number of threads assigned to each SM. In the G80, there are 16 kilobytes (kB) of shared memory in each SM. Keep in mind that shared memory is used by blocks, and recall that each SM can accommodate up to 8 blocks. In order to reach this maximum, each block must not use more than 2 kB of shared memory. If each block uses more than 2 kB of memory, the number of blocks that can reside in each SM is such that the total amount of shared memory used by these blocks does not exceed 16 kB; for example, if each block uses 5 kB of shared memory, no more than 3 blocks can be assigned to each SM.

For the matrix multiplication example, shared memory can become a limiting factor. For a tile size of 16×16, each block requires $16 \times 16 \times 4 = 1$ kB of storage for **Mds**. Another 1 kB is needed for **Nds**. Thus, each block uses 2 kB of shared memory. The 16-kB shared memory allows 8 blocks to simultaneous reside in an SM. Because this is the same as the maximum allowed by the threading hardware, shared memory is not a limiting factor for this tile size. In this case, the real limitation is the threading hardware limitation that only 768 threads are allowed in each SM. This limits the number of blocks in each SM to 3. As a result, only 3×2 kB $= 6$ kB of the shared memory will be used. These limits do change from device generation to the next but are properties that can be determined at runtime;

for example, the GT200 series of processors can support up to 1024 threads in each SM. See Appendix B for shared memory and other resource limitations in other types of GPU devices.

5.5 SUMMARY

In summary, CUDA defines registers, shared memory, and constant memory that can be accessed at higher speed and in a more parallel manner than the global memory. Using these memories effectively will likely require redesign of the algorithm. We used matrix multiplication as an example to illustrate tiled algorithms, a popular strategy to enhance the locality of data access and enable effective use of shared memory. We demonstrated that, with 16×16 tiling, global memory accesses are no longer the major limiting factor for matrix multiplication performance.

It is, however, important for CUDA programmers to be aware of the limited sizes of these types of memory. Their capacities are implementation dependent. Once their capacities are exceeded, they become limiting factors for the number of threads that can be simultaneously executing in each SM. The ability to reason about hardware limitations when developing an application is a key aspect of computational thinking. The reader is also referred to Appendix B for a summary of resource limitations of several different devices.

Although we introduced tiled algorithms in the context of CUDA programming, it is an effective strategy for achieving high performance in virtually all types of parallel computing systems. The reason is that an application must exhibit locality in data access in order to make effective use of high-speed memories in these systems. In a multicore CPU system, for example, data locality allows an application to effectively use on-chip data caches to reduce memory access latency and achieve high performance. Readers will find the tiled algorithm useful when they develop parallel applications for other types of parallel computing systems using other programming models.

Our goal for this chapter was to introduce the different types of CUDA memory. We introduced the tiled algorithm as an effective strategy for using shared memory, but we have not discussed the use of constant memory. We will explain the use of constant memory in Chapter 8. Furthermore, we will study a different form of tiling that enables more effective use of registers in Chapter 9.

5.6 **EXERCISES**

5.1 Consider the matrix addition where each element of the output matrix is the sum of the corresponding elements of the two input matrices. Can one use shared memory to reduce the global memory bandwidth consumption? *Hint:* Analyze the elements accessed by each thread and see if there is any commonality between threads.

5.2 Draw the equivalent of Figure 5.4 for an 8×8 matrix multiplication with 2×2 tiling and 4×4 tiling. Verify that the reduction in global memory bandwidth is indeed proportional to the dimension size of the tiles.

5.3 What type of incorrect execution behavior can happen if one forgets to use __syncthreads() function in the kernel of Figure 5.7? Note that there are two calls to __syncthreads(), each for a different purpose.

5.4 Assuming that capacity were not an issue for registers or shared memory, give one case that it would be valuable to use shared memory instead of registers to hold values fetched from global memory. Explain your answer.

CHAPTER

Performance Considerations

6

CHAPTER CONTENTS

INTRODUCTION

Although a CUDA™ kernel can run correctly on any CUDA device, its execution speed can vary greatly depending on the resource constraints of each device. In this chapter, we will discuss the major types of resource constraints in an actual CUDA device and how they can constrain the level of parallel execution in this device. In order to achieve their goals, programmers often have to find ways to achieve a required level of performance that is higher than that of an initial version of the application. In different applications, different constraints may dominate and become the limiting factors. One can improve the performance of an application on a particular CUDA device, sometimes dramatically, by trading one resource usage for another. This strategy works well if the resource constraint thus alleviated was actually the dominating constraint before the strategy was applied and the one thus exacerbated does not have negative effects on parallel execution. Without such understanding, performance tuning would be guesswork; plausible strategies may or may not lead to performance enhancements. Beyond insights into these resource constraints, this chapter further offers principles and case studies designed to cultivate intuition about the type of algorithms that can result in high-performance CUDA programs. It is also establishes idioms and ideas that will likely lead to good performance improvements during performance tuning efforts.

6.1 MORE ON THREAD EXECUTION

Let's first discuss some aspects of thread execution that can limit performance. Recall that launching a CUDA kernel generates a grid of threads that are organized as a two-level hierarchy. At the top level, a grid consists of a one- or two-dimensional array of blocks. At the bottom level, each block, in turn, consists of a one-, two-, or three-dimensional array of threads. In Chapter 4, we discussed the fact that blocks can execute in any order relative to each other, which allows for transparent scalability in parallel execution of CUDA kernels; however, we did not say much about the execution timing of threads within each block.

Conceptually, one should assume that threads in a block can execute in any order with respect to each other. Barrier synchronizations should be used whenever we want to ensure that all threads have completed a common phase of their execution before any of them begin the next phase. The correctness of executing a kernel should not depend on the fact that certain threads will execute in synchrony with each other. Having said this, we also want to point out that, due to various hardware cost considerations, the current generation of CUDA devices actually does bundle multiple threads for execution. Such implementation strategy leads to performance limitations for certain types of kernel function code constructs. It is advantageous for application developers to change these types of constructs to other equivalent forms that perform better.

As we discussed in Chapter 4, the NVIDIA® G80/GT200 implementation bundles several threads for execution. Each block is partitioned into *warps*. This implementation technique helps to reduce hardware costs and enable some optimizations in servicing memory accesses. In the foreseeable future, we expect that warp partitioning will remain as a popular implementation technique; however, the size of warps can easily vary from implementation to implementation. In the G80/GT200, each warp consists of 32 threads. We will use the G80/GT200 implementation to explain warp partitioning for the rest of this chapter.

Thread blocks are partitioned into warps based on thread indices. If a thread block is organized into a one-dimensional array (i.e., only `threadIdx.x` is used), then the partition is straightforward. The `threadIdx.x` values within a warp are consecutive and increasing. For a warp size of 32, warp 0 starts with thread 0 and ends with thread 31, warp 1 starts with thread 32 and ends with thread 63. In general, warp *n* starts with thread 32*n and ends with thread $32(n + 1) - 1$. For a block whose size is not a multiple of 32, the last warp will be padded with extra threads to fill up the 32 threads; for example, if a block has 48 threads, it will be partitioned into 2 warps, and its warp 1 will be padded with 16 extra threads.

For blocks that consist of multiple dimensions of threads, the dimensions will be projected into a linear order before partitioning into warps. The linear order is determined by lining up the row with larger *y* and *z* coordinates after those with lower ones. That is, if a block consists of two dimensions of threads, one would form the linear order by placing all threads whose `threadIdx.y` is 1 after those whose `threadIdx.y` is 0. Threads whose `threadIdx.y` is 2 will be placed after those whose `threadIdx.y` is 1, and so on.

Figure 6.1 shows an example of placing threads of a two-dimensional (2D) block into linear order. The upper part shows the 2D view of the block. Each thread is shown as T(x,y), with *x* being the `threadIdx.x` and *y* being `threadIdx.y` for the thread. The lower part shows the linear view of the block. The first four threads are those threads whose `threadIdx.y` is 0; they are placed with increasing `threadIdx.x` values. The next four threads are those threads whose `threadIdx.y` is 1. They are also placed with their increasing `threadIdx.x` values. For this example, all 16 threads form half a warp. The warp will be padded with another 16 threads to complete a 32-thread warp. Imagine a 2D block with 8×8 threads. The 64

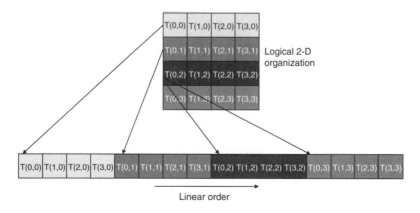

FIGURE 6.1

Placing threads into linear order.

threads will form 2 warps. The first warp starts from T(0,0) and ends with T(3,7). The second warp starts with T(4,0) and ends with T(7,7). It would be a useful exercise to draw out the picture as an exercise.

For a three-dimensional (3D) block, we first place all threads whose `threadIdx.z` is 0 into the linear order. Among these threads, they are treated as a 2D block, as shown in Figure 6.1. All threads whose `threadIdx.z` is 1 will then be placed into the linear order, and so on. For a $4 \times 8 \times 2$ block (4 in the x dimension, 8 in the y dimension, and 2 in the z dimension), the 64 threads will be partitioned into 2 warps, with T(0,0,0) through T(3,7,0) in the first warp and T(0,0,1) through T(3,7,1) in the second warp.

The hardware executes an instruction for all threads in the same warp, before moving to the next instruction. This style of execution, called *single-instruction, multiple-thread* (SIMT),[1] is motivated by hardware cost constraints, as it allows the cost of fetching and processing an instruction to be amortized over a large number of threads. It works well when all threads within a warp follow the same control flow path when working their data. For example, for an *if–then–else* construct, the execution works well when either all threads execute the *then* part or all execute the *else* part. When threads within a warp take different control flow paths, the simple execution style no longer works well. In our *if–then–else* example, when some threads execute the *then* part and others execute the *else* part, the SIMT execution style no longer works well. In such situations, the execution of the warp will require multiple passes through these divergent paths. One pass will be needed for those threads that follow the *then* part and another pass for those that follow the *else* part. These passes are sequential to each other, thus adding to the execution time.

When threads in the same warp follow different paths of control flow, we say that these threads *diverge* in their execution. In the *if–then–else* example, if some threads in a warp take the then path and some the else path, one pass will be used to execute all threads that take the then path.

---

[1]Note that SIMT is distinct from single-instruction, multiple-data (SIMD) implementation techniques, such as the popular Streaming SIMD Extensions (SSE) in CPUs. In an SSE implementation, the multiple data elements to be processed by a single instruction must be first collected and packed into a single register. Strict alignment requirements are involved that often require programmers to use additional instructions to satisfy. In SIMT, all threads process data in their own registers. There is much less burden on the programmers in terms of data collection and package. The option for control flow divergence in SIMT also simplifies the requirement for programmers to use extra instructions to handle control flow compared to SSE.

Another pass will be used to execute the others (ones that take the else path). Divergence also can arise in other constructs. For example, if threads in a warp execute a for loop which can iterate 6, 7, or 8 times for different threads. All threads will finish the first 6 iterations together. Two passes will be used to execute the 7th iteration, one pass for those that take the iteration and one for those that do not. Two passes will be used to execute all threads that need the 8th iteration, one pass for those that take the iteration and one for those that do not take the iteration.

An *if–then–else* construct can result in thread divergence when its decision condition is based on threadIdx values. For example, the statement if (threadIdx.x > 2) {} causes the threads to follow two divergent control flow paths; threads 0, 1, and 2 follow a different path than threads 3, 4, and 5, etc. Similarly, a loop can cause thread divergence if its loop condition is based on threadIdx values. Such usages arise naturally in some important parallel algorithms. We will use a reduction algorithm to illustrate this point.

A reduction algorithm extracts a single value from an array of values. The single value could be the sum, the maximal value, the minimal value, etc., among all elements. All of these types of reductions share the same computation structure. A reduction can be easily achieved by sequentially going through every element of the array. When an element is visited, the action to take depends on the type of reduction being performed. For a sum reduction, the value of the element being visited at the current step, or the current value, is added to a running sum. For a maximal reduction, the current value is compared to a running maximal value of all of the elements visited so far. If the current value is larger than the running maximal value, the current element value becomes the running maximal value. For a minimal reduction, the value of the element currently being visited is compared to a running minimal value. If the current value is smaller than the running minimal, the current element value becomes the running minimal. The sequential algorithm ends when all of the elements are visited.

When there are a large number of elements in the array, the time needed to visit all elements of an array becomes large enough to motivate parallel execution. A parallel reduction algorithm typically resembles that of a soccer tournament. In fact, the elimination process of the World Cup is a reduction of "maximal," where the maximal is defined as the team that beats all of the other teams. The tournament "reduction" is done by multiple rounds. The teams are divided into pairs. During the first round, all pairs play in parallel. Winners of the first round advance to the second round, whose winners advance to the third round, etc. With 16 teams entering a tournament, the 8 winners will emerge from the first round, 4 winners the second round, 2 winners the third round, and 1 final winner the fourth round. It should be easy to see that even with 1024 teams, it takes only 10 rounds to determine the final winner. The trick is to have enough soccer fields to hold the 512 games in parallel during the first round, 256 games in the second round, 128 games in the third round, and so on. With enough fields, even with 60,000 teams, we can determine the final winner in just 16 rounds. Of course, one would need to have enough soccer fields and enough officials to accommodate the 30,000 games in the first round.

Figure 6.2 shows a kernel function that performs parallel sum reduction. The original array is in the global memory. Each thread block reduces a section of the array by loading the elements of the section into the shared memory and performing parallel reduction. The code that loads the elements from global memory into the shared memory is omitted from Figure 6.2 for brevity. The reduction is done *in place*, which means that the elements in the shared memory will be replaced by partial sums. Each iteration of the while loop in the kernel function implements a round of reduction. The −syncthreads() statement in the for loop ensures that all partial sums for the previous iteration have been generated and thus all threads are ready to enter the current iteration before any thread is allowed to do so. This way, all threads that enter the second iteration will be using the values produced in the first iteration. After the first round, the even elements will be replaced by the partial sums generated in the first round. After the second round, the elements whose indices are multiples of four will be replaced with the partial sums. After the final round, the total sum of the entire section will be in element 0. In Figure 6.2, Line 3 initializes the stride variable to 1. During the first iteration, the *if* statement in Line 7 is used to select only the even threads to perform addition between two neighboring elements.

```
1. __shared__ float partialSum[]

2. unsigned int t = threadIdx.x;
3. for (unsigned int stride = 1;
4.     stride < blockDim.x; stride *= 2)
5. {
6.   __syncthreads();
7.   if (t % (2*stride) == 0)
8.     partialSum[t] += partialSum[t+stride];
9. }
```

FIGURE 6.2

A simple sum reduction kernel.

The execution of the kernel is illustrated in Figure 6.3. The threads and array elements are shown in the figure as columns, and the contents of the array at the end of iterations are shown as rows. Time progresses from top to bottom. As shown in row 1 in Figure 6.3, the even elements of the array now hold the pair-wise partial sums after iteration 1. Before the second iteration, the value of the stride variable is doubled to 2. During the second iteration, only those threads whose indices are multiples of four in Figure 6.3, will execute the add statement in Line 8 of Figure 6.2. Each thread generates a partial sum that covers 4 elements, as shown in row 2 of Figure 6.2. With 512 elements in each section, the kernel function will generate the total for the entire section after 9 iterations. By using blockDim.x as the loop bound in Line 4 in Figure 6.2, the kernel assumes that the kernel is launched with the same number of threads as the number of elements in the section; that is, for a section size of 512, the kernel needs to be launched with 512 threads.[2]

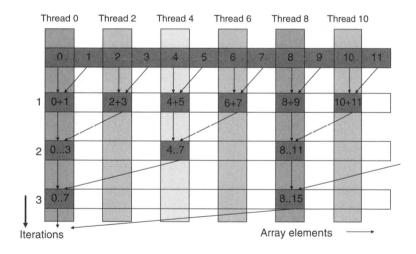

FIGURE 6.3

Execution of the sum reduction kernel.

---

[2]Note that using the same number of threads as the number of elements in a section is wasteful. Half of the threads in a block will never execute. The reader is encouraged to modify the kernel and the kernel launch execution configuration parameters to eliminate this waste (see Exercise 6.1).

The kernel in Figure 6.2 clearly has thread divergence. During the first iteration of the loop, only those threads whose `threadIdx.x` values are even will execute the add statement. One pass will be needed to execute these threads, and one additional pass will be needed to execute those that do not execute Line 8. In each successive iteration, fewer threads will execute Line 8, but two passes will still be needed to execute all of the threads. This divergence can be reduced with a slight change to the algorithm.

Figure 6.4 shows a modified kernel with a slightly different algorithm for sum reduction. Instead of adding neighbor elements in the first round, it adds elements that are half a section away from each other. It does so by initializing the stride to be half the size of the section. All of the pairs added during the first round are half the section size away from each other. After the first iteration, all the pair-wise sums are stored in the first half of the array. The loop divides the stride by 2 before entering the next iteration. This is done by shifting the stride value to the right by 1 bit, a less expensive way to implement "divide by 2" than by a real integer division. Thus, for the second iteration, the stride variable value is a quarter of the section size; that is, the algorithm adds elements that are a quarter section away from each other during the second iteration.

Note that the kernel in Figure 6.4 still has an *if* statement (Line 7) in the loop. The number of threads that execute Line 8 remains the same as in Figure 6.2. So, why should there be a performance difference between the two kernels? The answer lies in the positions of threads that execute Line 8 relative to those that do not.

Figure 6.5 illustrates the execution of the revised kernel. During the first iteration, all threads whose `threadIdx.x` values are less than half of the size of the section execute Line 8. For a section of 512 elements, threads 0 through 255 execute the add statement during the first iteration, while

```
1. __shared__ float partialSum[];

2. unsigned int t = threadIdx.x;
3. for (unsigned int stride = blockDim.x >> 1;
4.    stride > 0; stride >>= 1)
5. {
6.    __syncthreads();
7.    if (t < stride)
8.       partialSum[t] += partialSum[t+stride];
9. }
```

FIGURE 6.4

A kernel with less thread divergence.

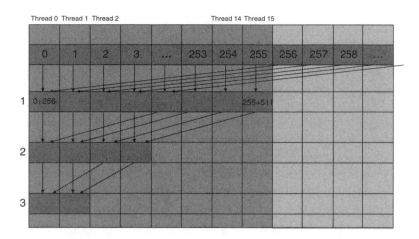

FIGURE 6.5

Execution of the revised algorithm.

threads 256 through 511 do not. The pair-wise sums are stored in elements 0 through 255 after the first iteration. Because a warp consists of 32 threads with consecutive `threadIdx.x` values, all threads in warps 0 through 7 execute the add statement, whereas warps 8 through 15 all skip the add statement. Because all of the threads in each warp take the same path, there is no thread divergence!

The kernel in Figure 6.4 does not completely eliminate the divergence due to the *if* statement. The reader should verify that, starting with the 5th iteration, the number of threads that execute Line 8 will fall below 32. That is, the final 5 iterations will have only 16, 8, 4, 2, and 1 threads performing the addition. This means that the code will still have divergence in these iterations.

6.2 GLOBAL MEMORY BANDWIDTH

One of the most important dimensions of CUDA kernel performance is accessing data in the global memory. CUDA applications exploit massive data parallelism; that is, CUDA applications typically process a massive amount of data from the global memory within a short period of time. In Chapter 5, we discussed tiling techniques that utilize shared memories to reduce the total amount of data that must be accessed by a collection of threads in the thread block. In this chapter, we will further discuss memory coalescing techniques that can more effectively move data from the global memory into shared memories and registers. Memory coalescing techniques are often used in conjunction with tiling techniques to allow CUDA devices to reach their performance potential by more efficiently utilizing the global memory bandwidth.[3]

Global memory in a CUDA system is typically implemented with dynamic random access memories (DRAMs). Data bits are stored in DRAM cells, which are very weak capacitors, where the presence or absence of a tiny amount of electrical charge distinguishes between 0 and 1. Reading data from a DRAM cell that contains a 1 requires the weak capacitor to share its tiny amount of charge to a sensor and set off a detection mechanism that determines whether a sufficient amount of charge is present in the capacitor. Because this is a very slow process, modern DRAMs use a parallel process to increase their rate of data access. Each time a location is accessed, many consecutive locations that includes the requested location are accessed. Many sensors are provided in each DRAM chip and they work in parallel, each sensing the content of a bit within these consecutive locations. Once detected by the sensors, the data from all of these consecutive locations can be transferred at very high speed to the processor. If an application can make use of data from multiple, consecutive locations before moving on to other locations, the DRAMs can supply the data at a much higher rate than if a truly random sequence of locations was accessed. To achieve anywhere close to the advertised peak global memory bandwidth, a kernel must arrange its data accesses so that each request to the DRAMs is for a large number of consecutive DRAM locations.

Recognizing the organization of modern DRAMs, the G80/GT200 designs employ a technique that allows the programmers to achieve high global memory access efficiency by organizing memory accesses of threads into favorable patterns. This technique takes advantage of the fact that threads in a warp execute the same instruction at any given point in time. When all threads in a warp execute a load instruction, the hardware detects whether the threads access consecutive global memory locations. That is,

---

[3]As we will discuss in Chapter 12, future CUDA devices will likely have a large on-chip cache for global memory data. Such a cache will automatically coalesce more of the kernel access patterns and reduce the need for programmers to manually rearrange their access patterns; however, with more than 100 million current and previous-generation CUDA devices in use, application programmers will still find coalescing techniques useful in the foreseeable future.

the most favorable access pattern is achieved when the same instruction for all threads in a warp accesses consecutive global memory locations. In this case, the hardware combines, or *coalesces*, all of these accesses into a consolidated access to consecutive DRAM locations. For example, for a given load instruction of a warp, if thread 0 accesses global memory location N,[4] thread 1 accesses location $N + 1$, thread 2 accesses location $N + 2$, etc., then all of these accesses will be coalesced, or combined into a single request for all consecutive locations when accessing the DRAMs. Such coalesced access allows the DRAMs to deliver data at a rate close to the peak global memory bandwidth.

Figure 6.6 illustrates the favorable versus unfavorable CUDA program matrix data access patterns for memory coalescing. Figure 6.6A illustrates the data access pattern of a loop where each thread reads a row of matrix **Md**. Assume that threads in a warp read adjacent rows; that is, during iteration 0, threads in a warp read element 0 of rows 0 through 31. During iteration 1, these same threads read element 1 of rows 0 through 31. None of the accesses will be coalesced. A more favorable access pattern is shown in Figure 6.6B, where each thread reads a column of **Nd**. During iteration 0, threads in warp 0 reads element 0 of columns 0 through 31. All of these accesses will be coalesced. In order to understand why the pattern in Figure 6.6B is more favorable than that in Figure 6.6A, we need to understand how these matrix elements are placed into the global memory.

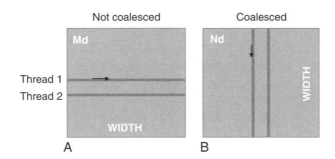

FIGURE 6.6

Memory access patterns for coalescing.

---

[4]N is also required to be aligned to 16-word boundaries; that is, the lower 6 bits of N should all be 0 bits. We will discuss techniques that address this alignment requirement in Chapter 9.

All locations in the global memory form a single, consecutive address space such that every location in the global memory has a unique address. This is analogous to a very long street where every house has a unique address. For example, if the global memory contains 1024 locations, these locations will be accessed by address 0 through 1023. The GT200 can have up to 4 GB (2^{32}) locations; the addresses range from 0 to $2^{32} - 1$. All variables of a CUDA program are placed into this linear address space and will be assigned an address.

As we showed in Chapter 3 (Figure 3.5), matrix elements in C and CUDA are placed into the linearly addressed locations according to the row major convention. That is, the elements of row 0 of a matrix are first placed in order into consecutive locations. They are followed by the elements of row 1 of the matrix, and so on. In other words, all elements in a row are placed into consecutive locations and entire rows are placed one after another. The term *row major* refers to the fact that the placement of data preserves the structure of rows; all adjacent elements in a row are placed into consecutive locations in the address space. The row major convention is illustrated in Figure 6.7 (same as Figure 3.5), where the 16 elements of 4×4 matrix **M** are placed into linearly addressed locations. The four elements of row 0 are first placed in their order of appearance in the row. Elements in row 1 are then placed, followed by elements of row 2, followed by elements of row 3. It should be clear that $\mathbf{M}_{0,0}$ and $\mathbf{M}_{0,1}$,

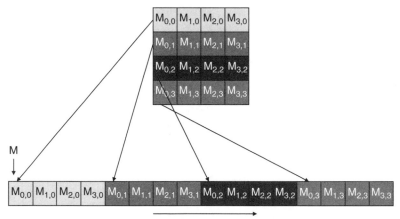

Linearized order in increasing address

FIGURE 6.7

Placing matrix elements into linear order.

although they appear to be consecutive in the 2D matrix, are placed four locations away in the linearly addressed memory.

Now that we have reviewed the placement of matrix elements into global memory, we are ready to discuss more about the favorable versus unfavorable matrix data access patterns in Figure 6.6. Figure 6.8 shows a small example of the favorable access pattern in accessing a 4×4 matrix. The arrow in the top portion of Figure 6.8 shows the access pattern of the kernel code for one thread. The accesses are generated by a loop where threads in a warp access the 0th elements of the columns in the first iteration. As shown in the bottom portion of Figure 6.8, these 0th elements are in consecutive locations in the global memory. The bottom portion also shows that these consecutive locations are accessed by the threads T(0) through T(3). The hardware detects that these accesses are to consecutive locations in the global memory and coalesces these accesses into a consolidated access. This allows the DRAMs to supply data at a high rate.

Figure 6.9 shows an example of a matrix data access pattern that is not coalesced. The arrow in the top portion of the figure shows that the kernel code for each thread accesses elements of a row in sequence. The accesses are generated by a loop where threads (T(0), T(1), T(2), T(3)) in the same warp access the 0th elements ($M_{0,0}$, $M_{0,1}$, $M_{0,2}$, $M_{0,3}$) of the four rows during the first iteration. As shown in the bottom portion of Figure 6.9, these elements are in locations that are four elements away from each other.

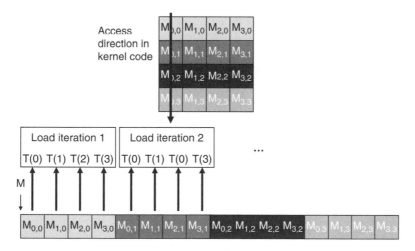

FIGURE 6.8

A coalesced access pattern.

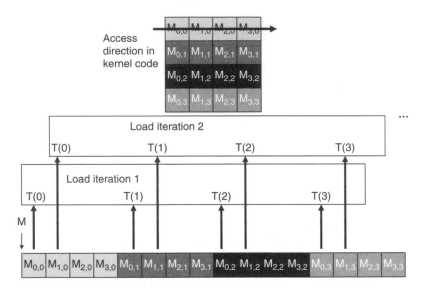

FIGURE 6.9

An uncoalesced access pattern.

The "Load iteration 1" box in the bottom portion shows how the threads access these nonconsecutive locations in the first iteration. The hardware will determine that accesses to these elements cannot be coalesced. As a result, when a kernel loop iterates through a row, the accesses to global memory are much less efficient than the case where a kernel iterates through a column.

If the algorithm intrinsically requires a kernel code to iterate through data within rows, one can use the shared memory to enable memory coalescing. The technique is illustrated in Figure 6.10 for matrix multiplication. Each thread reads a row from **Md**, a pattern that cannot be coalesced. Fortunately, a tiled algorithm can be used to enable coalescing. As we discussed in Chapter 5, threads of a block can first cooperatively load the tiles into the shared memory. Care can be taken to ensure that these tiles are loaded in a coalesced pattern. Once the data are in shared memory, they can be accessed on either a row basis or a column basis without any performance penalty because the shared memories are implemented as intrinsically high-speed, on-chip memory that does not require coalescing to achieve high data access rate.

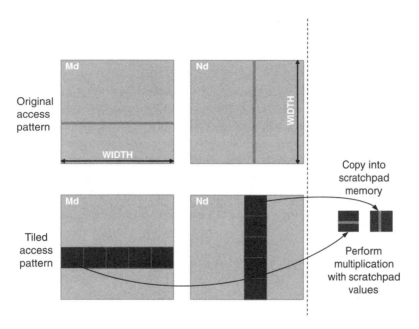

FIGURE 6.10

Using shared memory to enable coalescing.

We replicate Figure 5.7 here as Figure 6.11, where the matrix multiplication kernel loads two tiles of matrices **Md** and **Nd** into the shared memory. Note that each thread in a thread block is responsible for loading one **Md** element and one **Nd** element into **Mds** and **Nds** in each phase as defined by the for loop in Line 8. Recall that there are TILE_WIDTH^2 threads involved in each tile. The threads use threadIdx.y and threadIdx.y to determine the element of each matrix to load.

The **Md** elements are loaded in Line 9, where the index calculation for each thread uses m to locate the left end of the tile. Each row of the tile is then loaded by TILE_WIDTH threads whose threadIdx values differ in the *x* dimension. Because these threads have consecutive threadIdx.x values, they are in the same warp. Also, the index calculation Md[row * Width + m*TILE_WIDTH + tx] makes these threads access elements in the same row. The question is whether adjacent threads in the warp indeed access adjacent elements in the row. Because all terms of the index m*TILE_WIDTH + tx are identical for all threads except for tx and all threads in a warp have adjacent tx values. The hardware detects that these threads in the

```
__global__ void MatrixMulKernel(float* Md, float* Nd, float* Pd, int Width)
{
1.  __shared__float Mds[TILE_WIDTH][TILE_WIDTH];
2.  __shared__float Nds[TILE_WIDTH][TILE_WIDTH];

3.  int bx = blockIdx.x;  int by = blockIdx.y;
4.  int tx = threadIdx.x; int ty = threadIdx.y;

// Identify the row and column of the Pd element to work on
5.  int Row = by * TILE_WIDTH + ty;
6.  int Col = bx * TILE_WIDTH + tx;

7.  float Pvalue = 0;
// Loop over the Md and Nd tiles required to compute the Pd element
8.  for (int m = 0; m < Width/TILE_WIDTH; ++m) {

// Collaborative loading of Md and Nd tiles into shared memory
9.      Mds[ty][tx] = Md[Row*Width + (m*TILE_WIDTH + tx)];
10.     Nds[ty][tx] = Nd[(m*TILE_WIDTH + ty)*Width + Col];
11.     __syncthreads();

12.  for (int k = 0; k < TILE_WIDTH; ++k)
13.     Pvalue += Mds[ty][k] * Nds[k][tx];

14.  Pd[Row][Col] = Pvalue;
     }
 }
```

FIGURE 6.11

Tiled matrix multiplication kernel using shared memories.

same warp access consecutive locations in the global memory and combines them into a coalesced access.

In the case of **Nd**, all terms of the index (m*TILE_WIDTH + ty)*Width + Col have the same value for all threads in the same warp except for the tx term in Col. Note that all threads in the same warp have adjacent tx values; therefore, adjacent threads in a warp access adjacent elements in a row. The hardware detects that these threads in the same warp access consecutive location in the global memory and combine them into a coalesced access.

The reader will find it useful to draw a picture based on the kernel code in Figure 6.11 and identify the threadIdx.y and threadIdx.x values of the threads that load each element of the tile. Lines 5, 6, 9, 10 in Figure 6.11 form a frequently used programming pattern for loading matrix elements into shared memory in tiled algorithms. We would also like to encourage the reader to analyze the data access pattern by the dot-product loop in Lines 12 and 13. Note that the threads in a warp do not access consecutive location of **Mds**. This is not a problem, as **Mds** is in shared memory, which does not require coalescing to achieve high-speed data access.

6.3 DYNAMIC PARTITIONING OF SM RESOURCES

The execution resources in a streaming multiprocessor (SM) include registers, thread block slots, and thread slots. These resources are dynamically partitioned and assigned to threads to support their execution. In Chapter 4, we have seen that each GT200 SM has 1024 thread slots, each of which can accommodate one thread. These thread slots are partitioned and assigned to thread blocks during runtime. If each thread block consists of 256 threads, the 1024 threads slots are partitioned and assigned to four blocks. In this case, each SM can accommodate up to 4 thread blocks due to limitations on thread slots. If each thread block contains 128 threads, the 1024 thread slots are partitioned and assigned to 8 thread blocks. The ability to dynamically partition the thread slots among thread blocks makes the streaming multiprocessors versatile. They can either execute many thread blocks, each of which consists of few threads, or execute a few thread blocks, each of which consists of many threads. This is in contrast to a fixed partitioning method where each block receives a fixed amount of resource regardless of their real needs. Fixed partitioning results in wasted thread slots when a block has few threads and fails to support blocks that require more thread slots than the fixed partition allows.

Dynamic partitioning of resources can result in subtle interactions between resource limitations, which in turn can cause underutilization of resources. Such interactions can occur between block slots and thread slots. If each block has 64 threads, the 1024 thread slots can be partitioned and assigned to 16 blocks; however, because there are only 8 block slots in each SM, only 8 blocks will be allowed. This means that only 512 of the thread slots will be utilized. To fully utilize both the block slots and thread slots, one needs at least 128 threads in each block.

The register file is another dynamically partitioned resource. The number of registers in each CUDA device is not specified in the programming model and varies across implementations. In the G80, there is an 8192-entry register file in each SM. These registers are used to hold frequently used programmer and compiler-generated variables to reduce their access latency and to conserve memory bandwidth. As we mentioned in Chapter 5, the automatic variables declared in a CUDA kernel are placed into registers. Some kernels may use lots of automatic variables and others may use few of them. Thus, one should expect that some kernels require many registers and some require fewer. By dynamically partitioning the registers among blocks, the SM can accommodate more blocks if they require few registers and fewer blocks if they require more registers. One does, however, need to be aware of potential interactions between register limitations and other resource limitations.

In the matrix multiplication example, assume that the kernel code uses 10 registers per thread. If we have 16×16 thread blocks, how many threads can run on each SM? We can answer this question by first calculating the number of registers needed for each block, which is $10 \times 16 \times 16 = 2560$. The number of registers required by three blocks is 7680, which is under the 8192 limit. Adding another block would require 10,240 registers, which exceeds the limit; therefore, as shown in Figure 6.12A, the register limitation allows 3 blocks that altogether have 768 threads to run on each SM, which also fits within the limit of 8 block slots and 768 thread slots.

Now assume that the programmer declares another automatic variable in the kernel and bumps the number of registers used by each thread to 11. Assuming the same 16×16 blocks, each block now requires $11 \times 16 \times 16 = 2816$ registers. The number of registers required by 3 blocks is now 8448, which exceeds the register limitation. As shown in Figure 6.12B, the SM deals with this situation by reducing the number of blocks by 1, thus reducing the number of registered required to 5632. This, however, reduces the number of threads running on an SM from 768 to 512; that is,

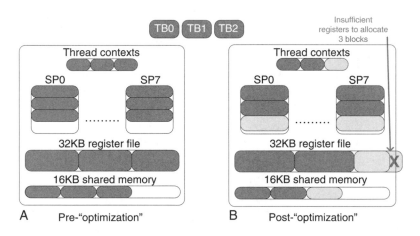

FIGURE 6.12

Interaction of resource limitations.

by using 1 extra automatic variable, the program saw a 1/3 reduction in the warp parallelism in G80 execution! This is sometimes referred to as a *performance cliff*, where a slight increase in resource usage can result in a dramatic reduction in parallelism and performance achieved. The reader is referred to the CUDA *Occupancy Calculator* [NVIDIA 2009], which is a downloadable Excel sheet that calculates the actual number of threads running on each SM for a particular device implementation given the usage of resources by a kernel.

In some cases, adding an automatic variable may allow the programmer to improve the execution speed of individual threads by initiating time consuming memory accesses early, as we will explain in more detail in Section 6.4. The improvement within each thread may be sufficient to overcome the loss of thread-level parallelism. For example, assume that in the original kernel, there are four independent instructions between a global memory load and its use. In the G80, each instruction takes 4 clock cycles to process, so the 4 independent instructions give a 16-cycle slack for the memory access. With a 200-cycle global memory latency, we need to have at least $200/(4 \times 4) = 14$ warps available for zero-overhead scheduling to keep the execution units fully utilized.

Assume that the additional register allows the programmer or the compiler to use a program transformation technique to increase the number of independent instructions from 4 to 8. These independent instructions give a 32-cycle slack for the memory access. With the same 200-cycle global memory latency, we now need to have only $200/(4 \times 8) = 7$ warps available for zero-overhead scheduling to keep the execution units fully utilized. Even though we just reduced the number of blocks from 3 to 2, and thus the number of warps from 24 to 16, we may have enough warps to fully utilize the execution units in each SM. Thus, the performance may actually increase! A programmer typically needs to experiment with each alternative and choose the best performing code. This can be a labor-intensive, tedious process. Ryoo et al. [Ryoo 2008] have proposed a methodology for automating the experimentation process to reduce the programming efforts required to reach an optimal arrangement for each variety of CUDA hardware.

6.4 DATA PREFETCHING

One of the most important resource limitations for parallel computing in general is that global memory has limited bandwidth in serving data accesses, and these accesses take a long time to complete. The tiling techniques for using shared memory address the problem of limited global memory bandwidth. The CUDA threading model tolerates long memory access latency by allowing some warps to make progress while others wait for their memory access results. This is a very powerful mechanism, but it may not be sufficient in some cases where all threads are waiting for their memory access results. Such a situation can arise if all threads have a very small number of independent instructions between memory access instructions and the consumer of the data accessed.

A useful, complementary solution to the problem is to prefetch the next data elements while consuming the current data elements, which increases the number of independent instructions between the memory accesses and the consumers of the data accessed. Prefetch techniques are often combined with tiling to simultaneously address the problems of limited bandwidth and long latency. We show such a combined approach in Figure 6.13.

The algorithm in Figure 6.13A corresponds to the tiled matrix multiplication kernel in Figure 6.10. Lines 9 and 10 in Figure 6.11 correspond to "Load current tile to shared memory" in Figure 6.13A. This is the part that loads data from global memory into shared memory. The statement in Line 9 actually has two parts. The first part loads an **Md** element from a global memory location into a register. The second part stores the register content into a shared memory location. Note that there are no independent instructions between these two parts. The warps that load their

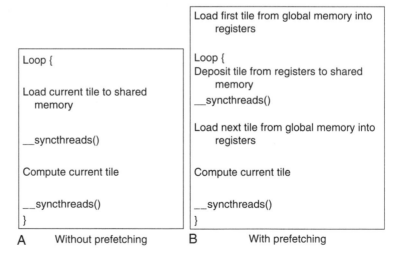

A   Without prefetching   B   With prefetching

FIGURE 6.13

Data prefetching.

current tiles will likely need to wait for a long time before they can compute the current tile; therefore, we will likely need a lot of warps to keep the floating-point units busy.

Figure 6.13B shows a prefetch version of a matrix multiplication kernel. Before we enter the `while` loop, we load the first tile into registers. Once we enter the loop, we move the loaded data into shared memory. Because this is a consumer of the loaded data, the threads will likely remain inactive, waiting for their loaded data while other threads make progress. As data arrive, warps are selected for execution, and they deposit the tile data from their registers to the shared memory. When all threads of a block complete depositing their data, they pass the barrier synchronization point and begin to load the next tile into their registers. The key is that the next tile data loaded are not immediately consumed; rather, the current block is processed from the shared memory by the dot-product loop of Lines 12 and 13 in Figure 6.11.

When the loop iterates, the "next tile" in the current iteration becomes the "current tile" of the next iteration. Thus, the deposit of the "current tile" into the shared memory corresponds to the "next tile" loaded in the previous iteration. The execution of the dot-product loop provides many independent instructions between the two parts. This reduces the amount of time the threads will have to wait for their global memory access data.

We would like to encourage the reader to revise the kernel in Figure 6.11 to use prefetch. In addition to using twice the amount of shared memory, data prefetch also uses two additional automatic variables (registers). As we discussed in Section 6.3, using additional registers can reduce the number of blocks that can run on an SM; however, this technique can still win if it significantly reduces the amount of time each thread waits for its global memory load data.

6.5 INSTRUCTION MIX

In current-generation CUDA graphics processing units (GPUs), each processor core has limited instruction processing bandwidth. Every instruction consumes instruction processing bandwidth, whether it is a floating-point calculation instruction, a load instruction, or a branch instruction. Figure 6.14A shows the dot-product loop of the matrix multiplication kernel. The loop incurs extra instructions to update loop counter k and performs conditional branch at the end of each iteration. Furthermore, the use of loop counter k to index the **Ms** and **Ns** matrices incurs address arithmetic instructions. These instructions compete against floating-point calculation

```
for (int k = 0; k < BLOCK_SIZE; ++k)
    Pvalue += Ms[ty][k] * Ns[k][tx];
```

(a) Loop incurs overhead instructions

```
Pvalue += Ms[ty][0] * Ns[0][tx] + …
              Ms[ty][15] * Ns[15][tx];
```

(b) Loop unrolling improves instruction mix.

FIGURE 6.14

Instruction mix considerations.

instructions for the limited instruction processing bandwidth. For example, the kernel loop in Figure 6.14A executes two floating-point arithmetic instructions, one loop branch instruction, two address arithmetic instructions, and one loop counter increment instruction. That is, only 1/3 of the instructions executed are floating-point calculation instructions. With limited instruction processing bandwidth, this instruction mixture limits the achievable performance to no more than 1/3 of the peak bandwidth.

A commonly used method to improve the instruction mix is to unroll the loop, as shown in Figure 6.14B. Given a tile size, one can simply unroll all the iterations and express the dot-product computation as one long multiply–add expression. This eliminates the branch instruction and the loop counter update. Furthermore, because the indices are constants rather than k, the compiler can use the addressing mode offsets of the load instructions to eliminate address arithmetic instructions. As a result, the long expression can execute at close to peak performance!

Ideally, loop unrolling should be automatically done by the compiler. This is one of the areas where compiler technology will likely be improved rapidly in the near future. Until the tools mature, many programmers will still unroll loops in their source code to achieve high performance.

6.6 THREAD GRANULARITY

An important algorithmic decision in performance tuning is the granularity of threads. It is often advantageous to put more work into each thread and use fewer threads. Such advantage arises when some redundant work exists between threads. Figure 6.15 illustrates such an opportunity in matrix multiplication. The tiled algorithm in Figure 6.11 uses one thread to compute

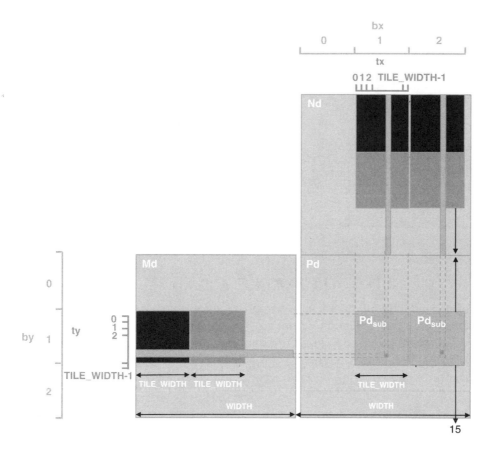

FIGURE 6.15

Increased thread granularity with rectangular tiles.

one element of the output **Pd** matrix. This requires a dot product between one row of **Md** and one column of **Nd**.

The opportunity for thread granularity adjustment comes from the fact that multiple blocks redundantly load each **Md** tile. As shown in Figure 6.15, the calculation of two **Pd** elements in adjacent tiles uses the same **Md** row. With the original tiled algorithm, the same **Md** row is redundantly loaded by the two blocks assigned to generate these two **Pd** tiles. One can eliminate this redundancy by merging the two thread blocks into one. Each thread in the new thread block now calculates two **Pd** elements. This is done by revising the kernel so each two dot products are computed by the kernel. Both dot products use the same **Mds** row but different **Nds** columns. This reduces the global memory access by 1/4. It also increases the number of independent instructions in the case of a prefetch algorithm in Figure 6.14, as there are two dot products calculated between the loading of the tiles into registers and depositing these tiles into shared memories. The reader is encouraged to write the new kernel.

The potential downside is that the new kernel now uses even more registers and shared memory. Thus, the number of blocks that can be running on each SM may decrease. It also reduces the total number of thread blocks by half, which may result in insufficient amount of parallelism for matrices of smaller dimensions. For the G80/GT200, we found that combining four adjacent horizontal blocks to compute for adjacent horizontal tiles gives the best performance for a 2048×2048 matrix multiplication.

6.7 MEASURED PERFORMANCE AND SUMMARY

The combined effects of various performance-enhancement techniques on the matrix multiplication kernel are shown in Figure 6.16. The techniques covered are tiling, loop unrolling, data prefetching, and thread granularity. The left side of the graph shows 8×8 tiling and the right side 16×16. For each tile size, we show the base code, the code after merging two blocks,

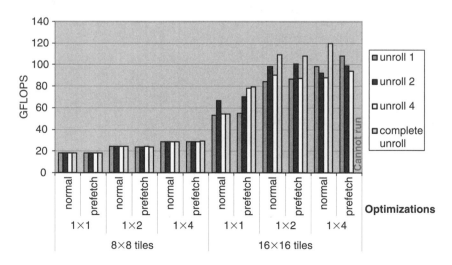

FIGURE 6.16

Measured performance with various techniques.

and the code after merging four blocks in granularity adjustment. Within each granularity, we show unrolling effects and prefetching effects. We can make at least four observations.

First, the tile size plays a major role in performance. Until the tile size reaches 16×16, neither loop unrolling nor data prefetch helps. This is reflected by the fact that all eight bars in each granularity bracket are of the same height. For small tile sizes such as 8×8, the saturated global memory bandwidth so severely limits the execution performance that transformations such as loop unrolling and data prefetching simply do not matter. On the other hand, because granularity adjustment can reduce global memory accesses, one should expect that it should improve performance. That is, 1×2 rectangular tiling reduces the global memory access by 1/4 and resulted and 1×4 tiling by 3/8. Note that 1×8 would have reduced the global traffic by only 7/16, a diminishing return that makes it much less attractive than using a larger tile size. The reductions in global memory accesses indeed help improve the performance shown in Figure 6.16.

Second, when the tile size becomes sufficiently large (16×16, in this case) to alleviate the saturation of global memory bandwidth, loop unrolling and data prefetching become much more important. In most cases, completely unrolling the loop can result in more than 20% performance improvement.

The third observation is that, although data prefetching is very beneficial for 1×1 tiling, it does not help much for 1×2 rectangular tiling. In fact, for 1×4 rectangular tiling, the register usage by one 16×16 block of the data prefetching kernel exceeds the total number of registers in the SM. This makes the code not executable in the G80! This is a good illustration of the fact that, as one applies multiple techniques to a kernel, these techniques will likely interact by reducing the resources available to other techniques.

Finally, the appropriate combinations of performance tuning techniques can make a tremendous difference in the performance achieved by the matrix multiplication kernel. In Figure 6.16, the speed of the kernel executing on the G80 increased from 18 gigaflops to 120 GFLOPS; however, the programming efforts required to search through these combinations is currently quite large. See Ryoo et al. [RRB2008] for a more extensive study of performance enhancement effects. Much work is being done in both academia and industry to reduce the amount of programming efforts needed to achieve these performance improvements with automation tools.

6.8 EXERCISES

6.1 The kernels in Figure 6.2 and 6.4 are wasteful in their use of threads; half of the threads in each block never execute. Modify the kernels to eliminate such waste. Give the relevant execute configuration parameter values at the kernel launch. Is there a cost in terms of extra arithmetic operation needed? Which resource limitation can be potentially addressed with such modification? *Hints*: Line 2 and/or Line 4 can be adjusted in each case, and the number of elements in the section may increase.

6.2 Compare the modified kernels you wrote for Exercise 6.1. Which modification introduced fewer additional arithmetic operations?

6.3 Write a complete kernel based on Exercise 6.1 by: (1) adding the statements that load a section of the input array from global memory to shared memory, (2) using `blockIdx.x` to allow multiple blocks to work on different sections of the input array, and (3) writing the reduction value for the section to a location according to the `blockIdx.x` so all blocks will deposit their section reduction value to the lower part of the input array in global memory.

6.4 Design a reduction program based on the kernel you wrote for Exercise 6.3. The host code should: (1) transfer a large input array to the global memory, and (2) use a loop to repeatedly invoke the kernel you wrote for Exercise 6.3 with adjusted execution configuration parameter values so the reduction result for the input array will eventually be produced.

6.5 For the matrix multiplication kernel in Figure 6.11, draw the access patterns of threads in a warp of Lines 9 and 10 for a small 16×16 matrix size. Calculate the `tx` values and `ty` values for each thread in a warp and use these values in the **Md** and **Nd** index calculations in Lines 9 and 10. Show that the threads indeed access consecutive **Md** and **Nd** locations in global memory during each iteration.

6.6 Write a matrix multiplication kernel function that corresponds to the design illustrated in Figure 6.15.

6.7 The following scalar product code tests your understanding of the basic CUDA model. The following code computes 1024 dot products, each of which is calculated from a pair of 256-element vectors. Assume that the code is executed on the G80. Use the code to answer the questions that follow.

```
1  #define VECTOR_N 1024
2  #define ELEMENT_N 256
3  const int DATA_N          = VECTOR_N * ELEMENT_N;
4  const int DATA_SZ         = DATA_N * sizeof(float);
5  const int RESULT_SZ       = VECTOR_N * sizeof(float);
   ...
6  float *d_A, *d_B, *d_C;
   ...
7  cudaMalloc((void **)&d_A, DATA_SZ);
8  cudaMalloc((void **)&d_B, DATA_SZ);
9  cudaMalloc((void **)&d_C, RESULT_SZ);
   ...
10 scalarProd<<<VECTOR_N, ELEMENT_N>>>(d_C, d_A, d_B, ELEMENT_N);
11
12 __global__ void
13 scalarProd(float *d_C, float *d_A, float *d_B, int ElementN)
14 {
15     __shared__ float accumResult[ELEMENT_N];
16     //Current vectors bases
17     float *A = d_A + ElementN * blockIdx.x;
18     float *B = d_B + ElementN * blockIdx.x;
19     int tx = threadIdx.x;
20
21     accumResult[tx] = A[tx] * B[tx];
22
23     for(int stride = ElementN /2; stride > 0; stride >>= 1)
24     {
25         __syncthreads();
26         if(tx < stride)
27         accumResult[tx] += accumResult[stride + tx];
28     }
30     d_C[blockIdx.x] = accumResult[0];
31 }
```

   a. How many threads are there in total?
   b. How many threads are there in a warp?
   c. How many threads are there in a block?
   d. How many global memory loads and stores are done for each thread?

> **e.** How many accesses to shared memory are done for each block? (4 pts.)
>
> **f.** List the source code lines, if any, that cause shared memory bank conflicts. (2 pts.)
>
> **g.** How many iterations of the `for` loop (Line 23) will have branch divergence? Show your derivation.
>
> **h.** Identify an opportunity to significantly reduce the bandwidth requirement on the global memory. How would you achieve this? How many accesses can you eliminate?

6.8 In Exercise 4.2, out of the possible range of values for BLOCK_SIZE, for what values of BLOCK_SIZE will the kernel completely avoid uncoalesced accesses to global memory?

6.9 In an attempt to improve performance, a bright young engineer changed the CUDA code in Exercise 6.8 into the code below.

```
__shared__ float partialSum[];
unsigned int tid = threadIdx.x;
for (unsigned int stride = n>>1; stride >= 32; stride >>= 1) {
    __syncthreads();
    if (tid < stride)
        shared[tid] += shared[tid + stride];
}
__syncthreads();
if (tid < 32) { // unroll last 5 predicated steps
    shared[tid] += shared[tid + 16];
    shared[tid] += shared[tid + 8];
    shared[tid] += shared[tid + 4];
    shared[tid] += shared[tid + 2];
    shared[tid] += shared[tid + 1];
}
```

> **a.** Do you believe that the performance will improve on the G80? Why or why not?
>
> **b.** Should the engineer receive a reward or a lecture? Why?

References and Further Reading

CUDA occupancy calculator. Santa Clara, CA: NVIDIA Corp. (http://news. developer.nvidia.com/2007/03/cuda_occupancy_.html).

Ryoo, S., Rodrigues, C. I., Baghsorkhi, S. S., & Stone, S. S. (2008). Optimization principles and application performance evaluation of a multithreaded GPU using CUDA. In *Proceedings of the 13th ACM SIGPLAN Symposium on Principles and Practice of Parallel Programming* (pp. 73–82). Salt Lake City, UT.

Ryoo, S., Rodrigues, C. I., Stone, S. S., Baghsorkhi, S. S., Ueng, S. Z., Stratton, J. A., et al. (2008). Program pruning for a multithreaded GPU. In *Code generation and optimization: Proceedings of the Sixth Annual IEEE/ACM International Symposium on code generation and optimization* (pp. 195–204). Boston, MA.

Floating Point Considerations

7

CHAPTER CONTENTS

INTRODUCTION

In the early days of computing, floating-point arithmetic capability was found only in mainframes and supercomputers. Although many microprocessors designed in the 1980s started to have floating-point coprocessors, their floating-point arithmetic operations were extremely slow—about three orders of magnitude slower than that of mainframes and supercomputers. With advances in microprocessor technology, many microprocessors designed in the 1990s, such as Intel® Pentium® III and AMD® Athlon™, began to have high-performance floating-point capabilities that rivaled supercomputers. High-speed floating-point arithmetic has become a standard feature for microprocessors and graphics processing unit (GPUs) today. As a result, it has also become important for application programmers to understand and take advantage of floating-point arithmetic in developing their applications. In particular, we will focus on the accuracy of floating-point arithmetic, the precision of floating-point number representation, and how they should be taken into consideration in parallel computation.

7.1 FLOATING-POINT FORMAT

The original IEEE 754 floating-point standard, published in 1985, was an effort by the computer manufacturers to conform to a common representation and arithmetic behavior for floating-point data. Most, if not all, of the computer manufacturers in the world have accepted this standard. In particular, virtually all microprocessors designed in the future will either fully conform to or almost fully conform to the IEEE-754 floating-point standard and its more recent IEEE 754-2008 revision [IEEE 2008]. Therefore, it is important for application developers to understand the concept and practical considerations of this standard.

A floating-point number system starts with the representation of a numerical value as bit patterns. In the IEEE floating-point standard, a numerical value is represented in three groups of bits: sign (S), exponent (E), and mantissa (M). Each (S, E, M) pattern uniquely identifies a numeric value according to the following formula:

$$\text{Value} = (-1)^S \times M \times \{2^E\}, \text{ where } 1.0 \leq M < 2.0 \qquad (1)$$

The interpretation of S is simple: S = 0 indicates a positive number and S = 1 a negative number. Mathematically, any number, including −1, when raised to the power of 0, results in 1; thus, the value is positive. On the other hand, when −1 is raised to the power of 1, it is −1 itself. With a multiplication by −1, the value becomes negative. The interpretation of M and E bits are, however, much more complex. We will use the following example to help explain the interpretation of M and E bits.

Assume for the sake of simplicity that each floating-point number consists of a 1-bit sign, a 3-bit exponent, and a 2-bit mantissa. We will use this hypothetical 6-bit format to illustrate the challenges involved in encoding E and M. As we discuss numeric values, we will sometime need to express a number either as a decimal place value or as a binary place value. Numbers expressed as a decimal place value will have the subscript D and those expressed as a binary place value will have the subscript B. For example, 0.5_D (5×10^{-1}, as the place to the right of the decimal point carries a weight of 10^{-1}) is the same as 0.1_B (1×2^{-1}, as the place to the right of the decimal point carries a weight of 2^{-1}).

7.1.1 Normalized Representation of M

Formula (1) requires that $1.0_B \leq M < 10.0_B$, which makes the mantissa value for each floating-point number unique; for example, the only one mantissa value allowed for 0.5_D is M =1.0:

$$0.5_D = 1.0_B \times 2^{-1}$$

Another potential candidate would be $0.1_B \times 2^0$, but the value of the mantissa would be too small according to the rule. Similarly, $10.0_B \times 2^{-2}$ is not legal because the value of the mantissa is too large. In general, with the restriction that $1.0_B \leq M < 10.0_B$, every floating point number has exactly one legal mantissa value. The numbers that satisfy this restriction will be referred to as *normalized numbers*. Because all mantissa values that satisfy the restriction are of the form 1.*xx*, we can omit the "1." part from the representation; therefore, the mantissa value of 0.5 in a 2-bit mantissa representation is 00, which is derived by omitting "1." from 1.00. This makes a 2-bit mantissa effectively a 3-bit mantissa. In general, with the IEEE format, an *n*-bit mantissa is effectively an $(n+1)$-bit mantissa.

7.1.2 Excess Encoding of E

The number of bits used to represent E determines the range of numbers that can be represented. Large *positive* E values result in very large floating-point values; for example, if the E value is 64, the floating-point number being represented is between 2^{64} ($>10^{18}$) and 2^{65}. You would be extremely happy if this was the balance of your savings account! Large *negative* E values result in very small floating-point values; for example, if the E value is -64, the number being represented is between 2^{-64} ($<10^{-18}$) and 2^{-63}. This is a very tiny fractional number. The E field allows a floating-point number representation to represent a larger range of numbers. We will come back to this point when we look at the representable numbers of a format.

The IEEE standard adopts an encoding convention for E. If *n* bits are used to represent the exponent E, then $(2^{n-1} - 1)$ is added to the two's complement representation for the exponent to form its excess representation. A two's complement representation is a system where the negative value of a number can be derived by first complementing every bit of the value and adding 1 to the result. In our 3-bit exponent representation, there are three bits in the exponent; therefore, the value $2^{3-1} - 1 = 011$ will be added to the two's complement representation of the exponent value. Figure 7.1 shows the two's complement representation and the excess presentation of each decimal exponent value. In our example, the exponent for 0.5_D is -1. The two's complement representation of -1 can be derived by first complementing 001, the representation of 1, into 110 and then adding 001 to get 111. The excess presentation adds another 011 to the two's complement representation, as shown in the figure, which results in 010.

The advantage of excess representation is that an unsigned comparator can be used to compare signed numbers. As shown in Figure 7.2,

Two's Complement	Decimal Value	Excess Representation
000	0	011
001	1	100
010	2	101
011	3	110
100	Reserved pattern	111
101	−3	000
110	−2	001
111	−1	010

FIGURE 7.1

Excess-3 encoding, sorted by two's complement ordering.

Two's Complement	Decimal Value	Excess-3
100	(reserved pattern)	111
101	−3	000
110	−2	001
111	−1	010
000	0	011
001	1	100
010	2	101
011	3	110

FIGURE 7.2

Excess-3 encoding, sorted by excess-3 ordering.

the excess-3 code increases monotonically from −3 to 3 when viewed as unsigned numbers. The code from −3 is 000 and that for 3 is 110. Thus, if one uses an unsigned number comparator to compare excess-3 code for any number from −3 to 3, the comparator gives the correct comparison result in terms of which number is larger, smaller, etc. For example, if one compares excess-3 codes 001 and 100 with an unsigned comparator, 001 is smaller than 100. This is the correct conclusion, as the values that they represent (−2 and 1) have exactly the same relation. This is a desirable property for hardware implementation, because unsigned comparators are smaller and faster than signed comparators.

Now we are ready to represent 0.5_D with our 6-bit format:

$0.5_D = 0\ 010\ 00$, where S = 0, E = 010, and M = ~~(1.)~~00

That is, the 6-bit representation for 0.5_D is 001000.

In general, with normalized mantissa and excess-coded exponent, the value of a number with an n-bit exponent is

$$(-1)^S 1.M \times 2^{(E-(2^\wedge(n-1))+1)}$$

7.2 REPRESENTABLE NUMBERS

The representable numbers of a number format are the numbers that can be exactly represented in the format; for example, the representable numbers for a 3-bit unsigned integer format are shown in Figure 7.3. Neither -1 nor 9 can be represented in this format. We can draw a number line to identify all of the representable numbers, as shown in Figure 7.4, where all representable numbers of the 3-bit unsigned integer format are marked with stars.

The representable numbers of a floating-point format can be visualized in a similar manner. In Figure 7.5, we show all the representable numbers

000	0
001	1
010	2
011	3
100	4
101	5
110	6
111	7

FIGURE 7.3

Representable numbers of a 3-bit unsigned format.

FIGURE 7.4

Representable numbers of a 3-bit unsigned integer format.

E	M	No-Zero		Abrupt Underflow		Denorm	
		S = 0	S = 1	S = 0	S = 1	S = 0	S = 1
00	00	2^{-1}	$-(2^{-1})$	0	0	0	0
	01	$2^{-1} + (1 \times 2^{-3})$	$-[2^{-1} + (1 \times 2^{-3})]$	0	0	1×2^{-2}	$-(1 \times 2^{-2})$
	10	$2^{-1} + (2 \times 2^{-3})$	$-[2^{-1} + (2 \times 2^{-3})]$	0	0	2×2^{-2}	$-(2 \times 2^{-2})$
	11	$2^{-1} + (3 \times 2^{-3})$	$-[2^{-1} + (3 \times 2^{-3})]$	0	0	3×2^{-2}	$-(3 \times 2^{-2})$
01	00	2^0	$-(2^0)$	2^0	$-(2^0)$	2^0	$-(2^0)$
	01	$2^0 + (1 \times 2^{-2})$	$-[2^0 + (1 \times 2^{-2})]$	$2^0 + (1 \times 2^{-2})$	$-[2^0 + (1 \times 2^{-2})]$	$2^0 + (1 \times 2^{-2})$	$-[2^0 + (1 \times 2^{-2})]$
	10	$2^0 + (2 \times 2^{-2})$	$-[2^0 + (2 \times 2^{-2})]$	$2^0 + (2 \times 2^{-2})$	$-[2^0 + (2 \times 2^{-2})]$	$2^0 + (2 \times 2^{-2})$	$-[2^0 + (2 \times 2^{-2})]$
	11	$2^0 + (3 \times 2^{-2})$	$-[2^0 + (3 \times 2^{-2})]$	$2^0 + (3 \times 2^{-2})$	$-[2^0 + (3 \times 2^{-2})]$	$2^0 + (3 \times 2^{-2})$	$-[2^0 + (3 \times 2^{-2})]$
10	00	2^1	$-(2^1)$	2^1	$-(2^1)$	2^1	$-(2^1)$
	01	$2^1 + (1 \times 2^{-1})$	$-[2^1 + [1 \times 2^{-1})]$	$2^1 + (1 \times 2^{-1})$	$-[2^1 + (1 \times 2^{-1})]$	$2^1 + (1 \times 2^{-1})$	$-[2^1 + (1 \times 2^{-1})]$
	10	$2^1 + (2 \times 2^{-1})$	$-[2^1 + (2 \times 2^{-1})]$	$2^1 + (2 \times 2^{-1})$	$-[2^1 + (2 \times 2^{-1})]$	$2^1 + (2 \times 2^{-1})$	$-[2^1 + (2 \times 2^{-1})]$
	11	$2^1 + (3 \times 2^{-1})$	$-[2^1 + (3 \times 2^{-1})]$	$2^1 + (3 \times 2^{-1})$	$-[2^1 + (3 \times 2^{-1})]$	$2^1 + (3 \times 2^{-1})$	$-[2^1 + (3 \times 2^{-1})]$
11		Reserved pattern					

FIGURE 7.5

Representable numbers of no-zero, abrupt underflow, and denorm formats.

of what we have so far and two variations. We have used a 5-bit format to keep the size of the table manageable. The format consists of 1-bit S, 2-bit E (excess-1 coded), and 2-bit M (with "1." part omitted). The no-zero column gives the representable numbers of the format we discussed thus far. The reader is encouraged to generate at least part of the no-zero column based on the formula given in Section 7.1. Note that, with this format, 0 is not one of the representable numbers.

A quick look at how these representable numbers populate the number line, as shown in Figure 7.6, provides further insights about these representable numbers. In Figure 7.6, we show only the positive representable numbers. The negative numbers are symmetric to their positive counterparts on the other side of 0.

We can make five observations. First, the exponent bits define the major intervals of representable numbers. In Figure 7.6, there are three major intervals on each side of 0 because there are two exponent bits. Basically, the major intervals are between powers of twos. With two bits of exponents, there are three powers of two ($2^{-1} = 0.5_D$, $2^0 = 1.0_D$, $2^1 = 2.0_D$), and each starts an interval of representable numbers.

The second observation is that the mantissa bits define the number of representable numbers in each interval. With two mantissa bits, we have four representable numbers in each interval. In general, with N mantissa bits, we have 2^N representable numbers in each interval. If a value to be represented falls within one of the intervals, it will be rounded to one of these representable numbers. Obviously, the larger the number of representable numbers in each interval, the more precisely we can represent a value in the region; therefore, the number of mantissa bits determines the *precision* of the representation.

The third observation is that 0 is not representable in this format. It is missing from the representable numbers in the no-zero column of Figure 7.5. Because 0 is one of the most important numbers, not being able to represent 0 in a number representation system is a serious deficiency. We will address this deficiency later.

The fourth observation is that the representable numbers become closer to each other toward the neighborhood of 0. Each interval is half the size of

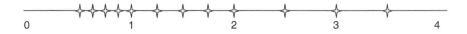

FIGURE 7.6

Representable numbers of the no-zero representation.

the previous interval as we move toward zero. In Figure 7.6, the right-most interval is of width 2, the next one is of width 1, and the next one is of width 0.5. Because every interval has the same representable numbers (four, in Figure 7.6), the representable numbers become closer to each other as we move toward zero. This is a desirable trend because as the absolute value of these numbers becomes smaller, it is more important to represent them more accurately. For example, if you have $1 billion in your bank account, you may not even notice a $1 rounding error in calculating your balance; however, if the total balance is $10, then having a $1 rounding error would be much more noticeable!

Having the representable numbers closer to each other makes it possible to represent numbers more accurately; for example, in Figure 7.6 there are four representable numbers. Unfortunately this trend does not hold for the very vicinity of 0, which leads to the fifth observation: There is a gap in representable numbers in the vicinity of 0. This is because the range of the normalized mantissa precludes 0. This is another serious deficiency. The representation introduces significantly larger ($4\times$) errors when representing numbers between 0 and 0.5 compared to the errors for the larger numbers between 0.5 and 1.0. In general, with N bits in the mantissa, this style of representation would introduce 2^N times more error in the interval closest to zero than the next interval. For numerical methods that rely on accurate detection of convergence conditions based on very small data values, such a deficiency can cause instability in execution time and accuracy of results. Furthermore, some algorithms generate small numbers and eventually use them as denominators. The errors in representing these small numbers can be greatly magnified in the division process and cause numerical instability in these algorithms.

One method that can accommodate 0 into a normalized floating-point number system is the *abrupt underflow* convention, which is illustrated in the second column of Figure 7.5. Whenever E is 0, the number is interpreted as 0. In our 5-bit format, this method takes away 8 representable numbers (4 positive and 4 negative) in the vicinity of 0 and makes them all 0. Due to its simplicity, some minicomputers in the 1980s used abrupt underflow. Although this method makes 0 a representable number, it creates an even larger gap between representable numbers in the vicinity of 0, as shown in Figure 7.7. It is obvious, when compared with Figure 7.6, that the gap of representable numbers has been enlarged significantly from 0.5 to 1.0. As we explained before, this is very problematic for many numerical algorithms whose correctness relies on accurate representation of small numbers near 0.

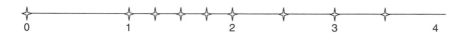

FIGURE 7.7

Representable numbers of the abrupt underflow format.

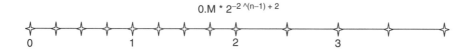

FIGURE 7.8

Representable numbers of a denormalization format.

The actual method adopted by the IEEE standard is called *denormalization*. The method relaxes the normalization requirement for numbers very close to 0. As shown in Figure 7.9, whenever $E = 0$, the mantissa is no longer assumed to be of the form $1.xx$. Rather, it is assumed to be $0.xx$. The value of the exponent is assumed to be the same as the previous interval. For example, in Figure 7.5, the denormalized representation 00001 has an exponent value of 00 and a mantissa value of 01. The mantissa is assumed to be 0.01, and the exponent value is assumed to be the same as that of the previous interval: 0 rather than -1. That is, the value that 00001 represents is $0.01 \times 2^0 = 2^{-2}$. Figure 7.8 shows the representable numbers for the denormalization format. The representation now has uniformly spaced representable numbers in the close vicinity of 0. Intuitively, the denormalized convention takes the four numbers in the last interval of representable numbers of a no-zero representation and spreads them out to cover the gap area. This eliminates the undesirable gap in the previous two methods. Note that the distances between representable numbers in the last two intervals are actually identical. In general, if the n-bit exponent is 0, then the value is

$$0.M \times 2^{-2^{\wedge}(n-1)+2}$$

In summary, the precision of a floating-point representation is measured by the maximal error that we can introduce to a floating-point number by representing that number as one of the representable numbers. The smaller the error is, the higher the precision. The precision of a floating-point representation can be improved by adding more bits to the mantissa.

Adding one bit to the representation in Figure 7.8 would improve the precision by reducing the maximal error by half; thus, a number system has higher precision when it uses more bits for mantissa.

7.3 SPECIAL BIT PATTERNS AND PRECISION

The actual IEEE format has one more special bit pattern. When all exponent bits are ones, the number represented is an infinity value if the mantissa is zero. It is a Not a Number (NaN) if the mantissa is not zero. All special bit patterns of the IEEE floating-point format are shown in Figure 7.9.

All other numbers are normalized floating-point numbers. Single-precision numbers have 1-bit S, 8-bit E, and 23-bit M. Double-precision numbers have 1-bit S, 11-bit E, and 52-bit M. Because a double-precision number has 29 more bits for the mantissa, the largest error for representing a number is reduced to $1/2^{29}$ of that of the single precision format! With the additional three bits of exponent, the double-precision format also extends the number of intervals of representable numbers. This extends the range of representable numbers to very large as well as very small values.

All representable numbers fall between $-\infty$ (negative infinity) and $+\infty$ (positive infinity). An ∞ can be created by overflow (e.g., divided by zero). Any representable number divided by $+\infty$ or $-\infty$ results in 0.

A NaN is generated by operations whose input values do not make sense—for example, $0/0$, $0 \times \infty$, ∞/∞, $\infty - \infty$. They are also used for data that have not been properly initialized in a program. There are two types of NaNs in the IEEE standard: signaling and quiet. Signaling NaNs (SNaNs)

Exponent	Mantissa	Meaning
11 ... 1	$\neq 0$	NaN
11 ... 1	$= 0$	$(-1)^S \times \infty$
00 ... 0	$\neq 0$	Denormalized
00 ... 0	$= 0$	0

FIGURE 7.9

Special bit patterns in the IEEE standard format.

are represented with the most significant mantissa bit cleared, whereas quiet NaNs are represented with the most significant mantissa bit set.

A signaling NaN causes an exception when used as input to arithmetic operations; for example, the operation (1.0 + SNaN) raises an exception. Signaling NaNs are used in situations where the programmer would like to make sure that the program execution is interrupted whenever any NaN values are used in floating-point computations. These situations usually mean that there is something wrong with the execution of the program. In mission-critical applications, the execution cannot continue until the validity of the execution can be verified with a separate means. For example, software engineers often mark all of the uninitialized data as signaling NaN. This practice ensures the detection of using uninitialized data during program execution. The current generation of GPU hardware does not support signaling NaN. This is due to the difficulty of supporting accurate signaling during massively parallel execution.

Quiet NaN generates a quiet NaN when used as input to arithmetic operations; for example, the operation (1.0 + quiet NaN) generates a quiet NaN. Quiet NaNs are typically used in applications where the user can review the output and decide if the application should be rerun with a different input for more valid results. When the results are printed, quiet NaNs are printed as "NaN" so the user can easily spot them in the output file. This is how one can detect data corruption in CUDA™ applications.

7.4 ARITHMETIC ACCURACY AND ROUNDING

Now that we have a good understanding of the IEEE floating-point format, we are ready to discuss the concept of arithmetic accuracy. Whereas the precision is determined by the number of mantissa bits used in a floating-point number format, the accuracy is determined by the operations performed on a floating number. The accuracy of a floating-point arithmetic operation is measured by the maximal error introduced by the operation. The smaller the error is, the higher the accuracy. The most common source of error in floating-point arithmetic is when the operation generates a result that cannot be exactly represented and thus requires rounding. Rounding occurs if the mantissa of the result value needs too many bits to be represented exactly. The cause of rounding is typically preshifting in floating-point arithmetic. When two input operands to a floating-point addition or subtraction have different exponents, the mantissa of the one with the smaller exponent is typically right-shifted until the exponents are equal. As a result, the final result can have more bits than the format can accommodate.

This can be illustrated with a simple example based on the 5-bit representation in Figure 7.5. Assume that we need to add 1.00×2^{-2} (0, 00, 01) to 1.00×2^1 (0, 10, 00); that is, we need to perform $(1.00 \times 2^1) + (1.00 \times 2^{-2})$. Due to the difference in exponent values, the mantissa value of the second number must be right shifted before being added to the first mantissa value; that is, the addition becomes $(1.00 \times 2^1) + (0.001 \times 2^1)$. The ideal result would be 1.001×2^1; however, we can see that this ideal result is not a representable number in a 5-bit representation. It would have required 3 bits of mantissa; thus, the best one can do is to generate the closest representable number, which is 1.01×2^1. By doing so, we introduce an error (0.001×2^1), which is half the place value of the least significant place. We refer to this as 0.5 unit in the last place (ULP). If the hardware is designed to perform arithmetic and rounding operations perfectly, the greatest error that one should introduce should be no more than 0.5 ULP. This is the accuracy achieved by the addition and subtraction operations in the NVIDIA® G80 and GT200.

In practice, some of the more complex arithmetic hardware units, such as division and transcendental functions, are typically implemented with iterative approximation algorithms. If the hardware does not perform a sufficient number of iterations, the result may have an error larger than 0.5 ULP. The inversion operation in the G80 and GT200 can introduce an error that is twice the place value of the least place of the mantissa, or 2 ULP. The arithmetic operations on newer generation GPUs are much more accurate.

7.5 ALGORITHM CONSIDERATIONS

Numerical algorithms often must sum up a large number of values. For example, the dot product in matrix multiplication needs to sum up pairwise products of input matrix elements. Ideally, the order of summing these values should not affect the final total, as addition is an associative operation; however, with finite precision, the order of summing these values can affect the accuracy of the final result, such as if we need to perform a sum reduction on 4 numbers in our 5-bit representation: $(1.00 \times 2^0) + (1.00 \times 2^0) + (1.00 \times 2^{-2}) + (1.00 \times 2^{-2})$. If we add up the numbers in strict sequential order, we have the following sequence of operations:

$$(1.00 \times 2^0) + (1.00 \times 2^0) + (1.00 \times 2^{-2}) + (1.00 \times 2^{-2})$$
$$= (1.00 \times 2^1) + (1.00 \times 2^{-2}) + (1.00 \times 2^{-2})$$
$$= (1.00 \times 2^1) + (1.00 \times 2^{-2})$$
$$= 1.00 \times 2^1$$

Note that in the second step and third step the smaller operands simply disappear because they are too small compared to the larger operands.

Now, let's consider a parallel algorithm where the first two values are added and the second two operands are added in parallel. The algorithm than add up the pairwise sum:

$$[(1.00 \times 2^0) + (1.00 \times 2^0)] + [(1.00 \times 2^{-2}) + (1.00 \times 2^{-2})]$$
$$= (1.00 \times 2^1) + (1.00 \times 2^{-1})$$
$$= 1.01 \times 2^1$$

Note that the results are different from the sequential result! This is because the sum of the third and fourth values is large enough that it can now affect the addition result. This discrepancy between sequential algorithms and parallel algorithms often surprises application developers who are not familiar with floating-point precision and accuracy considerations. Although we showed a scenario where a parallel algorithm produced a more accurate result than a sequential algorithm, the reader should be able to come up with a slightly different scenario where the parallel algorithm produces a less accurate result than a sequential algorithm. Experienced application developers either make sure that the variation in the final result can be tolerated or ensure that the data are sorted or grouped in such a way that the parallel algorithm results in the most accurate results.

A common technique to maximize floating-point arithmetic accuracy is to presort data before a reduction computation. In our sum reduction example, if we presort the data according to ascending numerical order, we will have the following:

$$(1.00 \times 2^{-2}) + (1.00 \times 2^{-2}) + (1.00 \times 2^0) + (1.00 \times 2^0)$$

When we divide up the numbers into groups in a parallel algorithm (say, the first pair in one group and the second pair in another group), it is guaranteed that numbers with numerical values close to each other are in the same group. Therefore, when we perform addition in these groups, we will likely have accurate results. Furthermore, the parallel algorithms will ultimately perform sequential operations within each group. Having the numbers sorted in ascending order allows a sequential addition to achieve greater accuracy. This is an important reason why sorting is frequently used in massively parallel numerical algorithms.

7.6 SUMMARY

This chapter has introduced the concepts of floating-point format and representable numbers that are foundational to the understanding of precision. Based on these concepts, we also explain the denormalized numbers and why they are important in many numerical applications. In early CUDA devices such as the G80, denormalized numbers were not supported; however, later hardware generations such as the GT200 support denormalized numbers. We have also explained the concept of the arithmetic accuracy of floating-point operations. It is important for CUDA programmers to understand the potentially lower accuracy of fast arithmetic operations implemented in the special function units. More importantly, the readers should now have a good understanding of why parallel algorithms often can affect the accuracy of calculation results and how one can potentially use sorting to improve the accuracy of their computation.

7.7 EXERCISES

7.1 Draw the equivalent of Figure 7.5 for a 6-bit format (1-bit sign, 3-bit mantissa, 2-bit exponent). Use your result to explain what each additional mantissa bit does to the set of representable numbers on the number line.

7.2 Draw the equivalent of Figure 7.5 for another 6-bit format (1-bit sign, 2-bit mantissa, 3-bit exponent). Use your result to explain what each additional exponent bit does to the set of representable numbers on the number line.

7.3 Assume that in a new processor design, due to technical difficulty, the floating-point arithmetic unit that performs addition can only do "round to zero" (rounding by truncating the value toward 0). The hardware maintains a sufficient number of bits so the only error introduced is due to rounding. What is the maximal ULP error value for add operations on this machine?

7.4 A graduate student wrote a CUDA kernel to reduce a large floating-point array to the sum of all its elements. The array will always be sorted with the smallest values to the largest values. To avoid branch divergence, he decided to implement the algorithm of Figure 6.4. Explain why this can reduce the accuracy of his results.

7.5 Assume that in a arithmetic unit design, the hardware implements an iterative approximation algorithm that generates two additional accurate mantissa bits of the result for the sin() function in each clock cycle. The architect decided to allow the arithmetic function to iterate nine clock cycles. Assume that the hardware fill in all remaining mantissa bits are 0. What would be the maximal ULP error of the hardware implementation of the sin() function in this design for the IEEE single-precision numbers? Assume that the omitted "1." mantissa bit must also be generated by the arithmetic unit.

Reference

IEEE Microprocessor Standards Committee. (2008). *Draft standard for floating-point arithmetic P754*. Piscataway, NJ: Institute of Electrical and Electronics Engineers.

Application Case Study: Advanced MRI Reconstruction

8

CHAPTER CONTENTS

INTRODUCTION

Application case studies teach computational thinking and practical programming techniques in a concrete manner. They also help demonstrate how the individual techniques fit into a top-to-bottom development process. Most importantly, they help us to visualize the practical use of these techniques in solving problems. In this chapter, we begin with the background and problem formulation of a relatively simple application. We show that parallel execution not only speeds up the existing approaches but also allows applications experts to pursue approaches that are known to provide benefit but were previously ignored due to their excessive computational requirements. We then use an example algorithm and its implementation source code from such an approach to illustrate how a developer can systematically determine the kernel parallelism structure, assign variables into CUDA™ memories, steer around limitations of the hardware, validate results, and assess the impact of performance improvements.

8.1 APPLICATION BACKGROUND

Magnetic resonance imaging (MRI) is commonly used by the medical community to safely and noninvasively probe the structure and function of biological tissues in all regions of the body. Images that are generated using MRI have had a profound impact in both clinical and research settings. MRI consists of two phases: acquisition (scan) and reconstruction. During the acquisition phase, the scanner samples data in the k-space domain (i.e., the spatial–frequency domain or Fourier transform domain) along a predefined trajectory. These samples are then transformed into the desired image during the reconstruction phase.

The application of MRI is often limited by high noise levels, significant imaging artifacts, and long data acquisition times. In clinical settings, short scan times not only increase scanner throughput but also reduce patient discomfort, which tends to mitigate motion-related artifacts. High image resolution and fidelity are important because they enable earlier detection of pathology, leading to improved prognoses for patients; however, the goals of short scan time, high resolution, and high signal-to-noise ratio (SNR) often conflict—improvements in one metric tend to come at the expense of one or both of the others. One needs new, disruptive technological breakthroughs to be able to simultaneously improve on all three dimensions. This study presents a case where massively parallel computing provides such a disruptive breakthrough.

The reader is referred to MRI textbooks such as Liang and Lauterbur [Liang 1999] for the physics principles behind MRI. For this case study, we will focus on the computational complexity in the reconstruction phase and how the complexity is affected by the k-space sampling trajectory. The k-space sampling trajectory used by the MRI scanner can significantly affect the quality of the reconstructed image, the time complexity of the reconstruction algorithm, and the time required for the scanner to acquire the samples. Equation (1) below shows a formulation that relates the k-space samples to the reconstructed image for a class of reconstruction methods.

$$\hat{m}(\mathbf{r}) = \sum_j W\left(\mathbf{k}_j\right) s\left(\mathbf{k}_j\right) e^{i2\pi \mathbf{k}_j \cdot \mathbf{r}} \tag{1}$$

In Equation (1), $\hat{m}(r)$ is the reconstructed image, $s(k)$ is the measured k-space data, and $W(k)$ is the weighting function that accounts for nonuniform sampling; that is, $W(k)$ decreases the influence of data from k-space regions with a higher density of sample points. For this class reconstructions,

$W(k)$ can also serve as an apodization function that reduces the influence of noise and reduces artifacts due to finite sampling.

If data are acquired at uniformly spaced Cartesian grid points in the k-space under ideal conditions, then the $W(k)$ weighting function is a constant and can thus be factored out of the summation in Equation (1). As a result, the reconstruction of $m(r)$ becomes an inverse fast Fourier transform (FFT) on $s(k)$, an extremely efficient computation method. A collection of data measured at such uniformly spaced Cartesian grid points is referred as a *Cartesian scan trajectory*. Figure 8.1A depicts a Cartesian scan trajectory. In practice, Cartesian scan trajectories allow straightforward implementation on scanners and are widely used in clinical settings.

Although the inverse FFT reconstruction of Cartesian scan data is computationally efficient, non-Cartesian scan trajectories often offer the advantages of reduced sensitivity to patient motion, better ability to provide self-calibrating field inhomogeneity information, and reduced requirements on scanner hardware performance. As a result, non-Cartesian scan trajectories such as spirals (shown in Figure 8.1C), radial lines (projection imaging), and rosettes have been proposed to reduce motion-related artifacts and address scanner hardware performance limitations.

Image reconstruction from non-Cartesian trajectory data presents both challenges and opportunities. The main challenge arises from the fact that

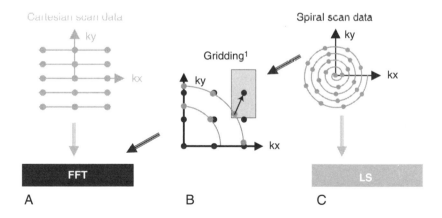

FIGURE 8.1

Scanner k-space trajectories and their associated reconstruction strategies: (A) Cartesian trajectory with FFT reconstruction, (B) spiral (or non-Cartesian trajectory in general) followed by gridding to enable FFT reconstruction, and (C) spiral (non-Cartesian) trajectory with linear-solver-based reconstruction.

the exponential terms are no longer uniformly spaced; the summation does not have the form of an FFT anymore. Therefore, one can no longer perform reconstruction by directly applying an inverse FFT to the k-space samples. In a commonly used approach called *gridding*, the samples are first interpolated onto a uniform Cartesian grid and then reconstructed using the FFT (see Figure 8.1B). For example, a convolution approach to gridding takes a k-space data point, convolves it with a gridding kernel, and accumulates the results on a Cartesian grid. Convolution is quite computationally intensive. Accelerating gridding computation on many-core processors facilitates the application of the current FFT approach to non-Cartesian trajectory data. Because we will be examining a convolution-style computation in Chapter 9, we will not cover it here.

In this chapter, we will cover an iterative, statistically optimal image reconstruction method that can accurately model imaging physics and bound the noise error in each image pixel value. This allows the reconstructed image pixel values to be used for measuring subtle phenomena such as tissue chemical anomalies before they become anatomical pathology. Figure 8.2 shows such a measurement that generates a map of sodium, a heavily regulated substance in normal human tissues. Because sodium is much less abundant than water molecules in human tissues, a reliable measure of sodium levels requires a higher SNR. An iterative, statistically optimal reconstruction method can be used to achieve the required level of SNR; however, such iterative reconstructions have been impractical for large-scale, three-dimensional (3D) problems due to their excessive computational requirements compared to gridding. Recently, these reconstructions have become viable in clinical settings when accelerated on graphics processing units (GPUs). In particular, we will show that an iterative reconstruction algorithm that used to take hours using a high-end sequential central processing unit (CPU) now takes only minutes using the NVIDIA® G80 to produce an image of moderate resolution, a delay acceptable in clinical settings.

8.2 ITERATIVE RECONSTRUCTION

Haldar and Liang proposed a linear-solver-based iterative reconstruction algorithm for non-Cartesian scan data, as shown in Figure 8.1C. The algorithm allows for explicit modeling and compensation for the physics of the scanner data acquisition process and can thus reduce the artifacts in the reconstructed image. It is, however, computation intensive.

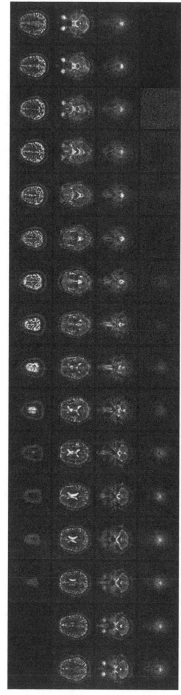

Courtesy of Keith Thulborn and Ian Atkinson, Center for MR Research, University of Illinois at Chicago

FIGURE 8.2

The use of non-Cartesian k-space sample trajectory and accurate linear-solver-based reconstruction has resulted in new MRI modalities with exciting medical applications. The improved SNR allows reliable collection of in vivo concentration data on such chemical substances as sodium in human tissues. The variation or shifting of sodium concentration is an early sign of disease development or tissue death; for example, the sodium map of a human brain can provide an early indication of brain tumor tissue responsiveness to chemotherapy protocols, thus enabling individualized medicine.

The reconstruction time on high-end sequential CPUs has been hours for moderate-resolution images; thus, this approach is impractical for clinical use. We use this as an example of innovative methods that have required too much computation time to be considered practical. We will show that massive parallelism in GPUs can reduce the reconstruction time to the order of a minute, so one can begin to deploy the new MRI modalities such as sodium imaging in clinical settings.

Figure 8.3 shows a solution of the quasi-Bayesian estimation problem formulation of the iterative linear-solver-based reconstruction approach, where ρ is a vector containing voxel values for the reconstructed image, $\mathbf{F}$ is a matrix that models the physics of the imaging process, $\mathbf{d}$ is a vector of data samples from the scanner, and $\mathbf{W}$ is a matrix that can incorporate prior information such as anatomical constraints. In clinical settings, the anatomical constraints represented in $\mathbf{W}$ are derived from one or more high-resolution, high-SNR water molecule scans of the patient. These water molecule scans reveal features such as the location of anatomical structures. The matrix $\mathbf{W}$ is derived from these reference images. The problem is to solve for ρ given all the other matrices and vectors.

On the surface, the computational solution to the problem formulation in Figure 8.3 should be very straightforward. It involves matrix–matrix multiplications and addition ($\mathbf{F}^H\mathbf{F} + \lambda\mathbf{W}^H\mathbf{W}$), matrix–vector multiplication ($\mathbf{F}^H\mathbf{d}$), matrix inversion ($\mathbf{F}^H\mathbf{F} + \lambda\mathbf{W}^H\mathbf{W})^{-1}$, and finally matrix–matrix multiplication [$(\mathbf{F}^H\mathbf{F} + \lambda\mathbf{W}^H\mathbf{W})^{-1}\mathbf{F}^H\mathbf{d}$]. However, the sizes of the matrices make this straightforward approach extremely time consuming. $\mathbf{F}^H$ and $\mathbf{F}$

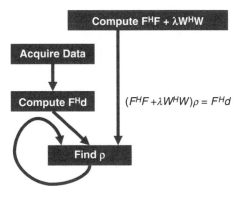

FIGURE 8.3

An iterative linear-solver-based approach to reconstruction of non-Cartesian *k*-space sample data.

are 3D matrices whose dimensions are determined by the resolution of the reconstructed image ρ. Even in a modest-resolution, 128^3-voxel reconstruction, there are 128^3 columns in **F** with N elements in each column, where N is the number of k-space samples used. Obviously, **F** is extremely large.

The sizes of the matrices involved are so large that the matrix operations required for a direct solution of the equation in Figure 8.3 is practically intractable. An iterative method for matrix inversion, such as the conjugate gradient (CG) algorithm, is therefore preferred. The conjugate gradient algorithm reconstructs the image by iteratively solving the equation in Figure 8.3 for ρ. During each iteration, the CG algorithm updates the current image estimate ρ to improve the value of the quasi-Bayesian cost function. The computational efficiency of the CG technique is largely determined by the efficiency of matrix–vector multiplication operations involving $\mathbf{F}^H\mathbf{F} + \lambda\mathbf{W}^H\mathbf{W}$ and ρ, as these operations are required during each iteration of the CG algorithm.

Fortunately, matrix **W** often has a sparse structure that permits efficient multiplication $\mathbf{W}^H\mathbf{W}$, and matrix $\mathbf{F}^H\mathbf{F}$ is a Toeplitz matrix that enables efficient matrix–vector multiplication via the FFT. Stone et al. [Stone 2008] presented a GPU accelerated method for calculating Q, a data structure that allows us to quickly calculate matrix–vector multiplication involving $\mathbf{F}^H\mathbf{F}$ without actually calculating $\mathbf{F}^H\mathbf{F}$ itself. The calculation of Q can take days on a high-end CPU core. It only has to be done once for a given trajectory and can be used for multiple scans.

The matrix–vector multiply to calculate $\mathbf{F}^H\mathbf{d}$ takes about one order of magnitude less time than Q but can still require about 3 hours for a 128^3-voxel reconstruction on a high-end sequential CPU. Because $\mathbf{F}^H\mathbf{d}$ needs to be computed for every image acquisition, it is desirable to reduce the computation time of $\mathbf{F}^H\mathbf{d}$ to minutes. We will show the details of this process. As it turns out, the core computational structure of Q is identical to that of $\mathbf{F}^H\mathbf{d}$. As a result, the same methodology can be used to accelerate the computation of both.

The "find ρ" step in Figure 8.3 performs the actual CG based on $\mathbf{F}^H\mathbf{d}$. As we explained earlier, precalculation of Q makes this step much less computationally intensive than $\mathbf{F}^H\mathbf{d}$ and accounts for less than 1% of the execution of the reconstruction of each image on a sequential CPU. As a result, we will leave it out of the parallelization scope and focus on $\mathbf{F}^H\mathbf{d}$ in this chapter. We will, however, revisit its status at the end of the chapter.

```
for (m = 0; m < M; m++) {

  phiMag[m] = rPhi[m]*rPhi[m] +
              iPhi[m]*iPhi[m];

  for (n = 0; n < N; n++) {
    expQ = 2*PI*(kx[m]*x[n] +
                 ky[m]*y[n] +
                 kz[m]*z[n]);

    rQ[n] +=phiMag[m]*cos(expQ);
    iQ[n] +=phiMag[m]*sin(expQ);
  }
}

        (A) Q computation
```

```
for (m = 0; m < M; m++) {

  rMu[m] = rPhi[m]*rD[m] +
           iPhi[m]*iD[m];
  iMu[m] = rPhi[m]*iD[m] -
           iPhi[m]*rD[m];

  for (n = 0; n < N; n++) {
    expFHd = 2*PI*(kx[m]*x[n] +
                   ky[m]*y[n] +
                   kz[m]*z[n]);

    cArg = cos(expFHd);
    sArg = sin(expFHd);

    rFHd[n] += rMu[m]*cArg -
               iMu[m]*sArg;
    iFHd[n] += iMu[m]*cArg +
               rMu[m]*sArg;
  }
}         (B) F^Hd computation
```

FIGURE 8.4

Computation of Q and $\mathbf{F}^H\mathbf{d}$.

8.3 COMPUTING $\mathbf{F}^H\mathbf{d}$

Figure 8.4A shows a sequential C implementation of the computations for computing Q, and Figure 8.4B shows that for $\mathbf{F}^H\mathbf{d}$. It should be clear from a quick glance at Figure 8.4A and Figure 8.4B that Q and $\mathbf{F}^H\mathbf{d}$ have identical structure. Both computations start with an outer loop, which encloses an inner loop. The only differences are the particular calculation done in each loop body and the fact that Q involves a much larger m, as it implements a matrix–matrix multiplication as opposed to a matrix–vector multiplication, thus requiring a much longer execution time. It suffices to discuss one of them here, and we will focus on $\mathbf{F}^H\mathbf{d}$, as this is the one that will have to be run for each image being reconstructed.

A quick glance at Figure 8.4B shows that the C implementation of $\mathbf{F}^H\mathbf{d}$ is an excellent candidate for acceleration on the GPU because it exhibits substantial data parallelism. The algorithm first computes the real and imaginary components of Mu (rMu and iMu) at each sample point in the k-space, then computes the real and imaginary components of $\mathbf{F}^H\mathbf{d}$ at each voxel in the image space. The value of $\mathbf{F}^H\mathbf{d}$ at any voxel depends on the values of all k-space sample points, but no voxel elements of $\mathbf{F}^H\mathbf{d}$ depend on any other elements of **F**^{H}**d**; therefore, all elements of **F**^{H}**d** can be computed in parallel. Specifically, all iterations of the outer loop can be done in parallel and all iterations of the inner loop can be done in parallel. The calculations of the inner loop, however, have a dependence on the calculation done by the preceding statements in the same iteration of the outer loop.

Despite the algorithm's abundant inherent parallelism, potential performance bottlenecks are evident. First, in the loop that computes the elements of **F**^{H}**d**, the ratio of floating-point operations to memory accesses is at best 3:1 and at worst 1:1. The best case assumes that the sin and cos trigonometry operations are computed using 5-element Taylor series that require 13 and 12 floating-point operations, respectively. The worst case assumes that each trigonometric operation is computed as a single operation in hardware. As we have seen in Chapter 5, a floating-point to memory access ratio of 16:1 or more is necessary for the kernel not to be limited by memory bandwidth. Thus, the memory accesses will clearly limit the performance of the kernel unless the ratio is drastically increased.

Second, the ratio of floating-point arithmetic to floating-point trigonometry functions is only 13:2; thus, GPU-based implementation must tolerate or avoid stalls due to long-latency `sin` and `cos` operations. Without a good way to reduce the cost of trigonometry functions, the performance will likely be dominated by the time spent in these functions.

We are now ready to take the steps to convert **F**^{H}**d** from sequential C code to CUDA kernel.

Step 1. Determine the Kernel Parallelism Structure

The conversion of a loop into a CUDA kernel is conceptually straightforward. Because all iterations of the outer loop of Figure 8.4B can be executed in parallel, we can simply convert the outer loop into a CUDA kernel by mapping its iterations to CUDA threads. Figure 8.5 shows a kernel from such a straightforward conversion. Each thread implements an iteration of the original outer loop; that is, we use each thread to calculate the contribution of one k-space sample to all **F**^{H}**d** elements. The original outer loop has M iterations, and M can be in the millions. We obviously need to have multiple thread blocks to generate enough threads to implement all of these iterations.

To make performance tuning easy, we declare a constant, FHd_THREADS_ PER_BLOCK, which defines the number of threads in each thread block when we invoke the cmpFHd kernel. Thus, we will use M/FHd_THREADS_PER_BLOCK

```
__global__ void cmpFHd(float* rPhi, iPhi, phiMag,
        kx, ky, kz, x, y, z, rMu, iMu, int N) {

    int m = blockIdx.x * FHd_THREADS_PER_BLOCK + threadIdx.x;

    rMu[m] = rPhi[m]*rD[m] + iPhi[m]*iD[m];
    iMu[m] = rPhi[m]*iD[m] - iPhi[m]*rD[m];

    for (n = 0; n < N; n++) {
        expFHd = 2*PI*(kx[m]*x[n] + ky[m]*y[n] + kz[m]*z[n]);

        cArg = cos(expFHd); sArg = sin(expFHd);

        rFHd[n] += rMu[m]*cArg - iMu[m]*sArg;
        iFHd[n] += iMu[m]*cArg + rMu[m]*sArg;
    }
}
```

FIGURE 8.5

First version of the FHd kernel. The kernel will not execute correctly due to conflicts between threads writing into rFHd and iFHd arrays. All arguments except N are of type float and the keyword float is omitted for most of them for brevity.

for the grid size (in terms of number of blocks) and FHd_THREADS_PER_BLOCK for block size (in terms of number of threads) for kernel invocation. Within the kernel, each thread calculates the original iteration of the outer loop that it is assigned to cover using the formula blockIdx.x*FHd_THREADS_PER_BLOCK + threadIdx.x. For example, assume that there are 65,536 k-space samples and we decided to use 512 threads per block. The grid size at kernel innovation would be 65,536/512 = 128 blocks. The block size would be 512. The calculation of m for each thread would be equivalent to blockIdx.x*512 + threadIdx.x.

Although the kernel of Figure 8.5 exploits ample parallelism, it suffers from a major problem: All threads write into all rFHd and iFHd voxel elements. This means that the kernel must use atomic operations in the global memory in the inner loop in order to keep threads from trashing each other's contributions to the voxel value. This can seriously affect the performance of a kernel. Note that, as is, the code will not even execute correctly because no atomic operation is used. We need to explore other options.

The other option is to use each thread to calculate one FHd value from all k-space samples. In order to do so, we need to first swap the inner loop and the outer loop so that each of the new outer-loop iterations processes one FHd element; that is, each of the new outer-loop iterations will execute the new inner loop that accumulates the contribution of all *k*-space samples to the FHd element handled by the outer-loop iteration. This transformation to the loop structure is called *loop interchange*. It requires a perfectly nested loop, meaning that there is no statement between the outer for loop statement and the inner for loop statement. This is, however, not true for the FHd code in Figure 8.4B. We need to find a way to move the calculation of rMu and iMu elements out of the way.

From a quick inspection of Figure 8.6A, which replicates Figure 8.4B, we see that the **F**^{H}**d** calculation can be split into two separate loops, as shown in Figure 8.6B, using a technique called *loop fission* or *loop splitting*. This transformation takes the body of a loop and splits it into two loops. In the case of **F**^{H}**d**, the outer loop consists of two parts: the statements before the inner loop and the inner loop. As shown in Figure 8.6B, we can perform loop fission on the outer loop by placing the statements before the inner loop into a loop and the inner loop into a second loop. The transformation changes the relative execution order of the two parts of the original outer loop. In the original outer loop, both parts of the first

```
for (m = 0; m < M; m++) {

   rMu[m] = rPhi[m]*rD[m] +
           iPhi[m]*iD[m];
   iMu[m] = rPhi[m]*iD[m] -
           iPhi[m]*rD[m];

   for (n = 0; n < N; n++) {
     expFHd = 2*PI*(kx[m]*x[n] +
               ky[m]*y[n] +
               kz[m]*z[n]);

   cArg = cos(expFHd);
   sArg = sin(expFHd);

   rFHd[n] += rMu[m]*cArg -
             iMu[m]*sArg;
   iFHd[n] += iMu[m]*cArg +
             rMu[m]*sArg;
   }
}
        (A) F^Hd computation
```

```
for (m = 0; m < M; m++) {

   rMu[m] = rPhi[m]*rD[m] +
           iPhi[m]*iD[m];
   iMu[m] = rPhi[m]*iD[m] -
           iPhi[m]*rD[m];
}
for (m = 0; m < M; m++) {
   for (n = 0; n < N; n++) {
     expFHd = 2*PI*(kx[m]*x[n] +
               ky[m]*y[n] +
               kz[m]*z[n]);

   cArg = cos(expFHd);
   sArg = sin(expFHd);

   rFHd[n] += rMu[m]*cArg -
             iMu[m]*sArg;
   iFHd[n] += iMu[m]*cArg +
             rMu[m]*sArg;
   }
}
        (B) after loop fission
```

FIGURE 8.6

Loop fission on the FHd computation.

iteration execute before the second iteration. After fission, the first part of all iterations will execute; they are then followed by the second part of all iterations. The reader should be able to verify that this change of execution order does not affect the execution results for $\mathbf{F}^H\mathbf{d}$. This is because the execution of the first part of each iteration does not depend on the result of the second part of any preceding iterations of the original outer loop. Loop fission is a transformation often done by advanced compilers that are capable of analyzing the (lack of) dependence between statements across loop iterations.

With loop fission, the $\mathbf{F}^H\mathbf{d}$ computation is now done in two steps. The first step is a single-level loop that calculates the rMu and iMu elements for use in the second loop. The second step corresponds to the loop that calculates the $\mathbf{F}^H\mathbf{d}$ elements based on the rMu and iMu elements calculated in the first step. Each step can now be converted into a CUDA kernel. The two CUDA kernels will execute sequentially with respect to each other. Because the second loop needs to use the results from the first loop, separating these two loops into two kernels that execute in sequence does not sacrifice any parallelism.

The cmpMu() kernel in Figure 8.7 implements the first loop. The conversion of the first loop from sequential C code to a CUDA kernel is straightforward; each thread implements one iteration of the original C code. Because the M value can be very big, reflecting the large number of k-space samples, such a mapping can result in a large number of threads, and, because each thread block can have only up to 512 threads, we will need to use multiple blocks to allow the large number of threads. This can be accomplished by having a number of threads in each block, specified by MU_THREADS_PER_BLOCK in Figure 8.7, and by employing M/MU_THREADS_PER_BLOCK blocks to cover all M iterations of the original loop. For example, if there are 65,536 k-space samples, the kernel could be invoked with a configuration of 512 threads per block and 65,536/512 = 128 blocks. This is done by

```
__global__ void cmpMu(float* rPhi, iPhi, rD, iD, rMu, iMu)
{
    int m = blockIdx.x * MU_THREADS_PER_BLOCK + threadIdx.x;

    rMu[m] = rPhi[m]*rD[m] + iPhi[m]*iD[m];
    iMu[m] = rPhi[m]*iD[m] - iPhi[m]*rD[m];
}
```

FIGURE 8.7

cmpMu kernel.

assigning 512 to MU_THREADS_PER_BLOCK and using MU_THREADS_PER_BLOCK as the block size and M/MU_THREADS_PER_BLOCK as the grid size during kernel innovation.

Within the kernel, each thread can identify the iteration assigned to it using its blockIdx and threadIdx values. Because the threading structure is one dimensional, only blockIdx.x and threadIdx.x need to be used. Each block covers a section of the original iterations, so the iteration covered by a thread is blockIdx.x*MU_THREADS_PER_BLOCK + threadIdx. Assume, for example, that MU_THREADS_PER_BLOCK = 512. The thread with blockIdx.x = 0 and threadIdx.x = 37 covers the 37th iteration of the original loop, whereas the thread with blockIdx.x = 5 and threadIdx.x = 2 covers the 2562nd (5*512 + 2) iteration of the original loop. Using this iteration number to access the **Mu**, **Phi**, and **D** arrays ensures that the arrays are covered by the threads in the same way they were covered by the iterations of the original loop. Because every thread writes into its own Mu element, there is no potential conflict between any of these threads.

Determining the structure of the second kernel requires a little more work. An inspection of the second loop in Figure 8.6B shows that we have at least three options when designing the second kernel. In the first option, each thread corresponds to one iteration of the inner loop. This option creates the most number of threads and thus exploits the greatest amount of parallelism; however, the number of threads would be $N*M$, with N in the range of millions and M in the range of hundreds of thousands. Their product would result in too many threads in the grid.

A second option is to use each thread to implement an iteration of the outer loop. This option employs fewer threads than the first option. Instead of generating $N*M$ threads, this option generates M threads. Because M corresponds to the number of k-space samples and a large number of samples (on the order of 100,000) is typically used to calculate $\mathbf{F}^H\mathbf{d}$, this option still exploits a large amount of parallelism. However, this kernel suffers the same problem as the kernel in Figure 8.5; that is, each thread will write into all rFHd and iFHd elements, thus creating an extremely large number of conflicts between threads. As is the case of Figure 8.5, the code in Figure 8.8 will not execute correctly without adding atomic operations that will significantly slow down the execution, thus this option does not work well.

A third option is to use each thread to compute one pair of rFHd and iFHd elements. This option requires us to interchange the inner and outer loops and then use each thread to implement an iteration of the new outer loop. The transformation is shown in Figure 8.9. Loop interchange is

```
__global__ void cmpFHd(float* rPhi, iPhi, phiMag,
        kx, ky, kz, x, y, z, rMu, iMu, int N) {

    int m = blockIdx.x * FHd_THREADS_PER_BLOCK + threadIdx.x;

    for (n = 0; n < N; n++) {
        float expFHd = 2*PI*(kx[m]*x[n]+ky[m]*y[n]+kz[m]*z[n]);

        float cArg = cos(expFHd);
        float sArg = sin(expFHd);

        rFHd[n] += rMu[m]*cArg - iMu[m]*sArg;
        iFHd[n] += iMu[m]*cArg + rMu[m]*sArg;
    }
}
```

FIGURE 8.8

Second option of the FHd kernel.

necessary because the loop being implemented by the CUDA threads must be the outer loop. Loop interchange makes each new outer loop iteration process a pair of rFHd and iFHd elements. Loop interchange is permissible here because all iterations of both levels of loops are independent of each other. They can be executed in any order relative to one another. Loop interchange, which changes the order of the iterations, is allowed when these iterations can be executed in any order. This option generates N threads. Because N corresponds to the number voxels in the reconstructed

```
for (m = 0; m < M; m++) {             for (n = 0; n < N; n++) {
  for (n = 0; n < N; n++) {             for (m = 0; m < M; m++) {
    expFHd = 2*PI*(kx[m]*x[n] +           expFHd = 2*PI*(kx[m]*x[n] +
                   ky[m]*y[n] +                          ky[m]*y[n] +
                   kz[m]*z[n]);                          kz[m]*z[n]);

    cArg = cos(expFHd);                   cArg = cos(expFHd);
    sArg = sin(expFHd);                   sArg = sin(expFHd);

    rFHd[n] += rMu[m]*cArg -              rFHd[n] += rMu[m]*cArg -
               iMu[m]*sArg;                          iMu[m]*sArg;
    iFHd[n] += iMu[m]*cArg +              iFHd[n] += iMu[m]*cArg +
               rMu[m]*sArg;                          rMu[m]*sArg;
  }                                     }
} (A) before loop interchange         } (B) after loop interchange
```

FIGURE 8.9

Loop interchange of the FHd computation.

image, the N value can be very large for higher resolution images. For a 128^3 image, there are $128^3 = 2{,}097{,}152$ threads, resulting in a large amount of parallelism. For higher resolutions, such as 512^3, we may need to invoke multiple kernels, with each kernel generating the value of a subset of the voxels. Note that these threads now all accumulate into their own rFHd and iFHd elements, as every thread has a unique n value. There is no conflict between threads. These threads can run totally in parallel. This makes the third option the best choice among the three options.

The kernel derived from the interchanged loops is shown in Figure 8.10. The threads are organized as a two-level structure. The outer loop has been stripped away; each thread covers an iteration of the outer (n) loop, where n is equal to blockIdx.x*FHd_THREADS_PER_BLOCK + threadIdx.x. Once this iteration (n) value is identified, the thread executes the inner loop based on that n value. This kernel can be invoked with a number of threads in each block, specified by a global constant, FHd_THREADS_PER_BLOCK. Assuming that N is the variable that gives the number of voxels in the reconstructed image, then N/FHd_THREADS_PER_BLOCK blocks cover all N iterations of the original loop. For example, if there are 65,536 k-space samples, the kernel could be invoked with a configuration of 512 threads per block and $65{,}536/512 = 128$ blocks. This is done by assigning 512 to FHd_THREADS_PER_BLOCK and using FHd_THREADS_PER_BLOCK as the block size and N/FHd_THREADS_PER_BLOCK as the grid size during kernel innovation.

```
__global__ void cmpFHd(float* rPhi, iPhi, phiMag,
      kx, ky, kz, x, y, z, rMu, iMu, int M) {

  int n = blockIdx.x * FHd_THREADS_PER_BLOCK + threadIdx.x;

  for (m = 0; m < M; m++) {
    float expFHd = 2*PI*(kx[m]*x[n]+ky[m]*y[n]+kz[m]*z[n]);

    float cArg = cos(expFHd);
    float sArg = sin(expFHd);

    rFHd[n] += rMu[m]*cArg - iMu[m]*sArg;
    iFHd[n] += iMu[m]*cArg + rMu[m]*sArg;
  }
}
```

FIGURE 8.10

Third option of the FHd kernel.

Step 2. Getting Around the Memory Bandwidth Limitation

The simple cmpFHd kernel in Figure 8.10 will provide limited speedup due to memory bandwidth limitations. A quick analysis shows that the execution is limited by the low compute-to-memory access ratio of each thread. In the original loop, each iteration performs at least 14 memory accesses: kx[m], ky[m], kz[m], x[n], y[n], z[n], rMu[m] twice, iMu[m] twice, rFHd[n] read and write, and iFHd[n] read and write. Meanwhile, about 13 floating-point multiply, add, or trigonometry operations are performed in each iteration; therefore, the compute-to-memory access ratio is approximately 1, which is too low according to our analysis in Chapter 5.

We can immediately improve the compute-to-memory access ratio by assigning some of the array elements to automatic variables. As we discussed in Chapter 5, the automatic variables will reside in registers, thus converting reads and writes to the global memory into reads and writes to on-chip registers. A quick review of the kernel in Figure 8.10 shows that for each thread, the same x[n], y[n], and z[n] elements are used across all iterations of the for loop. This means that we can load these elements into automatic variables before the execution enters the loop.[1] The kernel can then use the automatic variables inside the loop, thus converting global memory accesses to register accesses. Furthermore, the loop repeatedly reads from and writes into rFHd[n] and iFHd[n]. We can have the iterations read from and write into two automatic variables and only write the contents of these automatic variables into rFHd[n] and iFHd[n] after the execution exits the loop. The resulting code is shown in Figure 8.11. By increasing the number of registers used by 5 for each thread, we have reduced the memory access done in each iteration from 14 to 7. Thus, we have increased the compute-to-memory access ratio from 13:14 to 13:7. This is a very good improvement and a good use of the precious register resource.

Recall that the register usage can limit the number of blocks that can run in a streaming multiprocessor (SM). By increasing the register usage by 5 in the kernel code, we increase the register usage of each thread block by

---

[1]Note that declaring x[], y[], z[], rFHd[], and iFHd[] as automatic arrays will not work for our purposes here. Such a declaration would create private copies of all five arrays in the local memory of every thread! All we want is to have a private copy of one element of each array in the registers of each thread.

```
__global__ void cmpFHd(float* rPhi, iPhi, phiMag,
        kx, ky, kz, x, y, z, rMu, iMu, int M) {

    int n = blockIdx.x * FHd_THREADS_PER_BLOCK + threadIdx.x;

    float xn_r = x[n]; float yn_r = y[n]; float zn_r = z[n];
    float rFHdn_r = rFHd[n]; float iFHdn_r = iFHd[n];

    for (m = 0; m < M; m++) {
      float expFHd = 2*PI*(kx[m]*xn_r+ky[m]*yn_r+kz[m]*zn_r);

      float cArg = cos(expFHd);
      float sArg = sin(expFHd);

      rFHdn_r += rMu[m]*cArg - iMu[m]*sArg;
      iFHdn_r += iMu[m]*cArg + rMu[m]*sArg;
    }
    rFHd[n] = rFHd_r; iFHd[n] = iFHd_r;
}
```

FIGURE 8.11

Using registers to reduce memory accesses in the FHd kernel.

5*FHd_THREADS_PER_BLOCK. Assuming that we have 128 threads per block, we just increased the block register usage by 640. Because each SM can accommodate a combined register usage of 8192 registers among all blocks assigned to it, we need to be careful, as any further increase of register usage can begin to limit the number of blocks that can be assigned to an SM. Fortunately, the register usage is not a limiting factor to parallelism for the kernel.

We need to further improve the compute-to-memory access ratio to something closer to 10:1 by eliminating more global memory accesses in the cmpFHd kernel. The next candidates to consider are the k-space samples kx[m], ky[m], and kz[m]. These array elements are accessed differently than the x[n], y[n], and z[n] elements; different elements of kx, ky, and kz are accessed in each iteration of the loop in Figure 8.11. This means that we cannot load each k-space element into an automatic variable register and access that automatic variable off a register through all the iterations. So, registers will not help here; however, we should notice that the k-space elements are not modified by the kernel. This means that we might be able to place the k-space elements into the constant memory. Perhaps the cache for the constant memory can eliminate most of the memory accesses.

An analysis of the loop in Figure 8.11 reveals that the k-space elements are indeed excellent candidates for constant memory. The index used for accessing kx, ky, and kz is m, which is independent of threadIdx, which means that all threads in a warp will be accessing the same element of kx, ky, and kz. This is an ideal access pattern for cached constant memory; every time an element is brought into the cache, it will be used at least by all 32 threads in a warp in the G80. This means that for every 32 accesses to the constant memory, at least 31 of them will be served by the cache. This allows the cache to effectively eliminate 96% or more of the accesses to the constant memory. Better yet, each time a constant is accessed from the cache, it can be broadcast to all the threads in a warp. This means that no delays are incurred due to any bank conflicts in the access to the cache. This makes constant memory almost as efficient as registers for accessing k-space elements.[2]

There is, however, a technical issue involved in placing the k-space elements into the constant memory. Recall that constant memory has a capacity of 64 kB, but the size of the k-space samples can be much larger, on the order of hundreds of thousands or even millions. A typical way of working around the limitation of constant memory capacity is to break down a large dataset into chunks or 64 kB or smaller. The developer must reorganize the kernel so the kernel will be invoked multiple times, with each invocation of the kernel consuming only a chunk of the large dataset. This turns out to be quite easy for the cmpFHd kernel.

A careful examination of the loop in Figure 8.11 reveals that all threads will sequentially march through the k-space arrays. That is, all threads in the grid access the same k-space element during each iteration. For large datasets, the loop in the kernel simply iterates more times. This means that we can divide up the loop into sections, with each section processing a chunk of the k-space elements that fit into the 64-kB capacity of the constant memory.[3] The host code now invokes the kernel multiple times. Each time the host invokes the kernel, it places a new chunk into the constant memory before calling the kernel function. This is illustrated in Figure 8.12.

---

[2]The reason why a constant memory access is not exactly as efficient as a register access is that a memory load instruction is still needed to access the constant memory.

[3]Note that not all accesses to read-only data are as favorable for constant memory as what we have here. In Chapter 10, we present a case where threads in different blocks access different elements in the same iteration. This more diverged access pattern makes it much more difficult to fit enough of the data into the constant memory for a kernel launch.

```
__constant__ float   kx_c[CHUNK_SIZE],
                     ky_c[CHUNK_SIZE], kz_c[CHUNK_SIZE];
...
__ void main() {

  int i;
  for (i = 0; i < M/CHUNK_SIZE; i++);
    cudaMemcpy(kx_c,&kx[i*CHUNK_SIZE],4*CHUNK_SIZE,
             cudaMemCpyHostToDevice);
    cudaMemcpy(ky_c,&ky[i*CHUNK_SIZE],4*CHUNK_SIZE,
             cudaMemCpyHostToDevice);
    cudaMemcpy(ky_c,&ky[i*CHUNK_SIZE],4*CHUNK_SIZE,
             cudaMemCpyHostToDevice);
    ...
    cmpFHd<<<FHd_THREADS_PER_BLOCK, N/FHd_THREADS_PER_BLOCK>>>
             (rPhi, iPhi, phiMag, x, y, z, rMu, iMu, int M);
  }
  /* Need to call kernel one more time if M is not */
  /* perfect multiple of CHUNK SIZE */
}
```

FIGURE 8.12

Chunking *k*-space data to fit into constant memory.

In Figure 8.12, the cmpFHd kernel is called from a loop. The code assumes that the kx, ky, and kz arrays are in the host memory. The dimension of kx, ky, and kz is given by *M*. At each iteration, the host code calls the cudaMemcpy() function to transfer a chunk of the *k*-space data into the device constant memory. The kernel is then invoked to process the chunk. Note that when *M* is not a perfect multiple of CHUNK_SIZE, the host code will need to have an additional round of cudaMemcpy and one more kernel invocation to finish the remaining *k*-space data.

Figure 8.13 shows the revised kernel that accesses the *k*-space data from constant memory. Note that pointers to kx, ky, and kz are no longer in the parameter list of the kernel function. Because we cannot use pointers to access variables in the constant memory, the kx_c, ky_c, and kz_c arrays are accessed as global variables declared under the __constant__ keyword, as shown Figure 8.12.[4] By accessing these elements from the constant

---

[4]As we will discuss in Chapter 12, future generations of CUDA architectures and programming models will likely allow pointers to constant memories. This will allow one to use the same kernel structure and launch statements for both situations and simplify the work needed when moving a data structure between global memory and constant memory.

```
__global__ void cmpFHd(float* rPhi, iPhi, phiMag,
        x, y, z, rMu, iMu, int M) {

    int n = blockIdx.x * FHd_THREADS_PER_BLOCK + threadIdx.x;

    float xn_r = x[n]; float yn_r = y[n]; float zn_r = z[n];
    float rFHdn_r = rFHd[n]; float iFHdn_r = iFHd[n];

    for (m = 0; m < M; m++) {
        float expFHd =
            2*PI*(kx_c[m]*xn_r+ky_c[m]*yn_r+kz_c[m]*zn_r);

        float cArg = cos(expFHd);
        float sArg = sin(expFHd);

        rFHdn_r += rMu[m]*cArg - iMu[m]*sArg;
        iFHdn_r += iMu[m]*cArg + rMu[m]*sArg;
    }
    rFHd[n] = rFHd_r; iFHd[n] = iFHd_r;
}
```

FIGURE 8.13

FHd kernel revised to use constant memory.

cache, the kernel now has effectively only four global memory accesses to the rMu and iMu arrays. The compiler will typically recognize that the four array accesses are made to only two locations. It will only perform two global accesses, one to rMu[m] and one to iMu[m]. The values will be stored in temporary register variables for use in the other two. This makes the final number of memory accesses two. The compute-to-memory access ratio is up to 13:2. This is still not quite the desired 10:1 ratio but is sufficiently high that the memory bandwidth limitation is no longer the only factor that limits performance. As we will see, we can perform a few other optimizations that make computation more efficient and further improve performance.

If we ran the code in Figures 8.12 and 8.13, we would find out that the performance enhancement was not as high as we expected. As it turns out, the code shown in these figures does not result in as much memory bandwidth reduction as we expected. The reason is because the constant cache does not perform very well for the code. This has to do with the design of the constant cache and the memory layout of the k-space data. As shown in Figure 8.14, each constant cache entry is designed to store multiple consecutive words. This design reduces the cost of constant cache hardware

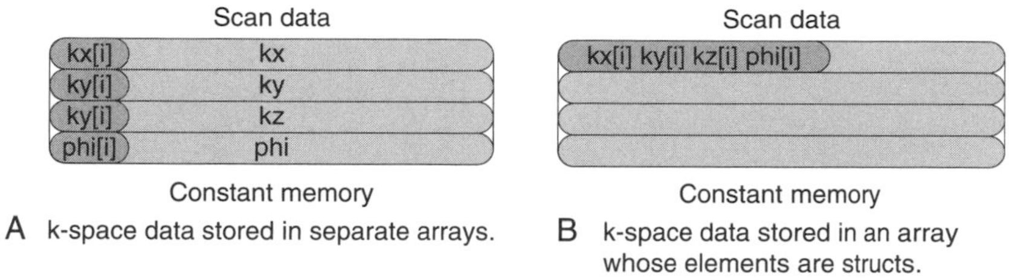

A k-space data stored in separate arrays.   **B** k-space data stored in an array whose elements are structs.

FIGURE 8.14

Effect of *k*-space data layout on constant cache efficiency.

design. If multiple data elements that are used by each thread are not in consecutive words, as illustrated in Figure 8.14A, they will end up taking up multiple cache entries. Due to cost constraints, the constant cache has only a very small number of entries. As shown in Figures 8.12 and 8.13, the *k*-space data is stored in three arrays: kx_c, ky_c, and kz_c. During each iteration of the loop, three entries of the constant cache are needed to hold the three *k*-space elements being processed. Because different warps can be at very different iterations, they may require many entries altogether. As it turns out, the G80 cache capacity was not sufficient to provide a sufficient number of entries for all the warps active in an SM.

The problem of inefficient use of cache entries has been well studied in the literature and can be solved by adjusting the memory layout of the *k*-space data. The solution is illustrated in Figure 8.14B and the code based on this solution in Figures 8.15. Rather than having the *x*, *y*, and *z* components of the *k*-space data stored in three separate arrays, the solution stores these components in an array whose elements as a struct. In the literature, this style of declaration is often referred to as an *array of structs*. The declaration of the array is shown at the top of Figure 8.15. By storing the *x*, *y*, and *z* components in the three fields of an array element, the developer forces these components to be stored in consecutive locations of the constant memory. Therefore, all three components used by an iteration can now fit into one cache entry, reducing the number of entries needed to support the execution of all the active warps. Note that, because we have only one array to hold all *k*-space data, we can just use one cudaMemcpy to copy the entire chunk to the device constant memory. The size of the transfer is adjusted from 4*CHUNK_SIZE to 12*CHUNK_SIZE to reflect the transfer of all the three components in one cudaMemcpy call.

```
struct kdata {
   float x, float y, float z;
} k;

__constant__ struct kdata k_c[CHUNK_SIZE];
...

__ void main() {

  int i;

  for (i = 0; i < M/CHUNK_SIZE; i++);
    cudaMemcpy(k_c,k,12*CHUNK_SIZE, cudaMemCpyHostToDevice);

    cmpFHd<<<FHd_THREADS_PER_BLOCK, N/FHd_THREADS_PER_BLOCK>>>
           (...);

}
```

FIGURE 8.15

Adjusting *k*-space data layout to improve cache efficiency.

With the new data structure layout, we also need to revise the kernel so the access is done according to the new layout. The new kernel is shown in Figure 8.16. Note that kx[m] has become k[m].x, ky[m] has become k[m].y, and so on. As we will see later, this small change to the code can result in significant enhancement of its execution speed.

```
__global__ void cmpFHd(float* rPhi, iPhi, phiMag,
       x, y, z, rMu, iMu, int M) {

  int n = blockIdx.x * FHd_THREADS_PER_BLOCK + threadIdx.x;

  float xn_r = x[n]; float yn_r = y[n]; float zn_r = z[n];
  float rFHdn_r = rFHd[n]; float iFHdn_r = iFHd[n];

  for (m = 0; m < M; m++) {
    float expFHd = 2*PI*(k[m].x*xn_r+k[m].y*yn_r+k[m].z*zn_r);

    float cArg = cos(expFHd);
    float sArg = sin(expFHd);

    rFHdn_r += rMu[m]*cArg - iMu[m]*sArg;
    iFHdn_r += iMu[m]*cArg + rMu[m]*sArg;
  }
  rFHd[n] = rFHd_r; iFHd[n] = iFHd_r;
}
```

FIGURE 8.16

Adjusting the *k*-space data memory layout in the FHd kernel.

Step 3. Using Hardware Trigonometry Functions

CUDA offers hardware mathematic functions that provide much higher throughput than their software counter parts. These functions are implemented as hardware instructions executed by the special function units (SFUs). The procedure for using these functions is quite easy. In the case of the cmpFHd kernel, we need to change the calls to sin and cos functions into their hardware versions: __sin and __cos. These are intrinsic functions that are recognized by the compiler and translated into SFU instructions. Because these functions are called in a heavily executed loop body, we expect that the change will result in a very significant performance improvement. The resulting cmpFHd kernel is shown in Figure 8.17.

We need to be careful about the reduced accuracy when switching from software functions to hardware functions. As we discussed in Chapter 7, hardware implementations currently have slightly less accuracy than software libraries. In the case of MRI, we need to make sure that the hardware implementation passes test cases that measure the SNR of the resulting image, as defined in Figure 8.18. The testing process involves a "perfect" image (I_0). We use a reverse process to generate corresponding "scanned" k-space data that are synthesized. The synthesized scanned data are then processed by the proposed reconstruction system to generate a

```
__global__ void cmpFHd(float* rPhi, iPhi, phiMag,
        x, y, z, rMu, iMu, int M) {

  int n = blockIdx.x * FHd_THREADS_PER_BLOCK + threadIdx.x;

  float xn_r = x[n]; float yn_r = y[n]; float zn_r = z[n];
  float rFHdn_r = rFHd[n]; float iFHdn_r = iFHd[n];

  for (m = 0; m < M; m++) {
    float expFHd = 2*PI*(k[m].x*xn_r+k[m].y*yn_r+k[m].z*zn_r);

    float cArg = __cos(expFHd);
    float sArg = __sin(expFHd);

    rFHdn_r += rMu[m]*cArg - iMu[m]*sArg;
    iFHdn_r += iMu[m]*cArg + rMu[m]*sArg;
  }
  rFHd[n] = rFHd_r; iFHd[n] = iFHd_r;
}
```

FIGURE 8.17

Using hardware __sin() and __cos() functions.

Netravali, A. N., & Haskell, B. G. (1995). *Digital pictures: Representation, compression, and standards* (2nd ed.). New York, NY: Plenum Press.

$$MSE = \frac{1}{mn} \sum_i \sum_j (I(i,j) - I_0(i,j))^2 \qquad A_s = \frac{1}{mn} \sum_i \sum_j I_0(i,j)^2$$

$$PSNR = 20 \log_{10}\left(\frac{\max(I_0(i,j))}{\sqrt{MSE}}\right) \qquad SNR = 20 \log_{10}\left(\frac{\sqrt{A_s}}{\sqrt{MSE}}\right)$$

FIGURE 8.18

Metrics used to validate the accuracy of hardware functions. I_0 is the perfect image; I is the reconstructed image. MSE, mean square error; PSNR, peak signal-to-noise ratio; SNR, signal-to-noise ratio.

reconstructed image (I). The values of the voxels in the perfect and recon-structed images are then plugged into the mean square error (MSE), peak signal-to-noise ratio (PSNR), and SNR formulas in Figure 8.18.

The criteria for passing the test depend on how the image will be applied. In our case, we worked with the MRI clinical experts to ensure that the SNR changes due to hardware functions is well within the accepted limits for their applications. In applications where the images are used by physicians for injury or disease evaluation, one also needs to have visual inspection of the image quality. Figure 8.19 shows the visual comparison of the original "true" image. It also illustrates that the PSNR achieved by both CPU double-precision and single-precision implementations was 27.6 dB, an acceptable level for the application. A visual inspection also shows that the reconstructed image does, indeed, correspond well with the original image.

The advantage of iterative reconstruction compared to a simple bilinear interpolation gridding/inverse fast Fourier transform (iFFT) is also obvious in Figure 8.19. The image reconstructed with the simple gridding/iFFT has a PSNR of only 16.8 dB, substantially lower than the PSNR of 27.6 dB achieved by the iterative reconstruction method. A visual inspection of the gridding/iFFT image in Part 2 of Figure 8.19 reveals severe artifacts that can significantly impact the usability of the image for diagnostic pur-poses. These artifacts do not occur in the images from the iterative recon-struction method.

When we moved from double-precision to single-precision arithmetic on the CPU, there was no measurable degradation of PSNR, which remained at 27.6 dB. When we moved the trigonometric function from the software library to the hardware units, we observed a negligible degradation of PSNR, from 27.6 dB to 27.5 dB. The slight loss of PSNR is within an acceptable range for the application. A visual inspection confirms that the

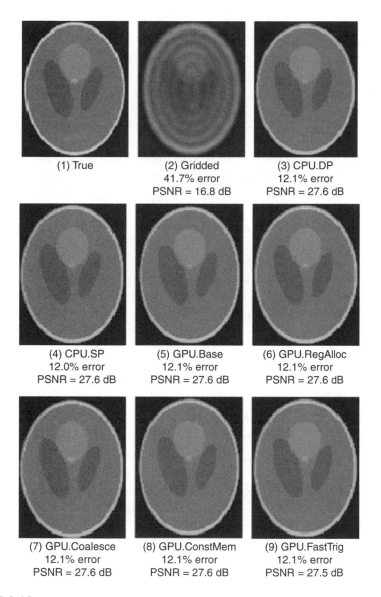

FIGURE 8.19

Validation of floating-point precision and accuracy of the different FHd implementations.

reconstructed image does not have significant artifacts compared to the original image.

Step 4. Experimental Performance Tuning

Up to this point, we have not determined the appropriate values for the configuration parameters for the kernel; for example, we need to determine the optimal number of threads for each block. On one hand, using a large number of threads in a block is necessary to fully utilize the thread capacity of each SM (given that only eight blocks can be assigned to each SM). On the other hand, having more threads in each block increases the register usage of each block and can reduce the number of blocks that can fit into an SM. Some possible values of number of threads per block are 32, 64, 128, 256, and 512. One could also consider non-power-of-two numbers.

One also needs to determine the number of k-space scan points per grid. All the scan point data consumed by a grid must fit into the 64-kB constant memory. This translates to 16 K single-precision floating point numbers. Because each scan point requires three single-precision, floating-point data, we can have up to 4 K scan points if we want to use power-of-two scan points in each grid for convenient loop control. Some possible numbers are 32, 64, 128, 256, 1024, 2048, and 4096. Intuitively, the larger numbers should be better because they require fewer kernel innovations.

Another kernel configuration parameter is the number of times one should unroll the body of the for loop. On one hand, unrolling the loop can reduce the number of overhead instructions and potentially reduce the number of clock cycles to process each k-space sample data. On the other hand, too much unrolling can potentially increase the usage of registers and reduce the number of blocks that can fit into an SM.

Note that the effects of these configurations are not isolated from each other. Increasing one parameter value can potentially use the resource that could be used to increase another parameter value. As a result, one must evaluate these parameters jointly in an experimental manner; that is, one may need to change the source code for each joint configuration and measure the run time. There can be a large number of source code versions to try. In the case of $\mathbf{F}^H\mathbf{d}$, the performance improves about 20% by systematically searching all the combinations and choosing the one with the best measured runtime, as compared to a heuristic tuning search effort that explores some promising trends. Ryoo et al. presented a Pareto-optimal-curve-based method to screen away most of the inferior combinations using [Ryoo 2008].

8.4 FINAL EVALUATION

To obtain a reasonable baseline, we implemented two versions of $\mathbf{F}^H\mathbf{d}$ on the CPU. Version CPU.DP uses double-precision for all floating-point values and operations, while version CPU.SP uses single-precision. Both CPU versions are compiled with the Intel® C++ Compiler (icc, version 10.1) using `flags -O3 -msse3 -axT -vec-report3 -fp-model fast = 2`, which (1) vectorizes the algorithm's dominant loops using instructions tuned for the Core 2 architecture, and (2) links the trigonometric operations to fast, approximate functions in the math library. Based on experimental tuning with a smaller dataset, the inner loops are unrolled by a factor of four and the scan data are tiled to improve locality in the L1 cache.

Each GPU version of $\mathbf{F}^H\mathbf{d}$ is compiled using the NVIDIA® CUDA compiler driver nvcc -O3 (version 1.1) and executed on a 1.35-GHz NVIDIA® Quadro® FX 5600. The Quadro card is housed in a system with a 2.4-GHz dual-socket, dual-core AMD® Opteron™ 2216 CPU. Each core has a 1-MB L2 cache. The CPU versions use p-threads to execute on all four cores of the 2.66-GHz Intel® Core™ 2 Extreme quad-core CPU, which has peak theoretical capacity of 21.2 gigaflops per core and a 4-MB L2 cache. The CPU versions perform substantially better on the Core 2 Extreme quad-core than on the dual-socket, dual-core Opteron; therefore, we will use the Core 2 Extreme quad-core results for the CPU.

All reconstructions use the CPU version of the linear solver, which executes 60 iterations on the Quadro FX 5600. Two versions of Q were computed on the Core 2 Extreme, one using double-precision and the other using single-precision. The single-precision Q was used for all GPU-based reconstructions and for the reconstruction involving CPU.SP, while the double-precision Q was used only for the reconstruction involving CPU.DP. As the computation of Q is not on the reconstruction's critical path, we give Q no further consideration.

To facilitate comparison of the iterative reconstruction with a conventional reconstruction, we also evaluated a reconstruction based on bilinear interpolation gridding and iFFT. Our version of the gridded reconstruction is not optimized for performance, but it is already quite fast.

All reconstructions were performed on sample data obtained from a simulated, three-dimensional, non-Cartesian scan of a phantom image. There were 284,592 sample points in the scan dataset, and the image was reconstructed at 1283 resolution, for a total of 221 voxels. In the first set of experiments, the simulated data contained no noise. In the second set of experiments, we added complex white Gaussian noise to the simulated data.

When determining the quality of the reconstructed images, the percent error and PSNR metrics were used. The percent error is the root-mean-square (RMS) of the voxel error divided by the RMS voxel value in the true image (after the true image had been sampled at 1283 resolution).

The data (runtime, gigaflops, and images) were obtained by reconstructing each image once with each implementation of the $\mathbf{F}^H\mathbf{d}$ algorithm described above. There are two exceptions to this policy. For GPU.Tune and GPU.Multi, the time required to compute $\mathbf{F}^H\mathbf{d}$ was so small that runtime variations in performance became non-negligible; therefore, for these configurations we computed $\mathbf{F}^H\mathbf{d}$ three times and reported the average performance.

As shown in Figure 8.20, the total reconstruction time for the test image using bilinear interpolation gridding followed by iFFT required less than 1 minute on a high-end sequential CPU. This confirms that there is little value in parallelizing this traditional reconstruction strategy. It is, however, obvious from Part 2 in Figure 8.19 that the resulting image exhibits an unacceptable level of artifacts.

The LS (CPU, DP) row in Figure 8.20 shows the execution timing of reconstructing the test image using double-precision, floating-point arithmetic on the CPU. The timing shows that the core step (Q) of calculating $\mathbf{F}^H\mathbf{F} + \lambda\mathbf{W}^H\mathbf{W}$. The first observation is that the Q computation for a moderate-resolution image based on a moderate number of k-space samples takes an unacceptable amount of time—more than 65 h on the CPU. Note

Reconstruction	Q		F^Hd		Total	
	Run time (m)	GFLOP	Run time (m)	GFLOP	Linear solver (m)	Recon. time (m)
Gridding + FFT (CPU,DP)	N/A	N/A	N/A	N/A	N/A	0.39
LS (CPU, DP)	4009.0	0.3	518.0	0.4	1.59	519.59
LS(CPU, SP)	2678.7	0.5	342.3	0.7	1.61	343.91
LS (GPU, Naïve)	260.2	5.1	41.0	5.4	1.65	42.65
LS (GPU, CMem)	72.0	18.6	9.8	22.8	1.57	11.37
LS (GPU, CMem, SFU, Exp)	7.5	178.9	1.5	144.5	1.69	3.19
	357X		228X			108X

FIGURE 8.20

Summary of performance improvements.

that this time is eventually reduced to 6.5 min on the GPU with all the optimizations described in Section 8.3. The second observation is that the total reconstruction time of each image requires more than 8 h, with only 1.59 min spent in the linear solver. This validates our decision to focus our parallelization effort on $\mathbf{F}^H\mathbf{d}$.

The LS (CPU, SP) row shows that we can reduce the execution time significantly when we convert the computation from double-precision, floating-point arithmetic to single-precision on the CPU. This is because the Streaming SIMD Extensions (SSE) instructions have higher throughput; that is, they calculate more data elements per clock cycle when executing in single-precision mode. The execution times, however, are still unacceptable for practical use.

The LS (GPU, Naïve) row shows that a straightforward CUDA implementation can achieve a speedup of about 10 times for Q and 8 times for the reconstruction of each image. This is a good speedup, but the resulting execution times are still unacceptable for practical use.

The LS (GPU, CMem) row shows that significant further speedup is achieved by using registers and constant cache to get around the global memory bandwidth limitations. These enhancements achieve about $4\times$ speedup over the naïve CUDA code! This demonstrates the importance of achieving optimal compute to global memory access (CGMA) ratios in CUDA kernels. These enhancements give the CUDA code about a $40\times$ speedup over the single-precision CPU code.

The LS (GPU, CMem, SPU, Exp) row illustrates the use of hardware trigonometry functions and experimental tuning together, which resulted in a dramatic speedup. A separate experiment, not shown here, shows that most of the speedup comes from hardware trigonometry functions. The total speedup over CPU single-precision code is very impressive: $357\times$ for Q and $108\times$ for the reconstruction of each image.

An interesting observation is that in the end, the linear solver actually takes more time than $\mathbf{F}^H\mathbf{d}$. This is because we have accelerated $\mathbf{F}^H\mathbf{d}$ dramatically ($228\times$). What used to be close to 100% of the per-image reconstruction time now accounts for less than 50%. Any further acceleration will now require acceleration of the linear solver, a much more difficult type of computation for massively parallel execution.

8.5 EXERCISES

8.1   Loop fission splits a loop into two loops. Use the `FHd` code in Figure 8.4B to enumerate the execution order of the two parts of the outer loop body, the statements before the inner loop, and the inner loop. (a) List the execution order of these parts from different iterations of the outer loop before fission. (b) List the execution order of these parts from the two loops after fission. (c) Determine if the execution results will be identical. The execution results are identical if all data required by a part are properly generated and preserved for their consumption before that part executes and the execution result of the part is not overwritten by other parts that should come after the part in the original execution order.

8.2   Loop interchange swaps the inner loop into the outer loop and vice versa. Use the loops from Figure 8.9 to enumerate the execution order of the instances of loop body before and after the loop exchange. (a) List the execution order of the loop body from different iterations before loop interchange; identify these iterations with the values of m and n. (b) List the execution order of the loop body from different iterations after loop interchange. Identify these iterations with the values of m and n. (c) Determine if the (a) and (b) execution results will be identical. The execution results are identical if all data required by a part are properly generated and preserved for their consumption before that part executes and the execution result of the part is not overwritten by other parts that should come after the part in the original execution order.

8.3   In Figure 8.11, identify the difference between the access to `x[]` and `kx[]` in the nature of indices used. Use the difference to explain why it does not make sense to try to load `kx[n]` into a register for the kernel shown in Figure 8.11.

8.4   During a meeting, a new graduate student told his advisor that he improved his kernel performance by using `cudaMalloc()` to allocate constant memory and `cudaMemcpy()` to transfer read-only data from the CPU memory to the constant memory. If you were his advisor, what would be your response?

References and Further Reading

Liang, Z. P., & Lauterbur, P. (1999). *Principles of magnetic resonance imaging: A signal processing perspective.* New York: Wiley.

Ryoo, S., Rodrigues, C. I., Stone, S. S., Stratton, J. A., Ueng, S. Z., Baghsorkhi, S. S., et al. (2008). Program optimization carving for GPU computing. *Journal of Parallel and Distributed Computing*, *68*(10), 1389–1401. http://www.gigascale.org/pubs/1313.html.

Stone, S. S., Haldar, J. P., Tsao, S. C., Hwu, W. M. W., Sutton, B. P., & Liang, Z. P. (2008). Accelerating advanced MRI reconstruction on GPUs. *Journal of Parallel and Distributed Computing*, *68*(10), 1305–1306. http://doi.acm.org/10.1145/1366230.1366276.

CHAPTER

Application Case Study: Molecular Visualization and Analysis

9

With special contributions from John Stone

CHAPTER CONTENTS

INTRODUCTION

The previous case study illustrated the process of selecting the appropriate level of a loop nest for parallel execution, the use of constant memory for magnifying the memory bandwidth for read-only data, the use of registers to reduce the consumption of memory bandwidth, and the use of special hardware functional units to accelerate trigonometry functions. In this case study, we use an application based on regular grid data structures to illustrate the use of additional practical techniques that achieve global memory access coalescing and improved computation throughput. We present a series of implementations of an electrostatic potential map calculation kernel, with each version improving upon the previous one. Each version adopts one or more practical techniques. The computation pattern of this application is one of the best matches for graphics processing unit (GPU) computing. This case study shows that the effective use of these practical techniques can significantly improve the execution throughput and is critical for the application to achieve its potential performance.

9.1 APPLICATION BACKGROUND

This case study is based on Visual Molecular Dynamics (VMD) [Humphrey 1996], a popular software system designed for displaying, animating, and analyzing biomolecular systems. As of 2009, VMD had more than 10,000 registered users. Although it has strong built-in support for analyzing biomolecular systems, such as calculating electrostatic potential values at spatial grid points of a molecular system, it has also been a popular tool for displaying other large datasets such as sequencing data, quantum chemistry simulation data, and volumetric data due to its versatility and user extensibility.

Although VMD is designed to run on a diverse range of hardware—laptops, desktops, clusters, and supercomputers—most users utilize VMD as a desktop science application for interactive three-dimensional (3D) visualization and analysis. For computation that runs too long for interactive use, VMD can also be used in a batch mode to render movies for later use. A motivation for using GPU acceleration in VMD is to make slow, batch-mode jobs fast enough for interactive use. This can drastically improve the productivity of scientific investigations. With CUDA™-enabled GPUs widely available on desktop PCs, such acceleration can have a broad impact on the VMD user community. To date, multiple aspects of VMD have been accelerated with CUDA, including electrostatic potential calculation, ion placement, molecular orbital calculation and display, and imaging of gas migration pathways in proteins.

The particular calculation used in this case study is that of electrostatic potential maps in a grid space. This calculation is often used in placement of ions into a structure for molecular dynamics simulation. Figure 9.1 shows the placement of ions into a protein structure in preparation for molecular dynamics simulation. In this application, the electrostatic potential map is used to identify spatial locations where ions (dark dots) can fit in according to physical laws. The function can also be used to calculate time-averaged potentials during molecular dynamics simulation, which is useful for the simulation process as well as the visualization and analysis of simulation results.

Among the several methods for calculating electrostatic potential maps, direct Coulomb summation (DCS) is a highly accurate method that is particularly suitable for GPUs [Stone 2007]. The DCS method calculates the electrostatic potential value of each grid point as the sum of contributions from all atoms in the system. This is illustrated in Figure 9.2. The contribution of atom i to lattice point j is the charge of that atom divided by the distance from lattice point j to atom i. Because this must be done for all grid

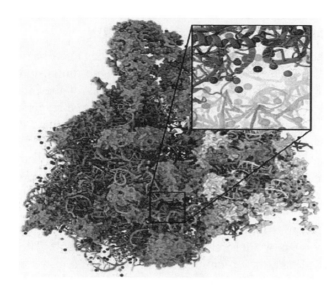

FIGURE 9.1

Electrostatic potential map used to build stable structures for molecular dynamics simulation.

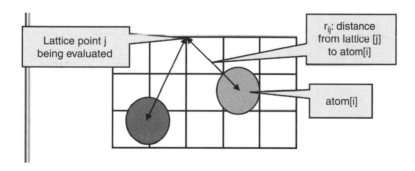

Lattice point j being evaluated

r_{ij}: distance from lattice [j] to atom[i]

atom[i]

FIGURE 9.2

The contribution of `atom[i]` to the electrostatic potential at lattice point *j* (`potential[j]`) is `atom[i].charge/rij`. In the direct Coulomb summation (DCS) method, the total potential at lattice point *j* is the sum of contributions from all atoms in the system.

points and all atoms, the number of calculations is proportional to the product of the total number of atoms in the system and the total number of grid points. For a realistic molecular system, this product can be very large; therefore, the calculation of the electrostatic potential map has been traditionally done as a batch job in VMD.

9.2 A SIMPLE KERNEL IMPLEMENTATION

Figure 9.3 shows the base C code of the DCS code. The function is written to process a two-dimensional (2D) slice of a three-dimensional grid. The function will be called repeatedly for all the slices of the modeled space. The structure of the function is quite simple, with three levels of `for` loops. The outer two levels iterate over the y-dimension and the x-dimension of the grid-point space. For each grid point, the innermost `for` loop iterates over all atoms, calculating the contribution of electrostatic potential energy from all atoms to the grid point. Note that each atom is represented by four consecutive elements of the `atoms[]` array. The first three elements store the x, y, and z coordinates of the atom and the fourth element the electrical charge of the atom. At the end of the innermost loop, the accumulated value of the grid point is written out to the grid data structure. The outer loops then iterate and take the execution to the next grid point.

Note that the DCS function in Figure 9.3 calculates the x and y coordinates of each grid point on the fly by multiplying the grid-point index values by the spacing between grid points. This is a uniform grid method, where all grid points are spaced at the same distance in all three dimensions. The function does take advantage of the fact that all the grid

```
void cenergy(float*energygrid, dim3 grid, float gridspacing, float z, const float *atoms,
             int numatoms) {
  int i,j,n;
  int atomarrdim = numatoms * 4;
  for (j=0; j<grid.y; j++) {
   float y = gridspacing * (float) j;
   for (i=0; i<grid.x; i++) {
    float x = gridspacing * (float) i;
    float energy = 0.0f;
    for (n=0; n<atomarrdim; n+=4) {  //calculate potential contribution of each atom
     float dx = x - atoms[n];
     float dy = y - atoms[n+1];
     float dz = z - atoms[n+2];
     energy += atoms[n+3]/sqrtf(dx*dx + dy*dy + dz*dz);
    }
    energygrid[grid.x*grid.y*k + grid.x*j + i] = energy;
   }
  }
}
```

FIGURE 9.3

Base Coulomb potential calculation code for a two-dimensional slice of the three-dimensional grid.

points in the same slice have the same z coordinate. This value is precalculated by the caller of the function and passed in as a function parameter (z).

Based on what we learned from the magnetic resonance imaging (MRI) case study, two attributes of the DCS method should be apparent. First, the computation is massively parallel; the computation of electrostatic potential for each grid point is independent of that of other grid points. There are two alternative approaches to organizing parallel execution. In the first option, we can use each thread to calculate the contribution of one atom to all grid points. This would be a poor choice, as each thread would be writing to all grid points, requiring extensive use of atomic memory operations to coordinate the updates done by different threads to each grid point. The second option uses each thread to calculate the accumulated contributions of all atoms to one grid point. This is a preferred approach, as each thread will be writing into its own grid point and it is not necessary to use atomic operations.

We will form a two-dimensional thread grid that matches the two-dimensional energy grid-point organization. In order to do so, we need to modify the two outer loops into perfectly nested loops so we can use each thread to execute one iteration of the two-level loop. We can either perform a loop fission (introduced in Section 8.3) or move the calculation of the y coordinate into the inner loop. The former would require us to create a new array to hold all y values and result in two kernels communicating data through global memory. The latter increases the number of times that the y coordinate will be calculated. In this case, we choose to perform the latter because there is only on calculation that can be easily accommodated into the inner loop without significant increase in execution time of the inner loop. The former would have added a kernel launch overhead for a kernel where threads do very little work. The selected transformation allows all i and j iterations to be executed in parallel. This is a tradeoff between the amount of calculation done and the level of parallelism achieved.

The second experience that we can apply from the MRI case study is that the electrical charge of every atom will be read by all threads. This is because every atom contributes to every grid point in the DCS method. Furthermore, the values of the atomic electrical charges and their positions are not modified during the computation. This means that the atomic charge and position values (the contents of the `atoms[]` array) can be efficiently stored in the constant memory (in the GPU box in Figure 9.4). Because there can be more than 64 kB of atom charges in the input, we need to partition them into 64-kB chunks in the same way that we did for the MRI case study.

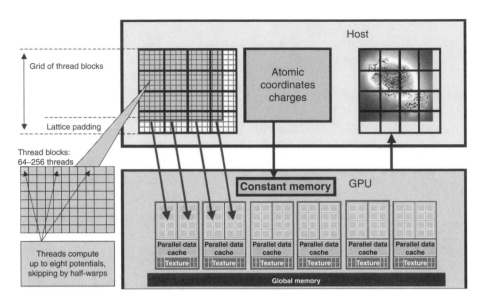

FIGURE 9.4

Overview of the DSC kernel design.

Figure 9.4 shows an overview of the DCS kernel design. The host program ("Host" box) inputs and maintains the atomic charges and their coordinates in the system memory. It also maintains the grid-point data structure in the system memory (left side of the "Host" box). The DCS kernel is designed to process a 2D slice of the energy grid-point structure (not to be confused with thread grids). The grid on the right side of the "Host" box shows an example of a 2D slice. For each 2D slice, the central processing unit (CPU) transfers its grid data to the device global memory. The atom information is divided into chunks to fit into the constant memory. For each chunk of the atom information, the CPU transfers the chunk into the device constant memory, invokes the DCS kernel to calculate the contribution of the current chunk to the current slice, and prepares to transfer the next chunk. After all chunks of the atom information have been processed for the current slice, the slice is transferred back to update the grid-point data structure in the CPU system memory. The system then moves on to the next slice.

Within each kernel invocation, the thread blocks are organized to calculate the electrostatic potential of tiles of the grid structure. In the simplest kernel, each thread calculates the value at one grid point. In more sophisticated kernels, each thread calculates multiple grid points and exploits the redundancy between the calculations of the grid points to improve execution speed. This is illustrated in the left side of the figure, labeled as "Thread blocks."

Figure 9.5 shows the resulting CUDA kernel code. We omitted some of the declarations. As in the case the MRI case study, the `atominfo[]` array is the device code counter part of the `atoms[]` array in the host base code of Figure 9.3. The host code also needs to divide up the atom information into chunks that fit into the constant memory for each kernel invocation. This means that the kernel will be invoked multiple times when there are multiple chunks' worth of atoms. Because this is similar to the MRI case study, we will not show the details.

The outer two levels of the loop in Figure 9.3 have been removed from the kernel code and are replaced by the execution configuration parameters in the kernel invocation. This is also similar to one of the steps we took the MRI case study, so we will not show the kernel invocation but leave it as an exercise for the reader. The rest of the kernel code is straightforward and corresponds directly to the original loop body of the innermost loop.

One particular aspect of the kernel is somewhat subtle and worth mentioning. The kernel code calculates the contribution of a chunk of atoms to a grid point. The grid point must be preserved in the global memory and updated by each kernel invocation. This means that the kernel needs to read the current grid point value, add the contributions by the current

```
. . .
    float curenergy = energygrid[outaddr];        Start global memory reads
    float coorx = gridspacing * xIndex;           early. Kernel hides some of
    float coory = gridspacing * yindex;                 its own latency.
    int atomid;
    float energyval=0.0f;
    for (atomid=0; atomid<numatoms; atomid++) {
     float dx = coorx - atominfo[atomid].x;
     float dy = coory - atominfo[atomid].y;
     energyval += atominfo[atomid].w*
               rsqrtf(dx*dx + dy*dy + atominfo[atomid].z);
    }                                             Only dependency on global
    energygrid[outaddr] = curenergy + energyval;  memory read is at the end of
                                                        the kernel...
```

FIGURE 9.5

DCS Kernel Version 1.

chunk of atoms, and write the updated value to global memory. The code attempts to hide the global memory latency by loading the grid value at the beginning of the kernel and using it at the end of the kernel. This helps to reduce the number of warps needed by the streaming multiprocessor (SM) scheduler to hide the global memory latency.

The performance of the kernel in Figure 9.5 is quite good, having been measured at 186 gigaflops on an NVIDIA® G80. In terms of application-level performance, the implementation can process 18.6 billion atom evaluations per second. A quick glance over the code shows that each thread does nine floating-point operations for every four memory elements accessed. On the surface, this is not a very good ratio. We need a ratio of at least 8 to avoid global memory congestion; however, all four memory accesses are done to an `atominfo[]` array. These `atominfo[]` array elements for each atom are cached in a hardware cache memory in each SM and are broadcast to a large number of threads. A calculation similar to that in the MRI case study shows that the massive reuse of memory elements across threads makes the constant cache extremely effective, boosting the effective ratio of floating operations per global memory access much higher than 10:1. As a result, global memory bandwidth is not a limiting factor for this kernel.

9.3 INSTRUCTION EXECUTION EFFICIENCY

Although the kernel in Figure 9.5 avoids global memory bottleneck through constant caching, it still must execute four constant memory access instructions for every nine floating-point operations performed. These memory access instructions consume hardware resources that could be otherwise used to increase the execution throughput of floating point instructions. This section shows that we can fuse several threads together so the `atominfo[]` data can be fetched once from the constant memory, stored into registers, and used for multiple grid points. This idea is illustrated in Figure 9.6.

Furthermore, all grid points along the same row have the same y coordinate; therefore, the difference between the y coordinate of an atom and the y coordinate of any grid point along a row has the same value. In the DCS Kernel Version 1 in Figure 9.5, this calculation is redundantly done by all threads for all grid points in a row when calculating the distance between the atom and the grid points. We can eliminate this redundancy and improve the execution efficiency.

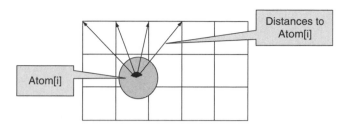

FIGURE 9.6

Reusing information among multiple grid points.

The idea is to have each thread to calculate the electrostatic potential for multiple grid points. In the kernel shown in Figure 9.7, each thread calculates four grid points. For each atom, the code calculates dy, the difference of the y coordinate in line 2. It then calculates the expression dy*dy plus the precalculated dz*dz information and saves it to the auto variable dysqpdzsq, which is assigned to a register by default. This value is the same for all four grid points; therefore, the calculation of energyvalx1 through energyvalx4 can just use the value stored in the register. Furthermore, the electrical charge information is also accessed from constant memory and stored in the automatic variable charge. Similarly, the x coordinate of the atom is also read from constant memory into auto variable x. Altogether, this kernel eliminates three accesses to constant memory for atominfo[atomid].y, three accesses to constant memory for atominfo [atomid].x, three accesses to constant memory for atominfo[atomid].w,

```
...for (atomid=0; atomid<numatoms; atomid++) {
    float dy = coory - atominfo[atomid].y;
    float dysqpdzsq = (dy * dy) + atominfo[atomid].z;
    float x = atominfo[atomid].x;
    float dx1 = coorx1 - x;
    float dx2 = coorx2 - x;
    float dx3 = coorx3 - x;
    float dx4 = coorx4 - x;
    float charge = atominfo[atomid].w;
    energyvalx1 += charge * rsqrtf(dx1*dx1 + dysqpdzsq);
    energyvalx2 += charge * rsqrtf(dx2*dx2 + dysqpdzsq);
    energyvalx3 += charge * rsqrtf(dx3*dx3 + dysqpdzsq);
    energyvalx4 += charge * rsqrtf(dx4*dx4 + dysqpdzsq);
    }
```

> Compared to non-unrolled kernel: memory loads are decreased by 4x, and FLOPS per evaluation are reduced, but register use is increased...

FIGURE 9.7

DCS Kernel Version 2.

three floating-point subtraction operations, five floating-point multiply operations, and nine floating-point add operations when processing an atom for four grid points. A quick inspection of the kernel code in Figure 9.7 should show that each iteration of the loop performs four constant memory accesses, five floating-point subtractions, nine floating-point additions, and five floating-point multiplications for four grid points.

The reader should also verify that the version of DCS kernel in Figure 9.5 performs 16 constant memory accesses, 8 floating-point subtractions, 12 floating-point additions, and 12 floating-point multiplications, a total of 48 operations for the same four grid points. Going from Figure 9.5 to Figure 9.7, there is a dramatic reduction from 48 operations down to 25 operations. This is translated into an increased execution speed from 186 gigaflops to 259 gigaflops. In terms of application-level throughput, the performance increases from 18.6 billion atom evaluations per second to 33.4 billion atom evaluations per second. The reason why the application-level performance improvement is higher than the floating-point operations per second (FLOPS) improvement is that some of the floating-point operations have been eliminated.

The cost of the optimization is that more registers are used by each thread. This reduces the number of threads that can be assigned to each SM. However, as the results show, this is a good tradeoff providing an excellent performance improvement.

9.4 MEMORY COALESCING

The performance of the DCS Kernel Version 2 shown in Figure 9.7 is quite high, but a quick profiling run reveals that the threads perform memory writes inefficiently. As shown in Figures 9.6 and 9.7, each thread calculates four neighboring grid points. This seems to be a reasonable choice; however, as we illustrate in Figure 9.8, the access pattern of threads will result in uncoalesced global memory writes.

We can identify two problems that are causing the uncoalesced writes in DCS Kernel Version 2. First, each thread calculates four adjacent neighboring grid points; thus, for each statement that access the `energygrid[]` array, the threads in a warp are not accessing adjacent locations. Note that two adjacent threads access memory locations that are three elements apart. Thus, the 16 locations to be written by all the threads in warp write are spread out, with three elements in between the loaded/written locations. This problem can be solved by assigning adjacent grid points to adjacent

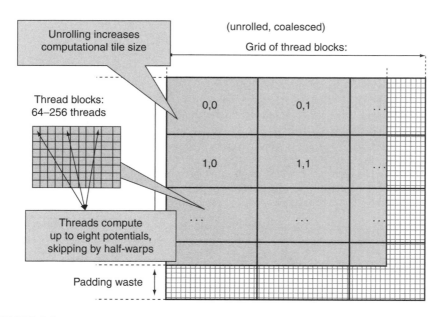

FIGURE 9.8

Organizing threads and memory layout for coalesced writes.

threads in each half warp. Assuming that we still want to have each thread calculate 4 grid points, we first assign 16 consecutive grid points to the 16 threads in a half-warp. We then assign the next 16 consecutive grid points to the same 16 threads. We repeat the assignment until each thread has the number of grid points desired. This assignment is illustrated in Figure 9.8. With some experimentation, the best number of grid points per thread turns out to be 8 for the G80.

The kernel code with warp-aware assignment of grid points to threads is shown in Figure 9.9. Note that the x coordinates used to calculate the distances are offset by the variable `gridspacing_coalescing`, which is the original grid spacing times the constant `BLOCKSIZEX` (in this case, 16). This reflects the fact that the x coordinates of the 8 grid points are 16 grid points away from each other. Also, after the end of the loop, memory writes to the `energygrid[]` array are indexed by `outaddr`, `outaddr+BLOCKSIZEX`,..., `outaddr+7*BLOCKSIZEX`. Each of these indices is one `BLOCKSIZEX` (16) away from the previous one. The detailed thread block organization for this kernel is left as an exercise. The reader should keep in mind that by setting the x-dimension size of the thread block to be equal to the half-warp size (16), we can simplify the indexing in the kernel.

```
...float coory = gridspacing * yindex;
  float coorx = gridspacing * xindex;
  float gridspacing_coalesce = gridspacing * BLOCKSIZEX;
  int atomid;
  for (atomid=0; atomid<numatoms; atomid++) {
    float dy = coory - atominfo[atomid].y;
    float dyz2 = (dy * dy) + atominfo[atomid].z;
    float dx1 = coorx – atominfo[atomid].x;
[...]
    float dx8 = dx7 + gridspacing_coalesce;
    energyvalx1 += atominfo[atomid].w * rsqrtf(dx1*dx1 + dyz2);
[...]
    energyvalx8 += atominfo[atomid].w * rsqrtf(dx8*dx8 + dyz2);
  }
  energygrid[outaddr                    ] += energyvalx1;
[...]
  energygrid[outaddr+7*BLOCKSIZEX] += energyvalx7;
```

> Points spaced for memory coalescing

> Reuse partial distance components dy^2 + dz^2

> Global memory ops occur only at the end of the kernel, decreases register use

FIGURE 9.9

DCS Kernel Version 3.

The other cause of uncoalesced memory writes is the layout of the energygrid[] array, which is a three-dimensional array. If the x-dimension of the array is not a multiple of half-warp size, the beginning location of the second row, as well as the beginning locations of the subsequent rows, will no longer be at the 16-word boundaries. This means that the half-warp accesses will not be coalesced, even though they write to consecutive locations. This problem can be corrected by padding each row with additional elements so the total length of the x-dimension is a multiple of 16. This can require adding up to 15 elements, or 60 bytes to each row, as shown in Figure 9.8. With the kernel of Figure 9.9, the number of elements in the x-dimension needs to be a multiple of $8 \times 16 = 128$. This is because each thread actually writes eight elements in each iteration. Thus, one may need to add up to 127 elements, or 1016 bytes, to each row.

Furthermore, there is a potential problem with the last row of thread blocks. Because the grid array may not have enough rows, some of the threads may end up writing outside the grid data structure. The grid data structure is a 3D array, so these threads will write into the next slice of grid points. One potential solution is to add a test in the kernel and avoid writing the array elements that are out of the known y-dimension size; however, this would have added a number of overhead instructions and incurred control divergence. A more desirable solution is to pad the *y*-dimension of the grid structure so it contains a multiple of tiles covered by thread blocks. This is shown in Figure 9.8 as the bottom padding in the grid structure. In general, one may need to add up to 15 rows due to this padding.

The cost of padding can be substantial for smaller grid structures. For example, if the energy grid has 100×100 grid points in each 2D slice, it would be padded into a 128×112 slice. The total number of grid points would increase from 10,000 to 14,336, or a 43% overhead. If we had to pad the entire 3D structure, the grid points would increase from $100 \times 100 \times 100 = 1,000,000$ to $128 \times 112 \times 112 = 1,605,632$, or a 60% overhead! This is part of the reason why we calculate the energy grids in 2D slices and use the host code to iterate over these 2D slices. Writing a single kernel to process the entire 3D structure would incur a lot more extra overhead. This type of tradeoff appears frequently in simulation models, differential equation solvers, and video processing applications.

The DCS Kernel Version 3 kernel shown in Figure 9.9 achieves about 291 gigaflops, or 39.5 billion atom evaluations per second. The measured speed of this kernel also has a slight enhancement from moving the read access to the `energygrid[]` array from the beginning of the kernel to the end of the kernel. The contributions to the grid points are first calculated in the loop. The code loads the original grid-point data after the loop, adds the contribution to them, and writes the updated values back. Although this movement exposes more of the global memory latency to each thread, it saves the consumption of eight registers. Because the kernel is already using many registers to hold the atom data and the distances, such saving in number of registers used relieves a critical bottleneck for the kernel. This allows more thread blocks to be assigned to each SM and achieves an overall performance improvement.

9.5 ADDITIONAL PERFORMANCE COMPARISONS

Figure 9.10 shows a summary of the performance comparison between the various DCS kernel implementations and how they compare with an optimized single-core CPU execution. One important observation is that the relative merit of the kernels varies with grid dimension lengths; however, DCS Kernel Version 3 (CUDA-Unroll8clx) from Figure 9.9 performs consistently better than all others once the grid dimension length is larger than 300. The notation Unroll8clx indicates that the kernel assigns 8 grid points to each thread and uses padding and strided grid point assignment to threads to ensure coalescing.

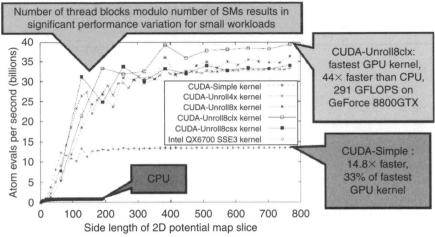

GPU computing. J. Owens, M. Houston, D. Luebke, S. Green, J. Stone, J. Phillips. *Proceedings of the IEEE*, 96:879-899, 2008.

FIGURE 9.10

Performance comparison of various DCS kernel versions.

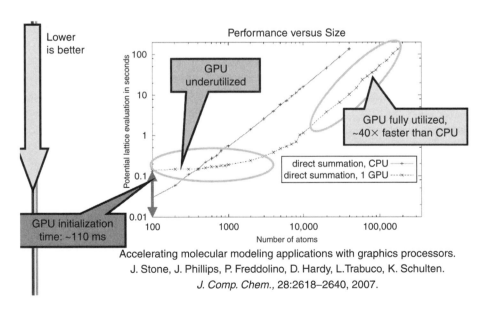

Accelerating molecular modeling applications with graphics processors. J. Stone, J. Phillips, P. Freddolino, D. Hardy, L.Trabuco, K. Schulten. *J. Comp. Chem.*, 28:2618–2640, 2007.

FIGURE 9.11

CPU versus CPU/GPU comparison.

A detailed comparison of the CPU performance and the CPU/GPU joint performance reveals a commonly observed tradeoff. Figure 9.11 shows a plot of the execution time of a medium-sized grid system for varying numbers of atoms to be evaluated. For 400 atoms or fewer, the CPU performs better. This is because the GPU has a fixed initialization overhead of 110 ms, regardless of the number of atoms to be evaluated. Also, for a small number of atoms, the GPU is underutilized, thus the curve of the GPU execution time is quite flat, between 100 and 1000 atoms.

The plot in Figure 9.11 reinforces a commonly held principle that GPUs perform better for large amounts of data. Once the number of atoms reaches 10,000, the GPU is fully utilized. The slopes of the CPU and the CPU/GPU execution times become virtually identical, with the CPU/GPU execution being consistently 44× faster than the CPU execution for all input sizes.

9.6 USING MULTIPLE GPUs

In Section 9.2, we gave an overview of the DCS kernel design. Recall that for each slice of the energy grid structure, the CPU first transfers the slice to the device memory and then streams the atom information through the device constant memory. This design provides a very straightforward path to using multiple GPUs to further improve the execution speed of the kernel.

For a multi-GPU design, the CPU first launches multiple p-threads. The CUDA runtime requires that each GPU must be associated with a separate p-thread running on the CPU. The CPU then forms a task pool, each task being the processing of one energy grid slice. When one of the GPUs becomes available, its corresponding p-thread picks up a task (slice), transfers the slice to the GPU, and begins to stream the atom information through the device constant memory of that GPU. In this way, the GPUs collaboratively process the pool of slices, thus increasing the rate of processing the grid. Using three GeForce® 8800 GTX GPUs, we have measured 863 gigaflops, or 117 billion atom evaluations per second. This is a 131× speedup over a single CPU core. This was measured from a PC with three GPU cards, as shown in Figure 9.12. With such speed, experiments that used to take a month on a PC box now take a few hours. This has been shown to greatly improve the productivity of researchers in the area of molecular science and medicine.

Although the use of multiple GPUs for the DCS kernel is conceptually simple, the detailed mechanics for creating CPU p-threads, creating a task pool, and handling errors and exception conditions can be tedious and error

FIGURE 9.12

A PC with three GeForce® 8800 GTX GPUs at 700 W of total system power.

prone. This has motivated the creation of the WorkForce framework and runtime to simplify the use of multiple GPUs. Interested readers should download WorkForce for their multiple-GPU applications.

9.7 EXERCISES

9.1 Complete the implementation of the DCS kernel shown in Figure 9.5. Fill in all of the missing declarations. Develop a kernel launch statement with all of the execution configuration parameters.

9.2 Compare the number of operations (memory loads, floating-point arithmetic, branches) executed in each iteration of the kernel shown in Figure 9.7 compared to that in Figure 9.5. Keep in mind that each iteration of the former corresponds to four iterations of the latter.

9.3 Complete the implementation of the DCS kernel shown in Figure 9.9. Explain in your own words how the thread accesses are coalesced in this implementation.

9.4 For the memory padding in Figure 9.8 and the DCS kernel shown in Figure 9.9, show why one needs to pad up to 127 elements in the x-dimension but only up to 15 elements in the y-dimension.

9.5 Give two reasons for adding extra "padding" elements to arrays allocated in the GPU global memory, as shown in Figure 9.8.

9.6 Give two potential disadvantages associated with increasing the amount of work done in each CUDA thread, as shown in Section 9.3.

References and Further Reading

Humphrey, W., Dalke, A., & Schulten, K. (1996). VMD: Visual molecular dynamics. *Journal of Molecular Graphics*, *14*, 33–38.

Stone, J. E., Phillips, J. C., Freddolino, P. L., Hardy, D. J., Trabuco, L. G., & Schulten, K. (2007). Accelerating molecular modeling applications with graphics processors. *Journal of Computational Chemistry*, *28*, 2618–2640.

Parallel Programming and Computational Thinking

10

CHAPTER CONTENTS

INTRODUCTION

We have so far concentrated on the practical experience of parallel programming, which consists of the CUDA™ programming model features, performance and numerical considerations, and systematic case studies. We will now switch gears to more abstract concepts. We will first generalize parallel programming into a process of decomposing a domain problem into well-defined, coordinated work units that can each be realized with efficient numerical methods and well-known algorithms. A programmer with strong computational thinking skills not only analyzes but also transforms the structure of a domain problem by determining which parts are inherently serial, which parts are amenable to high-performance parallel execution, and the tradeoffs involved in moving parts from the first category to the second. With good problem decomposition, the programmer has to select and implement algorithms that achieve an appropriate compromise among parallelism, computational efficiency, and memory bandwidth consumption. A strong combination of domain knowledge and computational thinking skills is often needed for creating successful computational solutions to challenging domain problems. This chapter will give the reader more insight into parallel programming and computational thinking in general.

10.1 GOALS OF PARALLEL PROGRAMMING

Before we discuss the fundamental concepts of parallel programming, it is important for us to first review the three main reasons why people adopt parallel computing. The first goal is to solve a given problem in less time. An investment firm, for example, may need to run a financial portfolio scenario risk analysis package on all of its portfolios during after-trading hours. Such an analysis may require 200 hours on a sequential computer; however, the portfolio management process may require that analysis be completed in 4 hours in order to make timely decisions based on the information. Using parallel computing may speed up the analysis and allow it to complete within the required time window.

The second goal of using parallel computing is to solve bigger problems within a given amount of time. In our financial portfolio analysis example, the investment firm may be able to run the portfolio scenario risk analysis on its current portfolio within an acceptable time window using sequential computing, but suppose the firm is planning on expanding the number of holdings in its portfolio. The enlarged problem size would cause the runtime of analysis under sequential computation to exceed the time window. Parallel computing that reduces the runtime of the bigger problem size can help accommodate the planned expansion to the portfolio.

The third goal of using parallel computing is to achieve better solutions for a given problem and a given amount of time. The investment firm may have been using an approximate model in its portfolio scenario risk analysis. Using a more accurate model may increase the computational complexity and increase the runtime based on sequential computing beyond the allowed window. A more accurate model may require consideration of interactions between more types of risk factors using a more numerically complex formula. Parallel computing that reduces the runtime of the more accurate model may complete the analysis within the allowed time window. In practice, the use of parallel computing may be driven by a combination of these three goals.

It should be clear from our discussion that parallel computing is primarily motivated by increased speed. The first goal is achieved by increased speed in running the existing model on the current problem size. The second goal is achieved by increased speed in running the existing model on a larger problem size. The third goal is achieved by increased speed in running a more complex model on the current problem size. Obviously, the increased speed through parallel computing can be used to achieve a combination of these goals; for example, parallel computing can reduce the runtime of a more complex model on a larger problem size.

It should also be clear from our discussion that applications that are good candidates for parallel computing typically involve large problem sizes and high modeling complexity. That is, these applications typically process a large amount of data, perform many iterations on the data, or both. For such a problem to be solved with parallel computing, the problem must be formulated in such a way that it can be decomposed into subproblems that can be safely solved at the same time. Under such formulation and decomposition, the programmer writes the code and organized data to solve these subproblems concurrently.

In Chapter 8, we presented a problem that is a good candidate for parallel computing. The magnetic resonance imaging (MRI) reconstruction problem involves a large amount of k-space sample data. Each k-space sample datum is also used many times for calculating its contributions to the reconstructed voxel data. For a reasonably high-resolution reconstruction, the sample data are used a very large number of times. We showed that a good decomposition of the F^HD problem in MRI reconstruction is to form subproblems that calculate the value of an F^HD element. All of these subproblems can be solved in parallel with each other, and we use a massive number of CUDA threads to solve them.

In Chapter 9, we presented another problem that is a good candidate for parallel computing. Figure 9.11 further showed that the electrostatic potential calculation problem should be solved with a massively parallel CUDA device only if there are 400 or more atoms. A realistic molecular dynamic system model typically involves at least hundreds of thousands of atoms and millions of energy grid points. The electrostatic charge information of each atom is used many times in calculating its contributions to the energy grid points. We showed that a good decomposition of the electrostatic potential calculation problem is to form subproblems to calculate the energy value of each grid point. Once again, all of these subproblems can be solved in parallel with each other, and we use a massive number of CUDA threads to solve them.

The process of parallel programming can typically be divided into four steps: problem decomposition, algorithm selection, implementation in a language, and performance tuning. The last two steps were the focus of previous chapters. In the next two sections, we will discuss the first two steps both generally and in depth.

10.2 PROBLEM DECOMPOSITION

Finding parallelism in large computational problems is often conceptually simple but can turn out to be challenging in practice. The key is to identify the work to be performed by each unit of parallel execution (a thread in CUDA) so the inherent parallelism of the problem is well utilized. For example, in the electrostatic potential map calculation problem, it is clear that all atoms can be processed in parallel and all energy grid points can be calculated in parallel; however, one must take care when decomposing the calculation work into units of parallel execution, which will be referred to as *threading arrangement*. As we discussed in Section 9.2, the decomposition of the electrostatic potential map calculation problem can be atom centric or grid centric. In an atom-centric threading arrangement, each thread is responsible for calculating the effect of one atom on all grid points. In contrast, a grid-centric threading arrangement uses each thread to calculate the effect of all atoms on a grid point.

Both threading arrangements lead to similar levels of parallel execution and the same execution results, but they can exhibit very different performance in a given hardware system. The grid-centric arrangement has a memory access behavior called *gather*, where each thread gathers or collects the effect of input atoms into a grid point. This is a desirable arrangement in CUDA devices because the threads can accumulate their results in their private registers. Also, multiple threads share input atom values and can effectively use constant memory caching or shared memory to conserve global memory bandwidth.

The atom-centric arrangement, on the other hand, exhibits a memory access behavior called *scatter*, where each thread scatters, or distributes, the effect of an atom into grid points. This is an undesirable arrangement in CUDA devices, because the multiple threads can write into the same grid point at the same time. The grid points must be stored in a memory that can be written by all the threads involved. Atomic operations must be used to prevent race conditions and loss of value during simultaneous writes to a grid point by multiple threads. These atomic operations are much slower than the register accesses used in the grid-centric arrangement.

A real application often consists of multiple modules that work together. The electrostatic potential map calculation is one such module in molecular dynamics applications. Figure 10.1 shows an overview of major modules of a molecular dynamics application. For each atom in the system, the application needs to calculate the various forms of forces—vibrational, rotational, and nonbonded—that are exerted on the atom. Each form of force is calculated by a different method. At the high level, a programmer needs to decide how the work is organized. Note that the amount of work can vary dramatically between these modules. The nonbonded force calculation typically involves interactions among many atoms and incurs much more calculation than the vibrational and rotational forces; therefore, these modules tend to be realized as separate

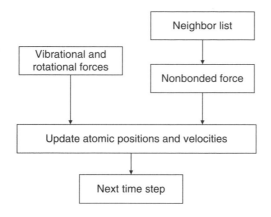

FIGURE 10.1

Major tasks of a molecular dynamics application.

passes over the force data structure. The programmer needs to decide if each pass is worth implementing in a CUDA device. For example, the programmer may decide that the vibrational and rotational force calculations do not involve a sufficient amount of work to warrant execution on a device. Such a decision would lead to a CUDA program that launches a kernel that calculates nonbonding forces for all the grid points while continuing to calculate the vibrational and rotational forces for the grid points on the host. The module that updates atomic positions and velocities may also run on the host. It first combines the vibrational and rotational forces from the host and the nonbonding forces from the device. It then uses the combined forces to calculate the new atomic positions and velocities.

The portion of work done by the device will ultimately decide the application-level speedup achieved by parallelization. Assume, for example, that the nonbonding force calculation accounts for 95% of the original sequential execution time, and it is accelerated by 100× using a CUDA device. Further assume that the rest of the application remains on the host and receives no speedup. The application-level speedup is $1/[5\% + (95\%/100)] = 1/(5\% + 0.95\%) = 1/(5.95\%) = 17\times$. This is a demonstration of Amdahl's law: The application speedup due to parallel computing is limited by the sequential portion of the application. In this case, even though the sequential portion of the application is quite small (5%), it limits the application level speedup to 17× even though the nonbonding force calculation has a speedup of 100×. This example illustrates a major challenge in decomposing large applications, in that the accumulated execution time of small activities that are not worth parallel execution on a CUDA device can become a limiting factor in the speedup seen by the end users.

Amdahl's law often motivates task-level parallelization. Although some of these smaller activities do not warrant fine-grained massive parallel execution, it may be desirable to execute some of these activities in parallel with each other when the dataset is large enough. This could be achieved by using a multicore host and executing each such task in parallel. This is a illustration of Gustafson's Law, which states that any sufficiently large problem can be effectively parallelized. When the data set is large enough and the more demanding calculation has been parallelized, one can effectively parallelize the less demanding calculation. Alternatively, we could try to simultaneously execute multiple small kernels, each corresponding to one task. The current CUDA devices do not support such parallelism, but the next-generation devices will.

An alternative approach to reducing the effect of sequential tasks is to exploit data parallelism in a hierarchical manner. In a typical Message Passing Interface (MPI) implementation, a molecular dynamics application would typically distribute large chunks of the spatial grids and their associated atoms to nodes of a networked computing cluster. By using the host of each node to calculate the vibrational and rotational force for its chunk of atoms, we can achieve speedup for these lesser modules. Each node can use a CUDA device to calculate the nonbonding force at higher-level of speedup. The nodes will need to exchange data to accommodate forces that go across chunks and atoms that move across chunk boundaries. Details of MPI programming is beyond the scope of this book. The main point here is that MPI and CUDA can be used in a complementary way in applications to achieve a higher level of speed with large datasets.

10.3 ALGORITHM SELECTION

An algorithm is a step-by-step procedure where each step is precisely stated and can be carried out by a computer. An algorithm must exhibit three essential properties: definiteness, effective computability, and finiteness. *Definiteness* refers to the notion that each step is precisely stated; there is no room for ambiguity as to what is to be done. *Effective computability* refers to the fact that each step can be carried out by a computer. *Finiteness* means that the algorithm must be guaranteed to terminate.

Given a problem, we can typically come up with multiple algorithms to solve the problem. Some require fewer steps to compute than others; some allow higher degrees of parallel execution than others; and some consume less memory bandwidth than others. Unfortunately, there is often not a single algorithm that is better than others in all three aspects. Given a problem and a decomposition strategy, a parallel programmer often needs to select an algorithm that achieves the best compromise for a given hardware system.

In our matrix multiplication example, we decided to decompose the matrix–matrix multiplication problem by having each thread compute the dot product for an output element. Given this decomposition, we presented two different algorithms. The algorithm in Section 3.5 is a straightforward algorithm where every thread simply performs an entire dot product. Although the algorithm fully utilizes the parallelism available in the decomposition, it consumes too much global memory bandwidth. In Section 5.3, we introduced tiling, an important algorithm strategy for conserving memory bandwidth. Note that the tiled algorithm partitions the dot products into phases. All threads involved in a tile must synchronize with each other so they can collaboratively load the tile of input data into the shared memory and collectively utilize the loaded data before they move on to the next phase. As we showed in Figure 5.7, the tiled algorithm requires each thread to execute more statements and incur more overhead in indexing the input arrays than the original algorithm; however, it runs much faster because it consumes much less global memory bandwidth. In general, tiling is one of the most important algorithm strategies for matrix applications to achieve high performance.

As we demonstrated in Sections 6.6 and 9.3, we can systematically merge threads to achieve higher levels of instruction and memory access efficiency. In Section 6.6, threads that handle in the same columns of neighboring tiles are combined into a new thread. This allows the new thread to access each **Md** element once in calculating multiple dot products, thus reducing the number of address calculation and memory load instructions executed. It also further reduces the consumption of global memory bandwidth. The same technique, when applied to the DCS kernel, further reduces the number of distance calculations while achieving a similar reduction in address calculations and memory load instructions.

One can often come up with even more aggressive algorithm strategies. An important algorithm strategy known as *cutoff binning* can significantly improve the execution efficiency of grid algorithms by sacrificing a small amount of accuracy. This is based on the observation that many grid calculation problems are based on physical laws where numerical contributions from particles or samples that are far away from a grid point can be negligible. This is illustrated for the electrostatic potential calculation in Figure 10.2. Figure 10.2(a) shows the direct summation algorithms discussed in Chapter 9. Each grid point receives contributions from all atoms.

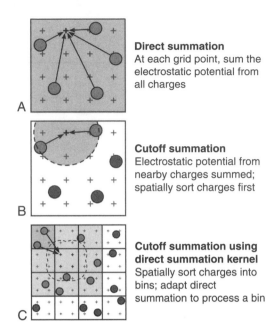

Direct summation
At each grid point, sum the electrostatic potential from all charges

Cutoff summation
Electrostatic potential from nearby charges summed; spatially sort charges first

Cutoff summation using direct summation kernel
Spatially sort charges into bins; adapt direct summation to process a bin

FIGURE 10.2

Cutoff summation algorithm.

Whereas this is a very parallel approach and achieves excellent speedup over CPU-only execution for moderate-sized energy grid systems, it does not scale well for very large energy-grid systems where the number of atoms increases proportional to the volume of the system. The amount of computation increases with the square of the volume. For large-volume systems, such an increase makes the computation excessively long even for massively parallel devices.

In practice, we know that each grid point needs to receive contributions from atoms that are close to it. The atoms that are far away from a grid point will have negligible contribution to the energy value at the grid point because the contribution is inversely proportional to the distance. Figure 10.2(b) illustrates this observation with a circle drawn around a grid point. The contributions to the grid point energy from atoms outside the large shaded circle are negligible. If we can devise an algorithm where each grid point only receives contributions from atoms within a fixed radius of its coordinate (+), the computational complexity of the algorithm would be reduced to linearly proportional to the volume of the system. This would make the computation time of algorithm linearly proportional to the volume of the system. Such algorithms have been used extensively in sequential computation.

In sequential computing, a cutoff algorithm handles one atom at a time. For each atom, the algorithm iterates through the grid points that fall within a radius of the atom's coordinate. This is a straightforward procedure, as the grid points are in an array that can be easily indexed as a function of their coordinates; however, this simple procedure does not carry easily to parallel execution. The reason is what we discussed in Section 10.2: The atom-centric decomposition does not work well due to it scatter memory access behavior.

We need to find a cutoff binning algorithm based on the grid-centric decomposition, where each thread calculates the energy value at one grid point. Fortunately, there is a well-known approach to adapting a direct summation algorithm, such as the one in Figure 9.5, into a cutoff binning algorithm. Rodrigues et al. [Rodrigues 2008] presented such an algorithm for the electrostatic potential problem.

The key idea of the algorithm is to first sort the input atoms into bins according to their coordinates. Each bin corresponds to a box in the grid space, and it contains all atoms whose coordinates fall into the box. We define a *neighborhood* of bins for a grid point to be the collection of bins that contain all the atoms that can contribute to the energy value of a grid point. If we have an efficient way to manage neighborhood bins for all grid points, we can calculate the energy value for a grid point by examining the neighborhood bins for the grid point. This is illustrated in Figure 10.2(c). Although Figure 10.2 shows only one layer of bins that immediately surround the bin containing a grid point as its neighborhood, a real algorithm will typically have multiple layers of bins in a grid's neighborhood. In this algorithm, all threads iterate through their own neighborhoods. They use their block and thread indices to identify the appropriate bins. Note that some of the atoms in the surrounding bins may not fall into the radius; therefore, when processing an atom, all threads need to check if the atom falls into its radius. This can cause some control divergence among threads in a warp.

The main source of improvement in computational efficiency comes from the fact that each thread now examines a much smaller set of atoms in a large grid system. This, however, makes constant memory much less attractive for holding the atom information. Because all thread blocks will be accessing different neighborhoods, it is not likely that the limited-size constant memory will be able to hold all the atoms that are needed by all active thread blocks. This motivates the use of global memory to hold a much larger set of atoms. To mitigate the bandwidth consumption, threads in a block collaborate in loading the atom information in the common neighborhood into the shared memory. All threads then examine the atoms out of shared memory. The reader is referred to Rodrigues et al. [Rodrigues 2008] for more details of this algorithm.

One subtle issue with binning is that bins may end up with different numbers of atoms. Because the atoms are statistically distributed in the grid system, some bins may have lots of atoms and some bins may end up with no atom at all. In order to guarantee memory coalescing, it is important that all bins are of the same size and aligned at appropriate coalescing boundaries. To accommodate the bins with the largest number of atoms, we would need to make the size of all other bins the same size. This would require us to fill many bins with dummy atoms whose electrical charge is 0, which causes two negative effects. First, the dummy atoms still occupy global memory and shared memory storage, and they consume data-transfer bandwidth to the device. Second, the dummy atoms extend the execution time of the thread blocks whose bins have few real atoms.

A well-known solution is to set the bin size at a reasonable level, typically much smaller than the largest possible number of atoms in a bin. The binning process maintains an overflow list. When processing an atom, if the atom's home bin is full, the atom is added to the overflow list instead. After the device completes a kernel, the result grid point energy values are transferred back to the host. The host executes a sequential cutoff algorithm on the atoms in the overflow list to complete the missing contributions from these overflow atoms. As long as the overflow atoms account for a small percentage of the atoms, the additional sequential processing of the overflow atoms is typically negligible. One can also design the kernel so each kernel invocation calculates the energy values for a subvolume of grid points. After each kernel completes, the host launches the next kernel and processes the overflow atoms for the completed kernel. Thus, the host will be processing the overflow atoms while the device executes the next kernel. This approach can hide most if not all of the delays in processing overflow atoms, as it is done in parallel with the execution of the next kernel.

Figure 10.3 shows a comparison of scalability and performance of the various electrostatic potential map algorithms. Note that the CPU-SSE3 curve is based on a sequential cutoff algorithm. For a map with small volumes (around 1000 Å^3), the host (CPU with SSE) executes faster than the direct summation kernel shown in Figure 9.9. For moderate volumes (between 2000 and 500,000 Å^3), the DCS kernel performs significantly

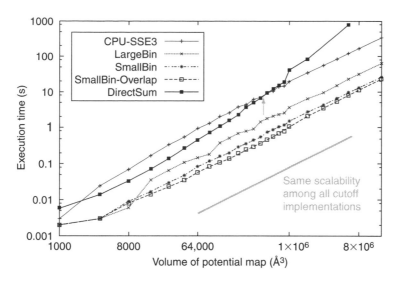

FIGURE 10.3

Scalability and performance of various algorithms for calculating electrostatic potential map.

better than the host due to its massive execution. As we anticipated, the DCS kernel scales poorly when the volume size reaches about 1,000,000 $Å^3$ and runs longer than the sequential algorithm on the CPU.

Figure 10.3 also shows the runtime of three binned cutoff algorithms. The LargeBin algorithm is a straightforward adaptation of the DCS kernel for cutoff. The kernel is designed to process a subvolume of the grid points. Before each kernel launch, the CPU transfers all atoms that are in the combined neighborhood of all the grid points in the subvolume. These atoms are still stored in the constant memory. All threads examine all atoms in the joint neighborhood. The advantage of the kernel is its simplicity. It is essentially the same as the DCS kernel with a preselected neighborhood of atoms. Note that the LargeBin approach performs reasonably well for moderate volumes and scales well for large volumes.

The SmallBin algorithm allows the threads running the same kernel to process different neighborhoods of atoms. This is the algorithm that uses global memory and shared memory for storing atoms. The algorithm achieves higher efficiency than the LargeBin algorithm because each thread needs to examine a smaller number of atoms. For moderate volumes (e.g., around 8000 $Å^3$), the LargeBin algorithm slightly outperforms SmallBin. The reason is that the SmallBin algorithm does incur more instruction overhead for loading atoms from global memory into shared memory. For a moderate volume, the entire system has a limited number of atoms. The ability to examine a smaller number of atoms does not provide sufficient advantage to overcome the additional instruction overhead; however, the difference is so small at 8000 Å^3 that the SmallBin algorithm is still a clear winner across all volume sizes. The SmallBin-Overlap algorithm overlaps the sequential overflow atom processing with the next kernel execution. It provides a slight but noticeable improvement in runtime over SmallBin. The SmallBin-Overlap algorithm achieves a 17× speedup for an efficiently implemented sequential CPU-SSE cutoff algorithm and maintains the same scalability for large volumes.

In summary, we have discussed the main dimensions of algorithm selection. The key lesson is that, given a problem decomposition decision, the programmer will typically have to select from a variety of algorithms. Some of these algorithms achieve different tradeoffs while maintaining the same numerical accuracy. Others involve sacrificing some level of accuracy to achieve much more scalable runtimes. The cutoff strategy is perhaps the most popular of such strategies. Even though we introduced cutoff in the context of electrostatic potential map calculation, it is used in many domains, including ray tracing in graphics and collision detection in games.

10.4 COMPUTATIONAL THINKING

Computational thinking is arguably the most important aspect of parallel application development [Wing 2006]. We define computational thinking as the thought process of formulating domain problems in terms of computation steps and algorithms. Like any other thought processes and problem-solving skills, computational thinking is an art. As we mentioned in the Introduction in Chapter 1, we believe that computational thinking is best taught with an iterative approach, where students bounce back and forth between practical experience and abstract concepts.

The electrostatic potential map example used in Chapters 9 and 10 serves as a good example of computational thinking. In order to develop an efficient parallel application that solves the electrostatic potential map problem, one must come up with a good high-level decomposition of the problem. As we showed in Sections 8.3, 9.2, and 10.2, one must have a clear understanding of the desirable (gather in CUDA) and undesirable (scatter in CUDA) memory access behaviors to make a wise decision.

Given a problem decomposition, the parallel programmer faces a potentially overwhelming task of designing algorithms to overcome major challenges in parallelism, execution efficiency, and memory bandwidth consumption. There is a very large volume of literature on a wide range of algorithm techniques that can be difficult to understand. It is beyond the scope of this book to provide comprehensive coverage of the available techniques, but we did discuss a substantial set of techniques that have broad applicability. Although these techniques are based on CUDA, they help the readers build up the foundation for computational thinking in general. We believe that humans understand best when we learn from the bottom up. That is, we must first learn the concepts in the context of a particular programming model, which provides us with solid footing, before we generalize our knowledge to other programming models. An in-depth experience with the CUDA model also enables us to gain maturity, which will help us learn concepts that may not even be pertinent to the CUDA model.

Myriad skills are needed for a parallel programmer to be an effective computational thinker. We summarize these foundational skills as follows:

- *Computer architecture*—Memory organization; caching and locality; memory bandwidth; single-instruction, multiple-thread (SIMT) versus single-program, multiple-data (SPMD) versus single-instruction, multiple-data (SIMD) execution; and floating-point precision versus accuracy. These concepts are critical in understanding the tradeoffs between algorithms.
- *Programming models and compilers*—Parallel execution models, types of available memories, array data layout and loop transformations, all concepts necessary for thinking through the arrangements of data structures and loop structures to achieve better performance.
- *Algorithm techniques*—Tiling, cutoff, binning, and other techniques that form the toolbox for designing superior parallel algorithms; understanding of the scalability, efficiency, and memory bandwidth implications of these techniques is essential in computational thinking.
- *Domain knowledge*—Numerical methods, models, accuracy requirements, and mathematical properties; an understanding of these ground rules allows a developer to be much more creative in applying algorithm techniques.

We believe that this book provides a solid foundation for all four areas. Readers should continue to broaden their knowledge in these areas after finishing this book. Most importantly, the best way to build up more computational thinking skills is to keep solving challenging problems with excellent computational solutions.

10.5 EXERCISES

10.1 Write a host function to perform binning of atoms. Determine the representation of the bins as arrays. Think about coalescing requirements. Make sure that every thread can easily find the bins it needs to process.

10.2 Write the part of the cutoff kernel function that determines if an atom is in the neighborhood of a grid point based on the coordinates of the atoms and the grid points.

References and Further Reading

Mattson, T. G., Sanders, B. A., & Massingill, B. L. (2004). *Patterns of parallel programming*. Upper Saddle River, NJ: Addison-Wesley Professional.

Message Passing Interface Forum. (2009). *MPI: A message-passing interface standard, Version 2.2*. http://www.mpi-forum.org/docs/mpi-2.2/mpi22-report.pdf

Rodrigues, C. I., Stone, J., Hardy, D., & Hwu, W. W. (2008). GPU acceleration of cutoff-based potential summation. In *Proceedings of the ACM international conference on computing frontiers (computing frontiers 2008)*, Ischia, Italy, May 5–7.

Wing, J. (2006). Computational thinking. *Communications of the ACM*, *49*(3), 33–35.

A Brief Introduction to OpenCL™

11

CHAPTER CONTENTS

INTRODUCTION

Now that you have learned high-performance parallel programming using CUDA™, we would like to introduce you to two new ways to exploit the parallel computing capabilities of graphics processing units (GPUs) and central processing units (CPUs). During the writing of this book, two new application programming interfaces (APIs) were introduced: OpenCL™ and DirectCompute™. In this chapter, we will give a brief overview of OpenCL to CUDA programmers. The fundamental programming model of OpenCL is so similar to CUDA that there is a one-to-one correspondence for most features. With your understanding of CUDA, you will be able to start writing OpenCL programs with the material presented in this chapter. In our opinion, the best way to learn OpenCL is actually to learn CUDA and then map the OpenCL features to their CUDA equivalent. We will then offer some pointers to introductory information about Microsoft's DirectCompute.

11.1 BACKGROUND

OpenCL is a standardized, cross-platform, parallel-computing API based on the C language. It is designed to enable the development of portable parallel applications for systems with heterogeneous computing devices.

The development of OpenCL was motivated by the need for a standardized high-performance application development platform for the fast-growing variety of parallel-computing platforms. In particular, it addresses significant limitations of the previous programming models for heterogeneous parallel-computing systems.

The CPU-based parallel programming models have typically been based on standards such as OpenMP™ but usually do not encompass the use of special memory types or SIMD execution by high-performance programmers. Joint CPU/GPU heterogeneous parallel programming models such as CUDA address complex memory hierarchies and SIMD execution but are typically platform, vendor, or hardware specific. These limitations make it difficult for an application developer to access the computing power of CPUs, GPUs, and other types of processing units from a single multiplatform source-code base.

The development of OpenCL was initiated by Apple® and developed by the Khronos Group, the same group that manages the OpenGL® standard. On one hand, it draws heavily on CUDA in the areas of supporting a single code base for heterogeneous parallel computing, data parallelism, and complex memory hierarchies. This is the reason why a CUDA programmer will find these aspects of OpenCL familiar once we connect the terminologies. The reader will especially appreciate the similarities between OpenCL and the low-level CUDA driver model.

On the other hand, OpenCL has a more complex platform and device management model that reflects its support for multiplatform and multivendor portability. OpenCL implementations already exist on AMD® ATI™ and NVIDIA® GPUs as well as x86 CPUs. In principle, one can envision OpenCL implementations on other types of devices such as digital signal processors (DSPs) and field-programmable gate arrays (FPGAs). Whereas the OpenCL standard is designed to support code portability across devices produced by different vendors, such portability does not come free. OpenCL programs must be prepared to deal with much greater hardware diversity and thus will exhibit more complexity. Also, many OpenCL features are optional and may not be supported on all devices, so a portable OpenCL code must avoid using these optional features. Some of these optional features, though, allow applications to achieve significantly more performance in devices that support them. As a result, a portable OpenCL code may not be able to achieve its performance potential on any of the devices; therefore, one should expect that a portable application that achieves high performance on multiple devices will employ sophisticated runtime tests and choose among multiple code paths according to the capabilities of the actual device used.

The objective of this chapter is not to provide full details on all programming features of OpenCL; rather, the objective is to give a CUDA programmer solid conceptual understanding of the OpenCL programming model features. With this foundation, the reader can immediately begin to program in OpenCL and consult the OpenCL specification [Khronos 2008] and programming guides [NVIDIA 2010, AMD 2009] on a needs basis.

11.2 DATA PARALLELISM MODEL

OpenCL employs a data parallelism model that has direct correspondence with the CUDA data parallelism model. An OpenCL program consists of two parts: kernels that execute on one or more OpenCL devices and a host program that manages the execution of kernels. Figure 11.1 summarizes the mapping of OpenCL data parallelism concepts to their CUDA equivalents. Like CUDA, the way to submit work for parallel execution in OpenCL is for the host program to launch kernel functions. We will discuss the additional kernel generation, device selection, and management work that an OpenCL host program must do as compared to its CUDA counterpart in Section 11.4.

When a kernel function is launched, its code is run by *work items*, which correspond to CUDA threads. An index space defines the work items and how data are mapped to the work items; that is, OpenCL work items are identified by global dimension index ranges (NDRanges). Work items form *work groups*, which correspond to CUDA thread blocks. Work items in the same work group can synchronize with each other using barriers that are equivalent to `syncthreads()` in CUDA. Work items in different work groups cannot synchronize with each other except by terminating the kernel function and launching a new one. As we discussed in Chapter 4, this limited scope of barrier synchronization enables transparent scaling.

OpenCL parallelism concept	CUDA equivalent
Kernel	Kernel
Host program	Host program
NDRange (index space)	Grid
Work item	Thread
Work group	Block

FIGURE 11.1

Mapping between OpenCL and CUDA data parallelism model concepts.

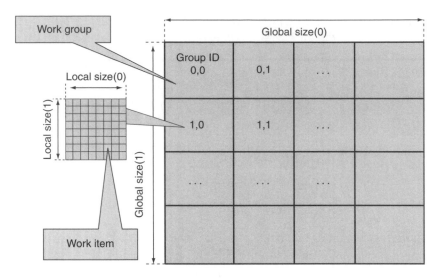

FIGURE 11.2

Overview of the OpenCL parallel execution model.

Figure 11.2 illustrates the OpenCL data parallelism model. The reader should compare Figure 11.2 with Figure 9.8 for similarities. The NDRange (CUDA grid) contains all work items (CUDA threads). For this example, we assume that the kernel is launched with a two-dimensional (2D) NDRange.

All work items have their own unique global index values. There is a minor difference between OpenCL and CUDA in the way they manage these index values. In CUDA, each thread has a `blockIdx` value and a `threadIdx` value. The two values are combined to form a global thread ID value for the thread. For example, if a CUDA grid and its blocks are organized as 2D arrays, the kernel code can form a unique global thread index value in the x-dimension as `blockIdx.x × blockDim.x + threadIdx.x`. These `blockIdx` and `threadIdx` values are accessible in a CUDA kernel as predefined variables.

In an OpenCL kernel, a thread can get its unique global index values by calling an API function, `get_global_id()`, with a parameter that identifies the dimension. See the `get_global_id(0)` entry in Figure 11.3. The calls `get_global_id(0)` and `get_global_id(1)` return the global thread index values in the x-dimension and the y-dimension, respectively. The global index value in the x-dimension is equivalent to the `blockIdx.x × blockDim.x + threadIdx.x` in CUDA. See Figure 11.3 for the `get_local_id(0)` function,

OpenCL API call	Explanation	CUDA equivalent
get_global_id(0);	Global index of the work item in the x-dimension	blockIdx.x×blockDim.x+threadIdx.x
get_local_id(0)	Local index of the work item within the work group in the x-dimension	threadIdx.x
get_global_size(0);	Size of NDRange in the x-dimension	gridDim.x ×blockDim.x
get_local_size(0);	Size of each work group in the x-dimension	blockDim.x

FIGURE 11.3

Mapping of OpenCL dimensions and indices to CUDA dimensions and indices.

which is equivalent to threadIdx.x. We did not show the higher dimension parameter values in Figure 11.3; they are 1 for the y-dimension and 2 for the z-dimension.

An OpenCL kernel can also call the API function get_global_size() with a parameter that identifies the dimensional sizes of its NDRanges. The calls get_global_size(0) and get_global_size(1) return the total number of work items in the x- and y-dimensions of the NDRanges. Note that this is slightly different from the CUDA gridDim values, which are in terms of blocks. The CUDA equivalent for the get_global_size(0) return value would be gridDim.x×blockDim.x.

11.3 DEVICE ARCHITECTURE

Like CUDA, OpenCL models a heterogeneous parallel computing system as a host and one or more *OpenCL devices*. The host is a traditional CPU that executes the host program. Figure 11.4 shows the conceptual architecture of an OpenCL device. Each device consists of one or more *compute units* (CUs) that correspond to CUDA streaming multiprocessors (SMs); however, a CU can also correspond to CPU cores or other types of execution units in compute accelerators such as DSPs and FPGAs.

Each CU, in turn, consists of one or more *processing elements* (PEs), which correspond to the streaming processors (SPs) in CUDA. Computation on a device ultimately happens in individual PEs. The reader should compare Figure 11.4 with Figure 3.7 for similarities between the

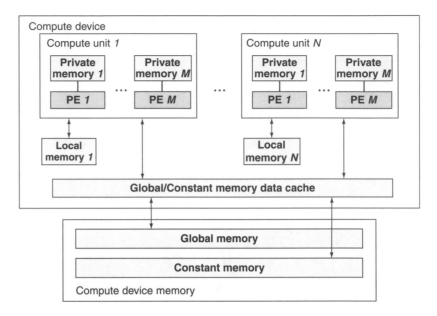

FIGURE 11.4

Conceptual OpenCL device architecture; the host is not shown.

OpenCL device architecture model and the CUDA device architecture model.

Like CUDA, OpenCL also exposes a hierarchy of memory types that can be used by programmers. Figure 11.4 illustrates these memory types: global, constant, local, and private. Figure 11.5 summarizes the supported use of OpenCL memory types and the mapping of these memory types to CUDA memory types. The OpenCL global memory corresponds to the

OpenCL Memory Types	CUDA Equivalent
global memory	global memory
constant memory	constant memory
local memory	shared memory
private memory	Local memory

FIGURE 11.5

Mapping of OpenCL memory types to CUDA memory types.

CUDA global memory. Like CUDA, the global memory can be dynamically allocated by the host program and supports read/write access by both host and devices.

Unlike CUDA, the constant memory can be dynamically allocated by the host. The constant memory supports read/write access by the host and read-only access by devices. To support multiple platforms, the size of constant memory is not limited to 64 kB in OpenCL. Instead, a device query returns the constant memory size supported by the device.

The mapping of OpenCL local memory and private memory to CUDA memory types is more interesting. The OpenCL local memory actually corresponds to CUDA shared memory. The OpenCL local memory can be dynamically allocated by the host and statically allocated in the device code. Like the CUDA shared memory, the OpenCL local memory cannot be accessed by the host and support shared read/write access by all work items in a work group. The private memory of OpenCL corresponds to the CUDA local memory.

11.4 KERNEL FUNCTIONS

OpenCL kernels have identical basic structure as CUDA kernels. All OpenCL kernel function declarations start with a __kernel keyword, which is equivalent to the __global keyword in CUDA. Figure 11.6 shows a simple OpenCL kernel function that performs vector addition. The function takes three arguments: pointers to the two input arrays and one pointer to the output array. The __global declarations in the function header indicate that the input and output arrays all reside in the global memory. Note that this keyword has the same meaning in OpenCL as in CUDA. The body of the kernel function is instantiated once for each work item. In Figure 11.6, each work item calls the get_global_id(0) function to receive its unique global index. This index value is then used by the work item to select the array elements to work on.

```
__kernel void vadd(__global const float *a,
    __global const float *b, __global float *result) {

    int id = get_global_id(0);
    result[id] = a[id] + b[id];
}
```

FIGURE 11.6

A simple OpenCL kernel example.

11.5 DEVICE MANAGEMENT AND KERNEL LAUNCH

OpenCL defines a much more complex model of device management than CUDA. The extra complexity stems from the OpenCL support for multiple hardware platforms. In OpenCL, devices are managed through *contexts*. Figure 11.7 illustrates the main concepts of device management in OpenCL. In order to manage one or more devices in the system, the OpenCL programmer first creates a context that contains these devices. This can be done by calling either `clCreateContext()` or `clCreateContextFromType()` in the OpenCL API. An application typically needs to use the `clGetDeviceIDs()` API function to determine the number and types of devices that exist in a system and to pass the information on to the `CreateContext` functions. The reader should read the OpenCL programming guide regarding the details of the parameters to be used for these functions.

To submit work for execution by a device, the host program must first create a command queue for the device. This can be done by calling the `clCreateCommandQueue()` function in the OpenCL API. Once a command queue is created for a device, the host code can perform a sequence of API function calls to insert a kernel along with its execution configuration parameters into the command queue. When the device is available for executing the next kernel, it removes the kernel at the head of the queue for execution.

Figure 11.8 shows a simple host programs that creates a context for a device and submits a kernel for execution by the device. Line 2 shows a call to create a context that includes all OpenCL available devices in

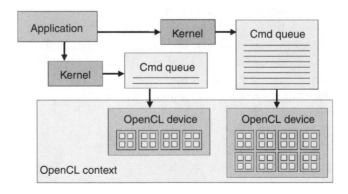

FIGURE 11.7

OpenCL context required to manage devices.

```
...
1. cl_int clerr = CL_SUCCESS;

2. cl_context clctx=clCreateContextFromType(0, CL_DEVICE_TYPE_ALL,
        NULL, NULL, &clerr);

3. size_t parmsz;
4. clerr= clGetContextInfo(clctx, CL_CONTEXT_DEVICES, 0, NULL, &parmsz);

5. cl_device_id* cldevs= (cl_device_id *) malloc(parmsz);
6. clerr= clGetContextInfo(clctx, CL_CONTEXT_DEVICES, parmsz,cldevs, NULL);

7. cl_command_queue clcmdq=clCreateCommandQueue(clctx,cldevs[0], 0, &clerr);
```

FIGURE 11.8

Creating an OpenCL context and command queue.

the system. Line 4 calls the clGetContextInfo() function to inquire about the number of devices in the context. Because Line 2 asks that all OpenCL available devices be included in the context, the application does not know the number of devices actually included in the context after the context is created. The second argument of the call in Line 4 specifies that the information being requested is the list of all devices included in the context; however, the fourth argument, which is a pointer to a memory buffer where the list should be deposited, is a NULL pointer. This means that the call does not want the list itself. The reason is that the application does not know the number of devices in the context and does not know the size of the memory buffer required to hold the list.

Line 4 provides a pointer to the variable parmsz, where the size of a memory buffer required to accommodate the device list is to be deposited; therefore, after the call in Line 4, the parmsz variable holds the size of the buffer needed to accommodate the list of devices in the context. The application now knows the amount of memory buffer needed to hold the list of devices in the context. It allocates the memory buffer using parmsz and assigns the address of the buffer to pointer variable cldevs at Line 5.

Line 6 calls clGetContextInfo() again with the pointer to the memory buffer in the fourth argument and the size of the buffer in the third argument. Because this is based on the information from the call at Line 4, the buffer is guaranteed to be the right size for the list of devices to be returned. The clGetContextInfo function now fills the device list information into the memory buffer pointed to by cldevs.

Line 7 creates a command queue for the first OpenCL device in the list. This is done by treating cldevs as an array whose elements are descriptors of OpenCL devices in the system. Line 7 passes `cldevs[0]` as the second argument into the `clCreateCommandQueue(0)` function; therefore, the call generates a command queue for the first device in the list returned by the `clGetContextInfo()` function.

The reader may wonder why we did not need to see this complex sequence of API calls in our CUDA host programs. The reason is that we have been using the CUDA runtime API that hides all of this complexity for the common case where there is only one CUDA device in the system. The kernel launch in CUDA handles all of the complexities on behalf of the host code. A developer who wants to have direct access to all CUDA devices in the system would need to use the CUDA driver API, where similar API calling sequences would be used. To date, OpenCL has not defined a higher level API that is equivalent to the CUDA runtime API. Until such a higher level interface is available, OpenCL will remain much more tedious to use than the CUDA runtime API.

11.6 ELECTROSTATIC POTENTIAL MAP IN OpenCL

We now present an OpenCL case study based on the DCS kernel in Figure 9.9. This case study is designed to give a CUDA programmer a practical, top to bottom experience with OpenCL. The first step in porting the kernel to OpenCL is to design the organization of the NDRange, which is illustrated in Figure 11.9. The design is a straightforward mapping of CUDA threads to OpenCL work items and CUDA blocks to OpenCL work groups. As shown in Figure 11.9, each work item will calculate up to eight grid points, and each work group will have 64–256 work items. The efficiency considerations in Chapter 9 apply.

The work groups are assigned to the computing units in the same way that CUDA blocks are assigned to the SMs. Such assignment is illustrated in Figure 11.10. One can use the same methodology demonstrated in Chapters 6 through 9 to derive a high-performance OpenCL DCS kernel. Although the syntax is different, the underlying thought process involved in developing a high-performance OpenCL kernel is very much the same as CUDA.

The OpenCL kernel function implementation closely matches the CUDA implementation. Figure 11.11 shows the key differences. One is the `__kernel` keyword in OpenCL versus the `__global` keyword in CUDA. The main difference lies in the way the data access indices are calculated.

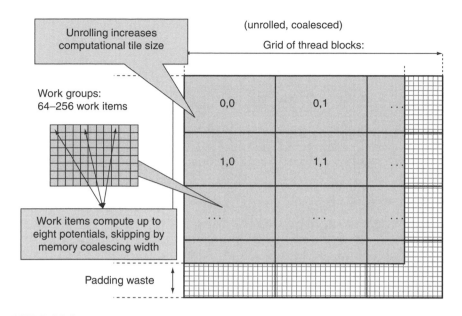

FIGURE 11.9

DCS Kernel Version 3 NDRange configuration.

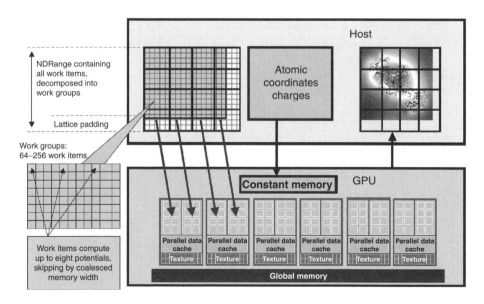

FIGURE 11.10

Mapping DCS NDRange to OpenCL device.

```
OpenCL:
__kernel voidclenergy( …) {

unsigned int xindex= (get_global_id(0) / get_local_id(0))* UNROLLX +
 get_local_id(0) ;
unsigned int yindex= get_global_id(1);
unsigned int outaddr= get_global_size(0) * UNROLLX *yindex+xindex;

CUDA:
__global__ void cuenergy(…) {
Unsigned int xindex= blockIdx.x *blockDim.x +threadIdx.x;
unsigned int yindex= blockIdx.y *blockDim.y +threadIdx.y;
unsigned int outaddr= gridDim.x *blockDim.x * UNROLLX*yindex+xindex
```

FIGURE 11.11

Data access indexing in OpenCL and CUDA.

In this case, the OpenCL `get_global_id(0)` function returns the equivalent of CUDA `blockIdx.x*blockDim.x + threadIdx.x`.

Figure 11.12 shows the inner loop of the OpenCL kernel. The reader should compare this inner loop with the CUDA code in Figure 9.9. The only difference is that the `__rsqrt()` call has been changed to a `native_rsqrt()` call, the OpenCL way to call an intrinsic function on a particular device.

OpenCL adopts a dynamic compilation model. Unlike CUDA, the host program needs to explicitly compile and create a kernel program. This is illustrated in Figure 11.13 for the DCS kernel. Line 1 declares the entire OpenCL DCS kernel source code as a string. Line 3 delivers the source

```
...for (atomid=0; atomid<numatoms; atomid++) {
float dy = coory -atominfo[atomid].y;
float dyz2= (dy * dy) + atominfo[atomid].z;
float dx1 = coorx -atominfo[atomid].x;
float dx2 = dx1 + gridspacing_coalesce;
float dx3 = dx2 + gridspacing_coalesce;
float dx4 = dx3 + gridspacing_coalesce;
float charge = atominfo[atomid].w;
energyvalx1 += charge* native_rsqrt(dx1*dx1 + dyz2);
energyvalx2 += charge* native_rsqrt(dx2*dx2 + dyz2);
energyvalx3 += charge* native_rsqrt(dx3*dx3 + dyz2);
energyvalx4 += charge* native_rsqrt(dx4*dx4 + dyz2);
}
```

FIGURE 11.12

Inner loop of the OpenCL DCS kernel.

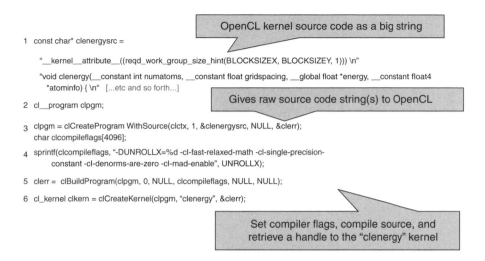

```
1  const char* clenergysrc =

   "__kernel__attribute__((reqd_work_group_size_hint(BLOCKSIZEX, BLOCKSIZEY, 1))) \n"

   "void clenergy(__constant int numatoms, __constant float gridspacing, __global float *energy, __constant float4
       *atominfo) { \n"  [...etc and so forth...]

2  cl__program clpgm;

3  clpgm = clCreateProgram WithSource(clctx, 1, &clenergysrc, NULL, &clerr);
   char clcompileflags[4096];

4  sprintf(clcompileflags, "-DUNROLLX=%d -cl-fast-relaxed-math -cl-single-precision-
       constant -cl-denorms-are-zero -cl-mad-enable", UNROLLX);

5  clerr = clBuildProgram(clpgm, 0, NULL, clcompileflags, NULL, NULL);

6  cl_kernel clkern = clCreateKernel(clpgm, "clenergy", &clerr);
```

OpenCL kernel source code as a big string

Gives raw source code string(s) to OpenCL

Set compiler flags, compile source, and retrieve a handle to the "clenergy" kernel

FIGURE 11.13

Building an OpenCL kernel.

code string to the OpenCL runtime system by calling the `clCreate-ProgramWithSource()` function. Line 4 sets up the compiler flags for the runtime compilation process. Line 5 invokes the runtime compiler to build the program. Line 6 requests that the OpenCL runtime create the kernel and its data structures so it can be properly launched. After Line 6, `clkern` points to the kernel that can be submitted to a command queue for execution.

As we explained in Section 11.5, OpenCL kernel has a much more complex device management model. We also discussed the creation of context and command queues in the host code. Figure 11.8 actually shows a simple host code that creates a context and command queue for a system with just one GPU to execute the kernel.

Figure 11.14 shows the host code that actually launches the DCS kernel. Line 1 and Line 2 allocate memory for the energy grid data and the atom information. The `clCreateBuffer` function corresponds to the `cudaMalloc()` function. The constant memory is implicitly requested by setting the mode of access to ready only for the `atominfo` array. Note that each memory buffer is associated with a context, which is specified by the first argument to the `clCreateBuffer` function call.

```
1. doutput= clCreateBuffer(clctx, CL_MEM_READ_WRITE,volmemsz,
       NULL, NULL);
2. datominfo= clCreateBuffer(clctx, CL_MEM_READ_ONLY,
       MAXATOMS *sizeof(cl_float4), NULL, NULL);
...
3. clerr= clSetKernelArg(clkern, 0,sizeof(int), &runatoms);
4. clerr= clSetKernelArg(clkern, 1,sizeof(float), &zplane);
5. clerr= clSetKernelArg(clkern, 2,sizeof(cl_mem), &doutput);
6. clerr= clSetKernelArg(clkern, 3,sizeof(cl_mem), &datominfo);
7. cl_event event;
8. clerr= clEnqueueNDRangeKernel(clcmdq,clkern, 2, NULL,
       Gsz,Bsz, 0, NULL, &event);
9. clerr= clWaitForEvents(1, &event);
10. clerr= clReleaseEvent(event);
...
11. clEnqueueReadBuffer(clcmdq,doutput, CL_TRUE, 0,
       volmemsz, energy, 0, NULL, NULL);
12. clReleaseMemObject(doutput);
13. clReleaseMemObject(datominfo);
```

FIGURE 11.14

OpenCL host code for kernel launch and .

Lines 3 through 6 in Figure 11.14 set up the arguments to be passed into the kernel function. In CUDA, the kernel functions are launched with C function call syntax extended with <<<>>>. In OpenCL, there is no explicit call to kernel functions, so one needs to use the clSetKernelArg() functions to set up the arguments for the kernel function.

Line 8 in Figure 11.14 submits the DCS kernel for launch. The arguments to the clEnqueueNDRangeKernel() function specify the command queue for the device that will execute the kernel, a pointer to the kernel, and the global and local sizes of the NDRange. Lines 9 and 10 check for errors if any. Line 11 transfers the contents of the output data back into the energy array in the host memory. The OpenCL clEnqueueReadBuffer () copies data from the device memory to the host memory and corresponds to the device to host direction of the cudaMemcpy() function.

The clReleaseMemObject() function is a little more sophisticated than cudaFree(). OpenCL maintains a reference count for data objects. OpenCL host program modules can retain (clRetainMemObject()) and release (clReleaseMemObject()) data objects. Note that clCreateBuffer() also serves as a retain call. With each retain call, the reference count of the object is incremented. With each release call, the reference count is decremented. When the reference count for an object reaches 0, the object is freed. This way, a library module can hang onto a memory object even though the other parts of the application no longer need the object and thus have released the object.

11.7 **SUMMARY**

OpenCL is a standardized, cross-platform API designed to support portable parallel application development on heterogeneous computing systems. Like CUDA, OpenCL addresses complex memory hierarchies and data-parallel execution. It draws heavily on the CUDA driver API experience. This is the reason why a CUDA programmer finds these aspects of OpenCL familiar. We have seen this through the mappings of the OpenCL data parallelism model concepts, NDRange API calls, and memory types to their CUDA equivalents.

On the other hand, OpenCL has a more complex platform and device management model that reflects its support for multiplatform and multivendor portability. Although the OpenCL standard is designed to support code portability across devices produced by different vendors, such portability does not come for free. OpenCL programs must be prepared to deal with much greater hardware diversity and thus will exhibit more complexity. We see that the OpenCL device management model, the OpenCL kernel compilation model, and the OpenCL kernel launch are much more complex than their CUDA counterparts.

We have by no means covered all the programming features of OpenCL. The reader is encouraged to read the OpenCL specification [Khronos 2008] and tutorials [Khronos 2010] for more OpenCL features. In particular, we recommend that the reader pay special attention to the device query, object query, and task parallelism model.

We would like to also point the reader to another important parallel programming API for heterogeneous computing systems. Microsoft's Direct-Compute is an API that takes advantage of the massively parallel processing power of a modern GPU to accelerate PC application performance in Microsoft® Windows Vista® or Windows 7 [Wikipedia]. DirectCompute is part of Microsoft's DirectX™ collection of APIs. Other DirectX APIs include Direct3D®, Direct2D, DirectWrite, DirectDraw®, DirectMusic®, DirectPlay®, and DirectSound®. DirectCompute is released with the DirectX 11 API but runs on both DirectX 10 and DirectX 11 GPUs. DirectCompute defines several versions of compute shader capabilities to ensure that applications can take advantage of GPUs. The reader should also expect that DirectCompute will have level of complexity similar to that of OpenCL in terms of device management and kernel launch models.

11.8 EXERCISES

11.1 Using the code base in Appendix A and examples in Chapters 3, 4, 5, and 6 to develop an OpenCL version of the matrix–matrix multiplication application.

11.2 Read the "OpenCL Platform Layer" section of the OpenCL specification. Compare the platform querying API functions with what you have learned in CUDA.

11.3 Read the "Memory Objects" section of the OpenCL specification. Compare the object creation and access API functions with what you have learned in CUDA.

11.4 Read the "Kernel Objects" section of the OpenCL specification. Compare the kernel creation and launching API functions with what you have learned in CUDA.

11.5 Read the "OpenCL Programming Language" section of the OpenCL specification. Compare the keywords and types with what you have learned in CUDA.

References and Further Reading

AMD. (2009). *Introductory tutorial to OpenCL™*. Sunnyvale, CA: Advanced Micro Devices. http://developer.amd.com/gpu/ATIStreamSDK/pages/TutorialOpenCL.aspx

Khronos OpenCL Working Group. (2008). Munshi, A. (Ed.), (2008). *The OpenCL specification*, Version 1.0, Document Revision 29. Beaverton, OR: Khronos Group. http://www.khronos.org/registry/cl/specs/opencl-1.0.29.pdf

Khronos Group. (2010). *OpenCL implementations, tutorials, and sample code*. Beaverton, OR: Khronos Group. http://www.khronos.org/developers/resources/opencl/

NVIDIA. (2010). *OpenCL GPU computing support on NVIDIA's CUDA architecture GPUs*. Santa Clara, CA: NVIDIA. http://www.nvidia.com/object/cuda_opencl.html

Wikipedia. (n.d.) *DirectCompute*. http://en.wikipedia.org/wiki/DirectCompute

Conclusion and Future Outlook

12

CHAPTER CONTENTS

INTRODUCTION

You made it! We have arrived at the finishing line. In this final chapter, we will briefly review the goals that we have achieved through this book. Instead of drawing a conclusion, we will offer our vision for the future evolution of massively parallel processor architectures and how the advancements will impact parallel application development.

12.1 GOALS REVISITED

As we stated in the Chapter 1, our primary goal is to teach you, the reader, how to program massively parallel processors to achieve high performance. We promised that it would become easy once you develop the right insight and go about it the right way. In particular, we promised to focus on *computational thinking* skills that would enable you to think about problems in ways that are amenable to parallel computing.

We delivered on these promises through an introduction to performance considerations for CUDA™ (Chapter 6), two detailed case studies (Chapters 8 and 9), and a chapter dedicated to computational thinking skills (Chapter 10). Through this process, we introduced the pertinent computer architecture knowledge needed to understand the hardware limitations that must be addressed in high-performance parallel programming. In particular, we focused on the memory bandwidth limitations that will remain as the primary performance limiting factor in massively parallel computing systems (Chapters 4–6 and 8–10). We also introduced the concepts of floating-point precision and accuracy and how they relate to parallel execution (Chapter 7). With these insights, high-performance parallel programming becomes a manageable process rather than a black art.

We stated that our second goal was to teach high-performance parallel programming styles that naturally avoid subtle correctness issues. To deliver on this promise, we showed that the simple data parallelism CUDA programming model (Chapters 3 and 4) based on barrier synchronization can be used to develop very high-performance applications. This disciplined approach to parallel programming naturally avoids the subtle race conditions that plague many other parallel programming systems (Chapter 4).

We promised to teach parallel programming styles that transparently scale across future hardware generations, which will be more and more parallel. With the CUDA threading model (Chapter 4), massive numbers of thread blocks can be executed in any order relative to each other. Your application will benefit from more parallel hardware coming in the future. We also presented algorithm techniques, such as tiling and cutoff, that allow your application scale naturally to very large datasets (Chapter 10).

Now that we have reviewed our promises, we would like to share our view of the coming evolution of the massively parallel processor architectures and how the advancements will likely impact application development. We hope that these outlooks will help you to peek into the future of parallel programming. Our comments reflect the new features in graphics processing units (GPUs) based on the NVIDIA® Fermi compute architecture that arrived at the market when this book went into press.

12.2 MEMORY ARCHITECTURE EVOLUTION
12.2.1 Large Virtual and Physical Address Spaces

Graphics processing units have traditionally used only a physical address space with up to 32 address bits, which limited the GPU dynamic random access memory (DRAM) to 4 gigabytes or less. This is because graphics applications have not demanded more than a few hundred megabytes of frame buffer and texture memory. This is in contrast to the 64-bit virtual space and 40+ bits of physical space that central processing unit (CPU) programmers have been taking for granted for many years.

Fermi adopts a CPU-style virtual memory architecture with a 64-bit virtual address space and a physical address space of at least 40 bits. The obvious benefit is that Fermi GPUs can incorporate more than 4 gigabytes of DRAM and that CUDA kernels can now operate on very large datasets, whether hosted entirely in onboard GPU DRAM or by accessing mapped host memory.

The Fermi virtual memory architecture also lays the foundation for a potentially profound enhancement to the programming model. The CPU system physical memory and the GPU physical memory can now be mapped within a single, shared virtual address space [Gelado 2009]. A shared global address space allows all variables in an application to have unique addresses. Such a memory architecture, when exposed by the programming tools and runtime system to applications, can result in several major benefits.

First, new runtime systems can be designed to allow CPUs and GPUs to access the entire volume of application data under traditional protection models. Such a capability would allow applications to use a single pointer system to access application variables, thus removing a confusing aspect of the current CUDA programming model where developers must not deference a pointer to the device memory in host functions.

These variables can reside in the CPU physical memory, the GPU physical memory, or even in both. The runtime can implement data migration and coherence support like the GPU Memory Access (GMAC) system [Gelado 2009]. If a CPU function dereferences a pointer and accesses a variable mapped to the GPU physical memory, the data access would still be serviced but perhaps at a longer latency. Such capability would allow the CUDA programs to more easily call legacy libraries that have not been ported to GPUs. In the current CUDA memory architecture, the developer must manually transfer data from the device memory to the host memory in order to use legacy library functions to process them on the CPU. GMAC is built on the current CUDA runtime application programming interface (API) and gives the developer the option to either rely on the runtime system to service such accesses or manually transfer data as a performance optimization. However, the GMAC system currently does not have a clean mechanism for supporting multiple GPUs. The new virtual memory capability would enable a much more elegant implementation.

Ultimately, the virtual memory capability will also enable a mechanism similar to the zero copy feature in CUDA 2.2 to allow the GPU to directly access very large physical CPU system memories. In some application areas such as computer-aided design (CAD), the CPU physical memory system may have hundreds of gigabytes of capacity. These physical memory systems are needed because the applications require the entire dataset to be "in core." It is not currently feasible for such applications to take advantage of GPU computing. With the ability to directly access very large CPU physical memories, it becomes feasible for GPUs to accelerate these applications.

The second potential benefit is that the shared global address space enables peer-to-peer direct data transfer between GPUs in a multi-GPU system. In current CUDA systems, GPUs must first transfer data to the CPU physical memory before delivering them to a peer GPU. A shared global address space enables the implementation of a runtime system to provide an API to directly transfer data from one GPU memory to another GPU memory. Ultimately, a runtime system can be designed to automate such transfers when GPUs reference data in each other's memory but which still allow the use of explicit data-transfer APIs as a performance optimization.

The third benefit is that one can implement I/O-related memory transfers directly in and out of the GPU physical memory. In current CUDA systems, the I/O data must first be transferred into the CPU physical memory before they can be copied into the GPU physical memory. The ability to directly transfer data in and out of the GPU physical memory can significantly reduce the copying cost and enhance the performance of applications that process large datasets.

12.2.2 Unified Device Memory Space

In the current CUDA memory model, constant memory, shared, memory, local memory, and global memory form their own separate address spaces. The developer can use pointers into the global memory but not others. In the Fermi architecture, these memories are now all parts of a unified address space. This makes it easier to abstract which memory contains a particular operand, allowing the programmer to deal with this only during allocation and making it simpler to pass CUDA data objects into other procedures and functions, irrespective of which memory area they come from. It makes CUDA code modules much more composable; that is, a CUDA device function can now accept a pointer that may point to any of these memories. The code would run faster if a function argument pointer points to a shared memory location and slower if it points to a global memory location. The programmer can still perform manual data placement and transfers as a performance optimization. This capability will significantly reduce the cost of building production-quality CUDA libraries.

12.2.3 Configurable Caching and Scratch Pad

The shared memory in previous CUDA systems served as programmer-managed scratch memory and increased the speed of applications where key data structures had localized, predictable access patterns. In Fermi, the shared memory has been enhanced to a larger on-chip memory that can be configured to be partially cache memory and partially shared memory, thus allowing coverage of both predictable and less predictable access patterns to benefit from on-chip memory. This configurability allows programmers to apportion the resources according to the best fit for their application.

Applications in an early design stage that are ported directly from CPU code will benefit greatly from enabling caching as the dominant part of the on-chip memory. This would further smooth the performance-tuning process by increasing the level of "easy performance" when a developer ports a CPU application to GPU.

Existing CUDA applications and those that have predictable access patterns will have the ability to increase their use of fast shared memory by a factor of 3 while retaining the same GPU "occupancy" they had on previous-generation devices. For CUDA applications whose performance or capabilities are limited by the size of the shared memory, the three times increase in size will be a welcome improvement. For example, in stencil computation, such as finite volume methods for computational fluid dynamics, the state loaded into the shared memory also includes "halo" cells from neighboring areas.

The relative portion of halo decreases as the size of the stencil increases. In three-dimensional simulation models, the halo cells can be comparable in data size to the main data for current shared memory sizes.

This can significantly reduce the effectiveness of the shared memory due to the significant portion of the memory bandwidth spent on loading of halo cells. For example, if the shared memory allows a thread block to load a 8^3 (=512)-cell stencil into the shared memory, with one layer of halo cells on every surface, then only 6^3 (=216) cells, or fewer than half of the loaded cells, are the main data. The bandwidth spent on loading the halo cells is actually bigger than that spent on the main data. A three times increase in shared memory size allows some of these applications to have a more favorable stencil size where the halo accounts for a much smaller portion of the data in shared memory. In our example, the increased size would allow an 11^3 (=1331)-cell stencil to be loaded by each thread block. With one layer of halo cells on each surface, a total of 9^3 (=729) cells, or more than half of the loaded cells, are the main data. This significantly improves the memory bandwidth efficiency and the performance of the application.

12.2.4 Enhanced Atomic Operations

The atomic operations in Fermi are much faster than those in previous CUDA systems. Atomic operations are frequently used in random scatter computation patterns such as histograms. Faster atomic operations reduce the need for complex algorithm transformations such as prefix scanning [Sengupta 2007] and sorting [Satish 2009] for implementing such random scattering computations in GPUs. These transformations tend to increase the number of kernel invocations needed to perform the target computation. Faster atomic operations can also reduce the need to involve the host CPU in algorithms that do collective operations or where multiple CUDA thread blocks update shared data structures, thus reducing the data transfer pressure between the CPU and GPU.

12.2.5 Enhanced Global Memory Access

The speed of random memory access is much faster in the Fermi architecture than previous CUDA systems. Programmers can be less concerned about memory coalescing. This allows more CPU algorithms to be directly used in the GPU as an acceptable base, further smoothing the path of porting applications that access a diversity of data structures such as ray tracing, and other applications that are heavily object oriented and may be difficult to convert into perfectly tiled arrays.

12.3 KERNEL EXECUTION CONTROL EVOLUTION

12.3.1 Function Calls within Kernel Functions

Previous CUDA versions did not allow function calls in kernel code. Although the source code of kernel functions can appear to have function calls, the compiler must be able to inline all function bodies into the kernel object so there are no function calls in the kernel function at runtime. Although this model works reasonably well for the performance-critical portions of many applications, it does not support the software engineering practices in more sophisticated applications. In particular, it does not support system calls, dynamically linked library calls, recursive function calls, and virtual functions in object-oriented languages such as C++.

Fermi supports function calls in kernel functions at runtime. The compiler is no longer required to inline the function bodies. It can still do so as a performance optimization. This capability is partly achieved by a cached, much faster local memory implementation that underlies a fast implementation of massively parallel call frame stacks for CUDA threads. It improves the composability of CUDA device code by allowing different authors to write different CUDA kernel components and assemble them all together without heavy redesign costs. In particular, it allows modern object-oriented techniques such as virtual function calls and software engineering practices such as dynamically linked libraries.

Support for function calls at runtime allows recursion and will significantly ease the burden on programmers as they transition from legacy CPU-oriented algorithms toward GPU-tuned approaches for divide-and-conquer types of computation. This also allows easier implementation of graph algorithms where data structure traversal often naturally involves recursion. In many cases, developers will be able to "cut and paste" CPU algorithms into a CUDA kernel and obtain a reasonably performing kernel, although continued performance tuning would still be needed.

12.3.2 Exception Handling in Kernel Functions

Previous CUDA systems did not support exception handling in kernel code. This was not a significant limitation for performance-critical portions of many high-performance applications, but it often incurs software engineering costs in production-quality applications that rely on exceptions to detect and handle rare conditions without executing code to explicitly test for such conditions. Also, it does not allow kernel functions to utilize operating system services, which is typically avoided in performance-critical portions of the applications, except during debugging situations.

With the availability of exception handling and function call support in Fermi, kernels can now call standard library functions such as `printf()` and `malloc()`, which can lead to system call traps. In our experience, the ability to call `printf()` in a kernel provides a subtle but important aid in debugging and supporting kernels in production software. Many end users are not technical and cannot be easily trained to run debuggers to provide developers with more details on what happened before a crash. The ability to execute `printf()` in the kernel allows the developers to add a mode to the application to dump the internal state so end users can submit meaningful bug reports.

12.3.3 Simultaneous Execution of Multiple Kernels

Previous CUDA systems allow only one kernel to execute on each GPU device at any point in time. Multiple kernel functions can be submitted for execution; however, they are buffered in a queue that releases the next kernel after the current one completes execution. Fermi allows multiple kernels from the same application to be executed simultaneously, which provides at least two user-level benefits.

First, multiple kernel execution reduces the pressure for the application developer to batch multiple kernel invocations into the launch of a larger kernel in order to more fully utilize the GPU. Second, parallel cluster applications often segment work into local and remote partitions, where remote work is involved in interactions with other nodes and resides on the critical path of global progress. In previous CUDA systems, kernels had to be large to keep the machine running efficiently, and one had to be careful not to launch local work such that global work could be blocked. Previously, this meant choosing between leaving the GPU idle while waiting for remote work to arrive or eagerly starting on local work to keep the GPU productive at the cost of increased latency for the completion of remote work units. With multiple kernel execution on Fermi, the application can use much smaller kernel sizes for launching work; as a result, when high-priority remote work arrives, it can start running with low latency instead of being stuck behind a large kernel of local computation.

12.3.4 Interruptible Kernels

Fermi allows running kernels to be canceled, thus easing the creation of CUDA-accelerated applications that allow the user to abort a long-running calculation at any time, without requiring significant design effort on the part of the programmer. When software support is available, this will enable implementation of user-level task scheduling systems that can better perform load balance between GPU nodes of a computing system and allow more graceful handling of cases where one GPU is heavily loaded and may be running slower than its peers [Stone 2009a].

12.4 CORE PERFORMANCE

12.4.1 Double-Precision Speed

The GPUs based on the NVIDIA GT200 architecture perform double-precision floating arithmetic in hardware but with significant speed reduction (around eight times slower) compared to single precision. The Fermi architecture's floating-point arithmetic units have been significantly strengthened to perform double-precision arithmetic at about half the speed of single precision. Applications that are intensive in double-precision, floating-point arithmetic will benefit tremendously. Other applications that use double precision carefully and sparingly will incur little or no noticeable performance cost.

In practice, the most significant benefit will likely be obtained by developers who are porting CPU-based numerical applications to GPUs. With the improved double-precision speed, they will have little incentive to spend the effort to evaluate whether their applications or portions of their applications can fit into single precision. This can significantly reduce the development cost for porting CPU applications to GPUs and addresses a major criticism of GPUs by the high-performance computing community.

12.4.2 Better Control Flow Efficiency

Fermi adopts a general compiler-driven predication technique [Mahlke 1995] that can more effectively handle control flow than previous CUDA systems. This technique was moderately successful in Very Long Instruction Word (VLIW) systems, but it can provide more dramatic speed improvements in GPU warp-style, single-instruction, multiple-data (SIMD) execution systems. This capability can potentially broaden the range of applications that can take advantage of GPUs. In particular, major performance benefits can potentially be realized for applications that are very data driven, such as ray tracing, quantum chemistry visualization, and cellular automata simulation.

12.5 **PROGRAMMING ENVIRONMENT**

The CUDA 3.0 software development kit (SDK) compiler generates standard object file formats used by standard CPU integrated development environments (IDEs). This enables integration of CUDA application debugging and profiling into standard IDEs such as Microsoft® Visual Studio®. Developers no longer need to leave the IDE in order to run the CUDA debugger or profiler. Also, through driver enhancements, when programmers are debugging on the graphics card the GPU will no longer crash or interfere with the host operating system or the windowing system.

Future CUDA compilers will include enhanced support for C++ templates and virtual function calls in kernel functions. Although hardware enhancements, such as runtime function calling capability, are in place, enhanced C++ language support in the compiler will take more time. The C++ try/catch features will also likely be fully supported in kernel functions in the near future. With these enhancements, future CUDA compilers will support most mainstream C++ features. The remaining features in kernel functions such as new, delete, constructors, and destructors will likely be available in later compiler releases.

12.6 **A BRIGHT OUTLOOK**

The new CUDA 3.0 SDK and the new GPUs based on the Fermi architecture mark the beginning of the third generation of GPU computing that places real emphasis on support for developer productivity and modern software engineering practices. With the new capabilities, the range of applications that will offer reasonable performance at minimal development costs will expand significantly. We expect that developers will immediately notice the reduction in application development, porting, and maintenance costs compared to previous CUDA systems. The existing applications developed with PyCUDA and similar high-level tools that automatically generate CUDA code will also likely get an immediate boost in their performance. Although the benefit of hardware enhancements in memory architecture, kernel execution control, and compute core performance will be visible in the associated SDK release, the true potential of these enhancements may take years to be fully exploited in the SDKs and runtimes. For example, the true potential of the hardware virtual memory capability will likely be fully achieved only when a shared global address space runtime that supports direct GPU I/O and peer-to-peer data transfer for multiple-GPU systems becomes widely available. We predict an exciting time for innovations from both industry and academia in programming tools and runtime environments for GPU computing in the next few years. Enjoy the ride!

References and Further Reading

Gelado, I., Navarro, N., Stone, J., Patel, S., & Hwu, W. W. (2009). *An asymmetric distributed shared memory model for heterogeneous parallel systems* (Technical Report). Urbana–Champaign: IMPACT Group, University of Illinois.

Mahlke, S. A., Hank, R. E., McCormick, J. E., August, D. I., & Hwu, W. W. (1995). A comparison of full and partial predicated execution support for ILP processors. In *Proceedings of the 22nd annual international symposium on computer architecture (ISCA '95),* Santa Margherita Ligure, Italy, June 22–24 (pp. 138–150). Piscataway, NJ: Institute of Electrical and Electronics Engineers.

Phillips, J. C., & Stone, J. E. (2009). Probing biomolecular machines with graphics processors. *Communications of ACM, 52*(10), 34–41.

Roberts, E., Stone, J. E., Sepulveda, L., Hwu, W. W., & Luthey-Schulten, Z. (2009). Long time-scale simulations of *in vivo* diffusion using GPU hardware. In *Proceedings of the 2009 IEEE international symposium on parallel & distributed processing (IPDPS '09)* (pp. 1–8). New York: IEEE Computer Society.

Rodrigues, C. I., Stone, J., Hardy, D., & Hwu, W. W. (2008). GPU acceleration of cutoff-based potential summation. In *Proceedings of the 2008 ACM international conference on computing frontiers (computing frontiers 2008)*, Ischia, Italy, May 5–7.

Satish, N., Harris, M., & Garland, M. (2009). Designing efficient sorting algorithms for manycore GPUs. In *Proceedings of the 2009 IEEE international symposium on parallel & distributed processing (IPDPS '09)* (pp. 1–10). New York: IEEE Computer Society.

Sengupta, S., Harris, M., Zhang, Y., & Owens, J. D. (2007). Scan primitives for GPU computing. In *Proceedings of the 22nd ACM SIGGRAPH/EUROGRAPHICS symposium on graphics hardware* (pp. 97–106). Aire-la-Ville, Switzerland: Eurographics Association.

Stone, J. E., & Hwu, W. W. (2009a). *WorkForce: A lightweight framework for managing multi-GPU computations* (Technical Report). Urbana–Champaign: IMPACT Group, University of Illinois.

Stone, J. E., Saam, J., Hardy, D. J., Vandivort, K. L., Hwu, W. W., & Schulten, K. (2009b). High-performance computation and interactive display of molecular orbitals on GPUs and multicore CPUs. In *Proceedings of the 2nd workshop on general-purpose processing on graphics processing units,* ACM International Conference Proceedings Series 383 (pp. 9–18). New York: ACM Press.

Matrix Multiplication Host-Only Version Source Code

APPENDIX CONTENTS

INTRODUCTION

This appendix shows a host-only source code that can be used as the base of your CUDA™ matrix multiplication code. We have already inserted timer calls in key places so you can use the measurement to isolate the execution time of the function that actually performs the matrix multiplication. It also has the code that you can use to print out the matrix contents and verify the results.

A.1 matrixmul.cu

```
/*****************************************************
    File Name    [matrixmul.cu]
    Synopsis     [This file defines the main function to do
        matrix-matrixmultiplication.]
    Description []
*****************************************************/
//----------------------------------------------------
// Included C libraries
//----------------------------------------------------
#include  <stdlib.h>
#include  <stdio.h>
```

```c
#include  <string.h>
#include  <math.h>
//-----------------------------------------------------
// Included CUDA libraries
//-----------------------------------------------------
#include <cutil.h>
//-----------------------------------------------------
// Included helper functions
//-----------------------------------------------------
#include "assist.h"
//-----------------------------------------------------
// Included host matrix-matrix multiplication function
prototype
//-----------------------------------------------------
#include "matrixmul.h"
/*========================================*/
/*                                        */
/*  Synopsis   [Main function]            */
/*  Description []                        */
/*                                        */
/*========================================*/
    int
main(int argc, char** argv)
{
    bool if_quiet = false;
    unsigned int timer_compute = 0;
    int i, j;
    char * matrix_id = NULL, * input_fn = NULL, * gold_fn = NULL;
    int Mw = 0, Mh = 0, Nw = 0, Nh = 0, Pw = 0, Ph = 0;

    if (argc == 2) {
        matrix_id = strdup(argv[1]);
    } else {
        fprintf(stderr, "Error: Wrong input parameter
        numbers.\n");
        fprintf(stderr, "Usage:\n"
                    "$> ./lab1.1-matrixmul <8, 128, 512,
                    3072, 4096>\n"
                    "Examples:\n"
```

```
                          " $> ./lab1.1-matrixmul 128\n"
                          );
      exit(1);
}
Mw = Mh = Nw = Nh = Pw = Ph = atoi(matrix_id);
input_fn = (char *) malloc(30*sizeof(char));
gold_fn = (char *) malloc(30*sizeof(char));
sprintf(input_fn, "matrix_%s.bin", matrix_id);
sprintf(gold_fn, "matrix_%s.gold", matrix_id);
if (Pw*Ph > 15*15) {
    if_quiet = true; // If not display matrix contents
}
printf("Input matrix size: %d by %d\n", Mw, Mh);
//----------------------------------------------------
// Setup host side
//----------------------------------------------------
printf("Setup host side environment:\n");

// allocate host memory for matrices M and N
printf(" Allocate host memory for matrices M and N.\n");
printf("   M: %d x %d\n", Mw, Mh);
printf("   N: %d x %d\n", Nw, Nh);
unsigned int size_M = Mw * Mh;
unsigned int mem_size_M = sizeof(float) * size_M;
float* hostM = (float*) malloc(mem_size_M);
unsigned int size_N = Nw * (Nh);
unsigned int mem_size_N = sizeof(float) * size_N;
float* hostN = (float*) malloc(mem_size_N);

// allocate memory for the result on host side
printf(" Allocate memory for the result on host side.\n");
unsigned int size_P = Pw * Ph;
unsigned int mem_size_P = sizeof(float) * size_P;
float* hostP = (float*) malloc(mem_size_P);

// Initialize the input matrices.
printf(" Generate input matrix data for matrix M and N.\n");
GenMatrixFile(input_fn, Pw, Ph, if_quiet);
unsigned int *matrix = ReadMatrixFile(input_fn, Pw, Ph, true);
```

```
for (i = 0; i < Mw; i++)
    for (j = 0; j < Nw; j++)
        hostM[i * Mw + j] = hostN[i * Mw + j] = (float)
        matrix[i*Mw + j];
free(matrix); matrix = NULL;
//========================================
// Do matrix-matrix multiplication
//========================================
printf(" Computing matrix multiplication M x N:\n");
if (Pw*Ph > 512*512) {
    printf(" (It takes time since matrix is larger than
    512by512.\n");
}
CUT_SAFE_CALL(cutCreateTimer(&timer_compute));
CUT_SAFE_CALL(cutStartTimer(timer_compute));

float* reference = (float*) malloc(mem_size_P);
computeGold(reference, hostM, hostN, Mh, Mw, Nw);
CUT_SAFE_CALL(cutStopTimer(timer_compute));

printf(" CPU Processing time : %f (ms)\n",
    cutGetTimerValue(timer_compute));
CUT_SAFE_CALL(cutDeleteTimer(timer_compute));

printf("Matrix data checksum : %g\n", CheckSum(reference,
Mw, Nw));

if (!if_quiet) {
   printf(" Matrix data contents :\n");
   printf("  ");
}
matrix = (unsigned int *) malloc(Pw * Ph * sizeof(unsigned int));
for (i = 0; i < Ph; i++) {
    for (j = 0; j < Pw; j++) {
        matrix[i*Pw + j] = (unsigned int) reference[i*Pw + j];
        if (!if_quiet) printf("%u ", matrix[i*Pw + j]);
    }
    if (!if_quiet) printf("\n  ");
}
```

```
    if (!if_quiet) printf("\n");

    WriteMatrixFile(gold_fn, matrix, Pw, Ph, 1);
    free(matrix); matrix = NULL;
    free(reference);

    // clean up memory
    free(hostM); free(hostN); free(hostP);
    free(input_fn); free(gold_fn);

    return 0;
}
```

A.2 matrixmul_gold.cpp

This "gold" version of the matrix multiplication function can be used to verify the results of your parallel implementation.

```
/********************************************************
    File Name   [matrixmul_gold.cpp]

    Synopsis   [This file defines the gold version matrix matrix
        multiplication.]

    Description []
********************************************************/
#include <stdio.h>
#include "matrixmul.h"
/*========================================*/
/*                                        */
/*  Synopsis  [Sequential/Gold version of matrix-matrix
    multiplication.]                      */
/*                                        */
/*  Description [This function computes multiplication
    of two matrix M and N,                */
/*  and stores the output to P.]          */
/*                                        */
/*========================================*/
    void
computeGold(
    float* P,    // Resultant matrix data
```

```
        const float* M,  // Matrix M
        const float* N,  // Matrix N
        int Mh,          // Matrix M height
        int Mw,          // Matrix M width
        int Nw)          // Matrix N width
{
    int i, j, k;
    float sum, a, b;

    for (i = 0; i < Mh; i++)
      for (j = 0; j < Nw; j++)
      {
        sum = 0;
        for (k = 0; k < Mw; k++)
        {
            a = M[i * Mw + k];
            b = N[k * Nw + j];
          //printf ("A[%d] * B[%d]\n", i * Mw + k, k * Nw + j);
            sum += a * b;
        }
        P[i * Nw + j] = (float)sum;
      }
}
```

A.3 `matrixmul.h`

```
/********************************************************
    File Name   [matrixmul.h]

    Synopsis   [This file defines the function prototype of
        the gold-versionmatrix-matrix multiplication.]

    Description []
********************************************************/
#ifndef MATRIXMUL_H
#define MATRIXMUL_H

extern "C"
void computeGold(
    float* P, const float* M, const float* N, int Mh, int Mw, int Nw);
#endif
```

A.4 assist.h

This file contains helper functions that assist in reading, writing, and verifying matrix data files to make your implementation easier.

```
/*******************************************************
    File Name   [assist.h]

    Synopsis   [This file defines the helper functions to assist
        In file access and result verification in matrix-
        matrix multiplication.]

    Description []
********************************************************/
    FILE *
OpenFile (const char * const fn_p,
    const char * const open_mode_p,
    const int if_silent              // If not show messages
    )
{
    FILE * f_p = NULL;

    if (fn_p == NULL) {
        printf ("Null file name pointer.");
        exit (−1);
    }
    if (!if_silent) {
        fprintf(stdout,"Opening the file %s ... ", fn_p);
    }

    f_p = fopen(fn_p, open_mode_p);
    if (f_p == NULL) {
        if (!if_silent) {
            fprintf(stdout,"failed.\n");
        } else {
            fprintf(stdout,"\nOpening the file %s ... failed.
            \n\n", fn_p);
        }
            exit (−1);
    }
    if (!if_silent) fprintf(stdout,"succeeded.\n");

    return (f_p);
}
```

```
    int
GenMatrixFile (
    const char * const matrix_fn_p,
    const unsigned int M_WIDTH,     // matrix width
    const unsigned int M_HEIGHT,     // matrix height
    const int if_silent     // If not show messages
    )
{
    FILE * matrix_fp = NULL;
    const unsigned int M_SIZE = M_WIDTH * M_HEIGHT;
    unsigned int * matrix = NULL;
    unsigned int i = 0, j = 0;
    matrix_fp = OpenFile (matrix_fn_p, "wb", 1);
    matrix = (unsigned int *) malloc (M_SIZE * sizeof
    (unsigned int));

    //if (!if_silent) fprintf (stdout, "Generated contents
    of matrix:\n");
    if (!if_silent) fprintf (stdout, "  ");
    for (i = 0; i < M_HEIGHT; i++) {
      for (j = 0; j < M_WIDTH; j++) {
        matrix[i*M_WIDTH + j] = i+j+1;
        if (!if_silent) fprintf (stdout, "%u ", matrix
        [i*M_WIDTH + j]);
        }
        if (!if_silent) fprintf (stdout, "\n  ");
      }
    if (!if_silent) fprintf (stdout, "\n");

    fwrite (matrix, 1, M_SIZE * sizeof (unsigned int),
    matrix_fp);

    fclose (matrix_fp);
    free (matrix); matrix = NULL;

    return (1);
}
    unsigned int *
ReadMatrixFile (
    const char * const matrix_fn_p,
    const unsigned int M_WIDTH,     // matrix width
    const unsigned int M_HEIGHT,     // matrix height
    const int if_silent     // If not show messages
```

```
    )
{
    FILE * matrix_fp = NULL;
    const unsigned int M_SIZE = M_WIDTH * M_HEIGHT;
    unsigned int * matrix = NULL;
    unsigned int i = 0, j = 0;

    matrix_fp = OpenFile(matrix_fn_p, "rb", if_silent);
    matrix = (unsigned int *) malloc(M_SIZE * sizeof
    (unsigned int));
    fread(matrix, 1, M_SIZE * sizeof (unsigned int),
    matrix_fp);

        if (!if_silent) {
            fprintf (stdout, "Read contents of matrix:\n");
            fprintf (stdout, "  ");
        for (i = 0; i < M_HEIGHT; i++) {
            for (j = 0; j < M_WIDTH; j++) {
                    fprintf (stdout, "%u ", matrix[i*M_WIDTH
                    + j]);
            }
            fprintf (stdout, "\n  ");
        }
        fprintf(stdout, "\n");
    }
    fclose (matrix_fp);

    return (matrix);
}
    int
WriteMatrixFile (
    const char * const matrix_fn_p,
    const unsigned int * const matrix,
    const unsigned int M_WIDTH,      // matrix width
    const unsigned int M_HEIGHT,     // matrix height
    const int if_silent      // If not show messages
    )
{
    FILE * matrix_fp = NULL;
    const unsigned int M_SIZE = M_WIDTH * M_HEIGHT;
    unsigned int i = 0, j = 0;
```

```
      matrix_fp = OpenFile (matrix_fn_p, "wb", if_silent);
      fwrite (matrix, 1, M_SIZE * sizeof (unsigned int),
      matrix_fp);

        if (!if_silent) {
            fprintf (stdout, "Written contents of matrix:\n");
        for (i = 0; i < M_HEIGHT; i++) {
            for (j = 0; j < M_WIDTH; j++) {
                fprintf (stdout, "%u ", matrix[i*M_WIDTH + j]);
            }
            fprintf (stdout, "\n");
        }
    }
    fclose (matrix_fp);

    return (1);
}
// Usage:
// CompareMatrixFile ("your output", "golden output", WC,
   HC, 1);

    void
CompareMatrixFile (
    const char * const matrix_fn_p1,
    const char * const matrix_fn_p2,
    const unsigned int M_WIDTH,      // matrix width
    const unsigned int M_HEIGHT,     // matrix height
    const int if_silent     // If not show messages
    )
{
    unsigned int i = 0, j = 0, wrong = 0;
    int check_ok = 1;
    unsigned int * m1 = ReadMatrixFile (matrix_fn_p1,
    M_WIDTH, M_HEIGHT, if_silent);
    unsigned int * m2 = ReadMatrixFile (matrix_fn_p2,
    M_WIDTH, M_HEIGHT, if_silent);
    printf (" Comparing file %s with %s ...\n", matrix_fn_p1,
    matrix_fn_p2);
    for (i = 0; i < M_HEIGHT && wrong < 15; i++) {
        for (j = 0; j < M_WIDTH && wrong < 15; j++) {
            //printf ("m1[%d][%d] ?= m2[%d][%d] : %d ?= %d\n",
```

```
                    // i,j,i,j, m1[i*M_WIDTH+j], m2[i*M_WIDTH+j]);
                if (m1[i*M_WIDTH+j] != m2[i*M_WIDTH+j]) {
                    printf ("m1[%d][%d] != m2[%d][%d] : %d != %d\n",
                            i,j,i,j, m1[i*M_WIDTH+j],
                            m2[i*M_WIDTH+j]);
                    check_ok = 0; wrong++;
                }
            }
        }
    printf ("  Check ok? ");
    if (check_ok) printf ("Passed.\n");
    else printf ("Failed.\n");
}


        float
CheckSum(const float *matrix, const int width, const int
height)
{
    int i, j;
    float s1, s2;

    for (i = 0, s1 = 0; i < width; i++) {
        for (j = 0, s2 = 0; j < height; j++) {
            s2 += matrix[i * width + j];
        }
        s1 += s2;
    }
    return s1;
}
```

A.5 EXPECTED OUTPUT

```
Input matrix size: 8 by 8
Setup host side environment:
    Allocate host memory for matrices M and N.
        M: 8 × 8
        N: 8 × 8
```

```
Allocate memory for the result on host side.
Generate input matrix data for matrix M and N.
    1 2 3 4 5 6 7 8
    2 3 4 5 6 7 8 9
    3 4 5 6 7 8 9 10
    4 5 6 7 8 9 10 11
    5 6 7 8 9 10 11 12
    6 7 8 9 10 11 12 13
    7 8 9 10 11 12 13 14
    8 9 10 11 12 13 14 15

Computing matrix multiplication M x N:
CPU Processing time   : 0.009000 (ms)
Matrix data checksum : 35456
Matrix data contents :
    204 240 276 312 348 384 420 456
    240 284 328 372 416 460 504 548
    276 328 380 432 484 536 588 640
    312 372 432 492 552 612 672 732
    348 416 484 552 620 688 756 824
    384 460 536 612 688 764 840 916
    420 504 588 672 756 840 924 1008
    456 548 640 732 824 916 1008 1100
```

GPU Compute Capabilities

B

APPENDIX CONTENTS

B.1 GPU COMPUTE CAPABILITY TABLES

As we discussed in Chapters 6–10, maximizing the kernel performance on a particular graphics processing unit (GPU) requires knowledge of the resource limitations in the GPU hardware. For this reason, the main hardware resource provisions in each GPU are typically exposed to applications in a standardized system called *compute capability*. The general specifications and features of a compute device depend on its compute capability. For CUDA™, the compute capability starts at Compute 1.0. Each higher level of compute capability indicates a newer generation of GPU devices with a higher number of features. In general, a higher level compute capability defines a superset of features of those at a lower level. Table B.1 shows the main dimensions of compute capability specifications. The table also gives the numerical value of each dimension for Compute 1.0. Each higher level of compute capability enhances one more of these dimensions as follows:

Compute Capability 1.1 adds support for atomic functions operating on 32-bit words in global memory.
Compute Capability 1.2 adds support for atomic functions operating in shared memory, atomic functions operating on 64-bit words in global memory, and warp vote functions. The number of registers per multiprocessor is increased to 16,384, the maximum number of active warps per multiprocessor is 32, and the maximum number of active threads per multiprocessor is 1024. Memory coalescing is improved (see below).
Compute Capability 1.3 adds support for double-precision, floating-point numbers and operations.

Table B.1 Main Dimensions of Compute Capability and the Attributes of Compute 1.0

Features	Compute 1.0
Number of stream processors per SM	8
Maximum number of threads per block	512
Maximum grid dimension (x, y)	65,535, 65,535
Maximum block dimension (x, y, z)	512, 512, 64
Threads in a warp	32
Registers per SM	8192 (8 K)
Shared memory per SM	16,384 (16 K)
Banks in shared memory	16
Total constant memory	65,536 (64 K)
Cache working set for constants per SM	8192 (8 K)
Local memory per thread	16,384 (16 K)
Cache working set for texture per SM	6 to 8 kB
Maximum number of active blocks per SM	8
Maximum active warps per SM	24
Maximum active threads per SM	768
1D texture bound to CUDA array—maximum width	2^{13}
1D texture bound to linear memory–maximum width	2^{27}
2D texture bound to linear memory or CUDA array—maximum dimension (x, y)	2^{16}, 2^{15}
3D texture bound to a CUDA array—maximum dimension (x, y, z)	2^{11}, 2^{11}, 2^{11}
Maximum kernel size	2 million microcode instructions

Depending on the time of its introduction, each GPU product supports up to a particular generation of compute capability. The compute capability and number of multiprocessors of all CUDA-enabled devices are given in Table B.2.

B.2 MEMORY COALESCING VARIATIONS

Each level of compute capability also specifies a different level of hardware memory coalescing capability. Knowing the compute capability, one can determine the number of global memory transactions that a load instruction

Table B.2 Many Device-Specific Features and Sizes Can Be Determined Calling the Runtime CUDA Function `cudaGetDeviceProperties()` (See *CUDA Programming Guide* for Details)

Product Name	Number of Multiprocessors	Compute Capability
GeForce®		
GTX 295	2 × 30	1.3
GTX 285, GTX 280, GTX275	30	1.3
GTX 260	24	1.3
9800 GX2	2 × 16	1.1
GTS 250, GTS 150, 9800 GTX, 9800 GTX+, 8800 GTS 512	16	1.1
8800 Ultra, 8800 GTX	16	1.0
9800 GT, 8800 GT, GTX 280 M, 9800 M GTX	14	1.1
GT 130, 9600 GSO, 8800 GS, 8800 M GTX, GTX 260 M, 9800 M GT	12	1.1
8800 GTS	12	1.0
9600 GT, 8800 M GTS, 9800 M GTS	8	1.1
9700 M GT	6	1.1
GT 120, 9500 GT, 8600 GTS, 8600 GT, 9700 M GT, 9650 M GS, 9600 M GT, 9600 M GS, 9500 M GS, 8700 M GT, 8600 M GT, 8600 M GS	4	1.1
G100, 8500 GT, 8400 GS, 8400 M GT	2	1.1
9500 M G, 9300 M G, 8400 M GS, 9400 mGPU, 9300 mGPU, 8300 mGPU, 8200 mGPU, 8100 mGPU, 9300 M GS, 9200 M GS, 9100 M G, 8400 M G	1	1.1
Tesla™		
S1070	4 × 30	1.3
C1060	30	1.3
S870	4 × 16	1.0
D870	2 × 16	1.0
C870	16	1.0
Quadro®		
Plex 2200 D2	2 × 30	1.3
Plex 2100 D4	4 × 14	1.1
Plex 2100 Model S4	4 × 16	1.0

(continued)

Table B.2 Many Device-Specific Features and Sizes Can Be Determined Calling the Runtime CUDA Function `cudaGetDeviceProperties()` (See *CUDA Programming Guide* for Details)—cont'd

Product Name	Number of Multiprocessors	Compute Capability
Plex 1000 Model IV	2 × 16	1.0
FX 5800	30	1.3
FX 4800	24	1.3
FX 4700 X2	2 × 14	1.1
FX 3700 M	16	1.1
FX 5600	16	1.0
FX 3700	14	1.1
FX 3600 M	12	1.1
FX 4600	12	1.0
FX 2700 M	6	1.1
FX 1700, FX 1700 M, FX 570, FX 570 M, NVS 320 M, FX 1600 M, FX 770 M	4	1.1
FX 370, NVS 290, NVS 140 M, NVS 135 M, FX 360 M	2	1.1
FX 370 M, NVS 130 M	1	1.1

in a warp will incur. In Compute 1.0 and Compute 1.1, memory transactions are done for memory 64- or 128-byte segments. Coalescing of accesses in a warp requires that the *k*th thread in a warp accesses the *k*th word in a 64-byte segment when accessing 32-byte words (or the *k*th word in two contiguous 128-byte segments when accessing 128-byte words). Not all threads need to participate for coalescing to work. In the top case in Figure B.1, one of the threads in a warp did not participate, but the accesses still coalesced into one transaction.

In particular, all accesses must be in sequence. If one or more of the accesses are out of sequence, the accesses will no longer be coalesced. In the middle part of Figure B.1, two of the accesses are out of sequence, and the accesses are not coalesced; 16 transactions to the global memory are necessary for the access.

In Compute 1.2 and above, the global memory transactions are issued in 32-, 64-, or 128-byte segments. Having a smaller segment size allows the hardware to reduce the waste of global memory bandwidth for some less coherent warp access patterns.

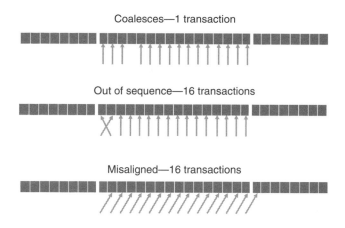

FIGURE B1

Memory coalescing in Compute 1.0 and 1.1.

Figure B.2 illustrates improvements in memory coalescing in Compute 1.2. The top part shows that warp accesses within a segment can be out of sequence and still be fully coalesced into one transaction. The middle part shows that the access can be nonaligned across a 128-byte boundary. One extra 32-byte segment transaction will be issued, and the accesses

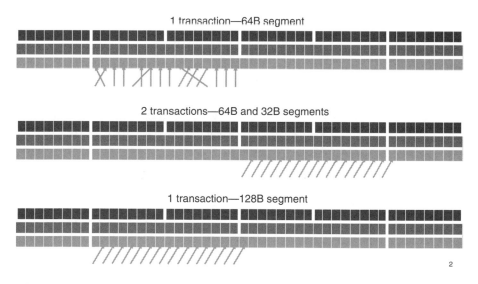

FIGURE B2

Memory coalescing in Compute 1.2 and above.

are still coalesced. The bottom part shows that, if warp accesses are not aligned but stay within a 128-byte boundary, a single 128-byte segment transaction will be used to access all of the words involved. In these two cases, the global memory bandwidth consumption is much less than that in Compute 1.0 or 1.1, where 16 transactions of 64-byte segments would be used.

Index

Page numbers followed by "*f*" indicate figures and "*t*" indicate tables.